PARTICIPATORY
DEMOCRACY

PARTICIPATORY DEMOCRACY

The Case of Parish Development Committees in Jamaica

Marc Anthony Thomas

The University of the West Indies Press

Jamaica • Barbados • Trinidad and Tobago

The University of the West Indies Press
7A Gibraltar Hall Road, Mona
Kingston 7, Jamaica
www.uwipress.com

A catalogue record of this book is available from the National Library of Jamaica.

ISBN: 978-976-640-854-1 (print)
978-976-640-855-8 (mobi)
978-976-640-856-5 (ePub)

Cover design by Robert Harris

Printed in the United States of America

To my family

Contents

Abbreviations

AGM	annual general meeting
CDC	community development committee
DAC	development area committee
JLP	Jamaica Labour Party
NAPDEC	National Association of Parish Development Committees
NGO	non-governmental organizations
PDC	parish development committee
PNP	People's National Party
SDC	Social Development Commission

1.

Planting the Seeds of Jamaica's Democracy

Parish development committees (PDCs) were set up to bolster Jamaica's democratization efforts yet, curiously, the committees rarely have leadership elections. One internal report lamented how undemocratic the committees were because of this fact, while government officials bewailed the "obvious" attempt by the leadership to hold on indefinitely to power. The traditional focus on idealized forms of democratic activity immediately casts organizations such as PDCs in a negative light. The careful investigation of each entity at a granular level, as in this study, revealed many and diverse reasons for relatively few elections. One PDC did not have elections in order to prevent partisan infiltration. In another instance, members delayed election efforts in order to identify a potential candidate who would be suitable not only by meeting constitutional expectations (a citizen of voting age, for example) but also by meeting the organization's needs as stipulated by the on-the-ground realities it was confronting. Such a candidate might have the financial wherewithal to assist the cash-strapped body or possess a reputation that would aid in recruiting efforts since membership was dwindling.

Delaying or denying an election was a shrewd tactic used to secure the very survival of the committee. In fact, this study found that the emergence, survival and ability to thrive of PDCs in Jamaica are determined largely by the extent to which such "emancipatory political tactics" are successfully applied by stakeholders to combat a number of continuing challenges in these committee's environments.

This work empirically expands the existing knowledge on participatory democracy through a study of Jamaica's PDCs. The present chapter will offer greater detail on the background, foci, methods and main research questions as well as offer an overview of how my finding are shared across the chapters.

Parish Development Committees

Jamaica's political system, an outgrowth of the country's colonial heritage, has traditionally provided few opportunities for the general population to participate in the nation's governance. The creation of parish development committees (throughout the book, both PDCs and "the experiment" refer to parish development committees) and other organizations aimed at eliciting citizen engagement in local governance in the Caribbean nation marked a departure from that history. A government report introducing this new participatory structure explained as follows:

> Parish Development Committees (PDCs), Development Area Committees (DACs) and Community Development Committees (CDCs) represent new institutional forms that have emerged in Jamaica's quest to create a new paradigm of participatory local governance, in which communities/civil society are made full partners in the quest for good governance and balanced/sustainable local development. They are key elements of the institutional framework for a new model of participatory governance that will vastly expand democratic practice in the society and help to renew/revitalize the political system – and create goodwill/commitment towards this system, by enabling the active participation of citizens in the policy/decision-making processes. It is also critical in empowering communities to have a greater say in managing their own affairs and determining their own destiny; in facilitating citizens to play a more active role in governance at the local level; and in unleashing the vast store of energy, talents, innovativeness and leadership that lie dormant in large sections of the population, but which are stifled by high levels of centralization and exclusion which limit their ability to contribute to local and national development.[1]

Schoburgh has nicely summarized the aims of this governance initiative: "Local government reform policy in Jamaica thus aimed to reorient the focus of local authorities from mere providers of local services to agents of social transformation."[2] The Department of Local Government report that introduced PDCs defined them as

> an inclusive, democratic, independent, non-political and voluntary organization which brings together all elements of civil society, governmental, quasi and non-governmental agencies and organizations in a parish or other local government jurisdiction. It is established for the primary purpose of facilitating local self-management and development processes within the parish, and promoting and facilitating the concepts, principles and practices of good governance and balanced and sustainable development within the local jurisdiction. It seeks to accomplish these goals by working through and in partnership with its corresponding Local Authority, and by promoting partnership, collaboration, coordination, cooperation and networking among all the diverse sectors, interest groups and stakeholders in the parish, and also by encouraging the adoption of positive values and attitudes, social harmony and stability, and respect for the parish's culture, heritage and unique character.[3]

As initially envisioned by the Office of the Prime Minister, PDCs were expected to "reverse adversarialism and tribalism, which are currently dominant characteristics of [Jamaica's] social and political relationships".[4] Caribbean scholars

Munroe and Buddan have also argued for more direct forms of participation in Jamaica, which they have suggested could serve as a mechanism for closing what they perceive to be the nation's democratic deficit.[5] The specific cause of this difficulty for Munroe particularly lies in the character of liberal democracy. As he has observed, "indirect representative democracy is concerned almost exclusively with institutional and procedural issues and mainly political inputs, participatory democracy is as much concerned with outcomes and substantive questions relating to the quality of social and economic life".[6] In his view, a more participatory form of local governance represented a necessary antidote to the existing situation: "The choice we face, particularly in the Anglophone Caribbean is not between retaining liberal democracy in its existing form or passing to some type of authoritarianism; it is between renewing and qualitatively transforming liberal democracy in a participatory direction on the one hand or observing its decay into one or another degree of disintegration and anarchy."[7]

With its 2008 report on local government reform, the Government of Jamaica formally acknowledged that despite the direct election of parish representatives to parish councils, a democratic deficit continued to exist at the local level. This reality created a scenario in which, "citizens feel outside of the decision-making processes, and receive very little information about the activities in their parish until implementation is well underway".[8] The state's solution to this situation was to bring civil society and local government representatives around the same table in a participatory space through the introduction of a structure of PDCs. The nation's leaders reasoned that information concerning government activities would filter down, and the will of the people would filter up the participatory structure of PDCs, development area committees (DACs) and community development committees (CDCs). This Jamaican solution was similar to ones posited across Latin America when other states in the region faced comparable challenges in recent years, including the introduction of participatory budgeting in Porto Alegre, Brazil, in 1989, and in Medellín, Colombia, in 2004.[9]

The Latin American Experience

Selee and Peruzzotti have argued that the emergence of outsider candidates, growth in anti-establishment discourse and decreasing voter turnout across Latin America are indicative of populations disaffected with representative democracy.[10] Hartlyn has suggested the following reasons for that disenchantment: limited vertical means of accountability, a history of authoritarian rule and radical policy changes from weak political parties resulting in policies that voters do not want.[11] Other analysts have argued that horizontal forms of accountability[12] are often inadequate as well, leading to poorly functioning representative institutions and a general difficulty in ensuring the rule of law.[13] Citizen discontent with the exigencies often imposed by market reforms undertaken in the 1990s has further fuelled widespread citizen disillusionment. In essence, while many nations in Latin America have come to practise popular rule, it is accompanied by what might be dubbed parochial tendencies.[14] Diamond has described the governance practices of many Central and South American nations as, "hollow, illiberal, poorly institutionalized democracy".[15] Since the 1980s, the region has sought to address the issue of voter disaffection that resulted in lack of citizen engagement in political processes by offering more direct forms of governance via participatory budgeting, planning and neighbourhood committees. The result of these steps has been a "wave of participation"[16] through such initiatives.

Hartlyn, along with Selee and Tulchin,[17] among others, have argued that more involvement in governance provides opportunities to bridge the divide between citizens and their representatives, determines the boundaries of voter responsibilities and often reduces the development of unsustainable governance forms, such as patron/client relations.[18] Hartlyn found that participatory initiatives can build meaningful relationships between elected representatives and citizens between elections. He also suggested that such efforts tend to receive broad popular support and have become an integral part of representational politics when they have been institutionalized.[19] Selee and Tulchin have argued that engaged citizens construct original shared concepts of what it means to exist as a collective.[20] This offers hope to many, cognizant of how important it is for voters to develop a common capacity for prudential judgements and a companion concern for the interests of their communities if they are to preserve free institutions. These scholars' findings support those of Pateman and Borkman more recently,[21] and, historically, those of de Tocqueville, who (in the 1830s) contended that active participation leads to an empowered citizenry.[22]

Scholars are not alone in their interest in participatory initiatives. International governmental bodies such as the World Bank and several major Western countries have embraced and are actively promoting broader public engagement in self-governance processes. Mohan and Stokke have contended, for example, that participatory poverty assessments are now an entrenched practice within the World Bank Group.[23] With the introduction of PDCs (and their companion structures, CDCs and DACs) Jamaica signalled that it, too, would pursue a participatory approach to governance. Unlike several of the initiatives that have been undertaken in Latin America aimed at this purpose, however, there are no empirical studies available on the ongoing Jamaican experiment with participatory democracy. That fact makes this study timely.

Assessing Participatory Democracy

A thorough examination of the roles and functions of PDCs in practice requires an investigation of Jamaica's participatory space. Gaventa has reminded readers that "rhetorical acceptance" of citizen participation does not necessarily result in more inclusive governance or significant improvements in social justice.[24] Indeed, Mohan and Stokke have argued that an oratorical shift towards local participatory engagement often masks "both local inequalities and power relations as well as [inegalitarian] national and transnational economic and political forces".[25] Miraftab has similarly observed that social inclusion can operate alongside material exclusion of marginalized groups.[26] This finding suggests that a wide-ranging contextual analysis of engagement initiatives is needed to ascertain if their intended outcomes are being achieved. In a similar vein, Cornwall and Gaventa have contended that scholars should examine the nature of power within participatory spaces while accepting their dynamic character.[27] Gaventa has defined power "as the network of social boundaries that delimit fields of possible action, and freedom refers to the ability to manipulate these boundaries". He further argued that actors within democratic arenas not only interact but also constantly shift perspectives as they relate to each other, with consequences for the character and outcomes of their engagement for governance.[28]

For their part, Mohan and Stokke have recommended that scholars "pay more attention to the politics of the local, that is, to the hegemonic production and representation of 'the local' and the use of 'the local' in counter-hegemonic collective mobilisation".[29] This reminder is useful, as community control historically has not automatically been positive for many citizens. Smaller populations have often proven susceptible to tyrannical control by the well-organized few with capacity and interest. Localized analysis, however, can also recognize when participation lends itself to serving as a site of "radical possibility".[30] This potential implies, as Foucault argued, that power relations innately afford opportunities for resistance.[31] Scott has shown that such opposition may not be overt, but may instead be offered in "hidden transcripts" by subalterns in the face of disproportionately powerful oppressors.[32] In keeping with this finding, this study followed Cornwall's advice "to generate new ethnographies of participation that help locate spaces for participation in the places in which they occur, framing their possibilities with reference to actual political, social, cultural and historical particularities rather than idealized models of democratic practice".[33] To gain a more nuanced understanding of Jamaica's PDCs as potential participatory spaces, I sought to observe and analyse these entities' "hidden transcripts". The result is an investigation of the PDCs selected for study as participatory spaces, with their hegemonic and counter-hegemonic forces highlighted and situated within the larger socio-economic and political conditions in which they operate.

By empirically examining four of Jamaica's fourteen PDCs,[34] I sought to ascertain the social, political, economic and cultural conditions in which direct and participatory forms of governance were more likely or less likely to emerge, sustain and thrive in the country. I explored whether supportive institutional, infrastructural and superstructural (referring to the society's culture and power configurations) conditions for their robust implementation were in place in Jamaica. I was also interested in learning more about who participates in the nation's PDCs and what factors motivate their engagement.

I translated these overarching areas of enquiry into the following questions, which I posed to PDC members and stakeholders:

- What factors influence the extent of citizen participation through the PDCs?
- How does one identify the types and extent of institutional support needed for citizen engagement experiments to thrive?
- In terms of infrastructure support for the nation's participatory bodies in the form of financial assistance, is there a reliable and sufficient source of funds available to maintain an office and secretariat?
- Is Jamaica's low level of social trust a deterrent to participatory democracy taking root?
- For policymakers and participants alike, are higher levels of social trust an expected outcome of the nation's current democratic experiment?
- What strategies do stakeholders employ to overcome challenges to accomplishing the goals of the PDCs?

The insight gained regarding these concerns deepened my understanding of the state of the government's participatory democracy initiative in Jamaica, enabling me to make predictions concerning the benefits and possibilities of the success of such future efforts, given prevailing social, political and economic conditions.

The concerns were best addressed by means of a qualitative research design that embraces local and contextualized knowledge.[35] To situate the enquiry, I undertook an extensive review of the literature concerning democracy, engagement and development to shed light on why and how participatory initiatives have emerged across the globe. Relevant scholarship also revealed the utility of the move away from a representative-centred democratic governance structure to one in which citizens have more of a say beyond selecting a legislator in an election every few years. To comprehend more fully the conditions that encourage the emergence and survival of robust participatory democracy, I examined a variety of empirical studies of such initiatives. That analysis was helpful in the development of the research design to study the Jamaican experiment. I chose to interview a variety of stakeholders engaged with the examined PDCs, including past PDC members, legislators, heads of interested civil society organizations, staff of the government's Social Development Commission (SDC), staff at the Ministry of Local Government and Community Development and Jamaican and other scholars with expertise concerning the nation's politics and culture. Past PDC members and other stakeholders were interviewed individually in person or by telephone, while most current members were engaged via focus groups. All participants were promised confidentiality but not anonymity, which involved minimizing access to the codes linking data to individuals, employing pseudonyms and, as best as possible, avoiding including information in discussions that could identify their source. In addition, the dates of the interviews were not displayed, and each interview was cited using a code (for example, VT032 represents an interview conducted with a former PDC member). The full list is provided in table 1.1.

I spoke to at least one representative of every PDC contacted (ten PDCs in total) and arranged focus groups for members of the four selected PDCs. The four PDCs were chosen on the basis of three criteria: (1) at least one urban PDC and one rural community PDC, (2) an established PDC that interviewees suggested would be broadly representative of the PDC universe regarding the types of concerns it addressed and the challenges it confronted, and (3) an emerging PDC into the four for which focus groups were organized. The profile of each selected PDC is as follows:

PDC 1: An established and exemplary PDC as described by all stakeholders with whom I spoke. It has a functioning secretariat and regular meetings. This PDC has attracted significant international funding not only for capacity building but also for several community projects, including efforts geared towards ensuring the financial viability of the group after donor funding. The parish is predominantly rural with significant investments in mining and manufacturing.

PDC 2: Also well established, this PDC has a functioning secretariat and holds regular meetings. It has not garnered as much international or local funding as PDC 1, but continues to make an impact through the small projects and initiatives in which it participates. The parish is urban in character and contains several manufacturing and agrobusiness firms.

Table 1.1. Codes and Titles of Interviewees

Code	Interviewees
VT037	PDC chairperson
VT120	PDC chairperson
VT076	PDC member
VT021	PDC member
VT064	PDC member
VT056	PDC staff (2 people)
VT012/VT014	PDC staff
VT059/VT122	PDC staff
VT123	PDC staff
VT105	Past PDC member
VT099	Past PDC member/chairperson
VT032	Past PDC member
VT034	Past PDC member
VT035	Past PDC member
VT073	Past PDC member/chairperson
VT080	Past PDC member
VT061	Past PDC member
VT066	Past PDC member
VT067	Past PDC member/chairperson
VT068	Past PDC member
VT070	Past PDC member
VT072	Past PDC member
VT111	Past PDC member/chairperson
VT109	Past PDC member
VT060	Community association/CDC member
VT069	Community association/CDC member
VT029	National Association of Parish Development Committees (NAPDEC) representative
VT053	SDC parish representative
VT010	SDC parish representative
VT030/VT124	SDC national representative
VT081	SDC parish representative
VT052	SDC parish representative

(*Continued*)

Table 1.1. (*continued*)

Code	Interviewees
VT036	Civil society group member
VT078	Civil society group member
VT026	Civil society group member
VT027	Civil society group member
VT040	Civil society group member
VT044	Civil society group member
VT050	Civil society group member
VT092	Academic
VT110	Academic
VT085	Academic
VT039	Academic
VT088	Legislator/mayor
VT107	Legislator/past member of Parliament
VT086	Legislator/member of Parliament
VT057	Legislator/former member of Parliament
VT023	Legislator/member of Parliament
VT013	Legislator/councillor as well as a former mayor (2 people)
VT084	Legislator/mayor
VT126	Legislator/former member of Parliament
VT033	Third-party president
VT112	Custos rotulorum*/civil society group member
VT038	Ministry of Local Government and Community Development senior staff
VT041	Ministry of Local Government and Community Development senior staff
VT042	Ministry of Local Government and Community Development senior staff
Focus Groups	
VT019	PDC 1 (13 people)
VT058	PDC 2 (8 people)
VT087	PDC 3 (9 people)
VT054	PDC 4 (8 people)

* Official website of the governor general of Jamaica, http://www.kingshouse.gov.jm /custodes. The custos rotulorum (Keeper of the Roll of the Justices of the Peace) presides at petty sessions court and is the chief magistrate for the parish.

PDC 3: Also established, this PDC has a functioning secretariat and holds regular meetings. It has not garnered as much international or local funding as PDC 1, but it is making significant inroads into specialized projects, in particular, those pertaining to the environment. The parish is considered rural and one of the poorest in the country. The leading industries within the parish are agriculture and tourism.

PDC 4: This PDC is fledgling and recently restarted following a long period of dormancy. It did not hold a meeting during the summer of 2012 and its members were largely concerned during the period with registering it and establishing functioning DACs. During my research period, this committee had an established secretariat but no formal office space. Like PDC 3, this parish is considered rural and is among the poorest in the country. The leading industries are agriculture and tourism.

I supplemented individual interviews with PDC members and the comments of participants in the focus groups with more than one hundred hours of personal observations of PDC activities and analysis of pertinent documents, including an assessment of Jamaica's relevant political history.

Through this last effort, in particular, I became aware of the persistent presence of emancipatory politics in the nation's culture. The term "emancipatory politics" captures the long-time desire of Jamaicans to attain self-determination. It recognizes that that process entails engaging all available avenues, including some that are neither sustainable nor immediately democratic. During the days of slavery, for example, flight was a common form of resistance.[36] Those enslaved resisted daily and imposed financial costs on planters by slowing production, destroying tools and pretending to be ill.[37] Davis has shown that Jamaica also had several armed insurrections during the period from 1670 to slavery's abolition on the island in 1838.[38] To circumvent the post-slavery challenges of poor wages and limited opportunities to purchase land, the subaltern created a sophisticated peasantry, remnants of which still exist today.[39] Through various forms of protest action, Jamaica's citizens continue to make it clear that they want a greater say in matters affecting their lives.[40] Knowledge of this history and its accompanying modus operandi allowed a more sensitive assessment of PDC activities. The result is an examination of an ongoing political experiment from which the conditions that support robust popular participation were inferred.

This project will immediately benefit affected stakeholders and policymakers by highlighting the strengths and weaknesses of existing policy concerning the PDCs, while providing a set of recommendations that can guide the design of a more effective course of action in the future. Considering the shared political history and economic plight of today's Caribbean states, the findings of this study should also be useful to civil society groups as well as governments across the region interested in deepening democracy via participatory programmes.

This introductory chapter has outlined the background, foci and main research questions that animated this enquiry. Chapter 2 situates the evolution of the PDCs in the context of Jamaica's political history. That chapter also reviews global participatory democratic programmes in order to identify the institutional, infrastructural and superstructural conditions (criteria) by which to assess the PDC experiment in Jamaica. Chapters 3 and 4 offer data analysis and principal findings. They capture the insights gleaned from the individual interviews, focus groups and observations of PDC operations and stakeholders primarily between May and August of 2012. These chapters explore the aims, structures and processes of the PDCs studied as well as the motivating factors and values articulated by the PDC members with whom I interacted. This study also charts the extent to which their collective efforts appear to be contributing to the survival and thriving of the PDCs and communities of which they are a part. These chapters also serve to examine the assumptions inherent in the Jamaican government's PDC policy design, the trials these bodies have faced and the actions their members have taken to address those challenges. The concluding chapter reviews the principal analytic findings and offers recommendations for more robust operation of the PDCs in Jamaica while reflecting on the conditions that support successful participatory democratic programmes not only in that nation but also across the Caribbean region.

2.

The Space for and the Characteristics of Participatory Democracy

Jamaica has used the referendum only once and has very few formal mechanisms beyond voting through which citizens may participate in governance. This situation is changing, evidenced by the introduction of PDCs in 1999, which allow residents to inform government policies and programmes at the grassroots level. This shift has not been reflected in an increase in the academic literature on direct and participatory democracy in Jamaica. Unfortunately, that scholarship remains sparse. This project seeks empirically to begin to remedy that lacuna and to expand knowledge of the roles, functions and processes of a sample of Jamaica's PDCs. This chapter provides a definition of participatory democracy, offers a historical account of major scholarship concerning it and highlights variations of such initiatives that have been placed into practice. The groundwork for this study of PDCs as an example of participatory democracy in Jamaica comes from the work of scholars and practitioners who have investigated such efforts. Of particular interest is the identification of the institutional, infrastructural or superstructural conditions that researchers have suggested allow participatory initiatives to emerge, survive and thrive.

Specifically, I derived the analytic framework for this study from Cornwall, Gaventa, and Mohan and Stokke, who have advocated for comprehensive contextual analysis of the relationship of power structures to engagement initiatives in order to gauge their relative effects and significance.[1] Cornwall, for example, as noted in chapter 1, has admonished researchers to "generate new ethnographies of participation that help locate spaces for participation in the places in which they occur, framing their possibilities with reference to actual political, social, cultural and historical particularities rather than idealized models of democratic practice".[2] This chapter's review of Jamaica's record in light of Cornwall's suggested analytical foci reveals a people constantly engaged in what I call "emancipatory politics". This terminology pays homage to the strategies and tactics used by the nation's residents since slavery to direct the course of their lives, be it running away from the plantation or creating an underground economy. While observing the PDCs for this study, I sought to identify these strategies or "hidden transcripts" in order to be as sensitive and nuanced as possible in the interpretation of citizen engagement efforts in PDCs. The discussion begins with how dissatisfaction with representative democracy has led to the development of recent participatory initiatives globally.

The Anaemic Liberal Democratic State?

Liberal democracy, or representative democracy, which offers voters the opportunity to provide a mandate (by election) to a small number of leaders to make decisions for them for a delimited term of office, appears to be losing favour with citizens across the globe. Widespread disaffection among Jamaicans with the relative efficacy of this approach was revealed in 2011 when a majority of those responding in a national poll suggested that the country would be better off under British rule.[3] Meanwhile, four years earlier, former Jamaican senator and professor of political science Trevor Munroe characterized the state of Caribbean democracy as in "undeniable decay".[4] Consider as well that in the United States, as with many other established democracies, slightly more than half the eligible population votes in national elections when given the opportunity.[5] (Turnouts of 58.23 per cent in 2008 and 54.87 per cent in 2012 are exemptions to a long downward trend.)[6] For its part, the US Congress, whose members are elected by state or by (frequently gerrymandered) districts, has seen its public approval plummet to an unprecedented low of 9 per cent.[7] LeDuc's public opinion surveys have captured the belief of people across the globe that representative governments are disengaged, remote, unresponsive and out of touch.[8] Large and growing citizen dissatisfaction and disenchantment across all the world's democracies is a critical issue.

This disaffection is not a recent development. In *Participatory Democracy: Developing Ideals of the Political Left*, Kramer cited a *London Times* report of 14 June 1968: "first year students at Nottingham College of Art and Design boycotted an examination as a protest over the present system of education . . . [also] [t]he British National Union of Students (NUS) informs university vice-chancellors and college principals that it will 'apply sanctions' unless they start to discuss the nine NUS demands before the end of the year".[9]

Kramer also noted that at the same time in France (specifically the spring of 1968), students, including those attending the Sorbonne in Paris, seized several universities during weeks of fighting with gendarmes. Discontent in France during this period went beyond university students as workers in some of that nation's largest factories rose up and took control of those locations. Around the same time, too, a general strike nearly shut the country down and succeeded in forcing French government leaders to promise new elections.

Belgium, Holland, West Germany and Sweden all experienced similar citizen discontent that year, but perhaps most memorable were the many riots by black individuals as well as various large-scale student protests against conscription and the Vietnam War in the United States during this time frame.

Ready explanations for this phenomenon at the time included students nervous about exams in England, low pay in France, people not wanting to go to war and racism in America. Kramer has argued that accepting these rationalizations misses the larger issue, "the most important point of those responsible for these acts of nonviolent and not-so-nonviolent civil disobedience all over [was] that those influenced by a set of policies should have a direct say in the determination of these policies and that this goal [was] undemocratically ignored by the institutions of today's liberal society".[10]

The National Union of Students at the time requested, "effective student presence on all relevant college committees, student-staff control of discipline and joint discussion of course content and teaching methods [and] student control of their own organizations".[11] The cry was for a more democratic order in which those affected by public policies and programmes could have a direct say in writing the laws they were expected to follow.

Lott concluded that representative government may have been a shining viable solution two hundred years ago, but it is no longer effective for today's vast and infinitely more complicated societies.[12] In light of this, he has also suggested that the only workable alternative to representative government is more direct forms of democracy.[13] This echoes similar popular calls on behalf of comparable goals articulated in Jamaica and many other nations.[14]

Participatory Democracy Defined

Barber described participatory democracy in this way: "politics in the participatory mode [is] where conflict is resolved in the absence of an independent ground through a participatory process of ongoing, proximate self-legislation and the creation of a political community capable of transforming dependent, private individuals into free citizens and partial and private interests into public goods".[15] The institutions needed to usher in this sort of "strong democracy", according to Barber, include the use of referenda, initiatives, the creation of neighbourhood assemblies and public sponsorship of local volunteer programmes.[16] This perspective is similar to de Tocqueville's vision of potential venues for deliberation, which included but was not limited to casual conversations between neighbours and formal meetings of community associations.[17] Such activities are at the heart of any practical programme to encourage the exercise of political power by an engaged citizenry and promote the public interest, which is the essence of a "strong democracy".[18] Such a definition is consonant with the role of the PDCs to provide a platform by which residents may consider the impacts of public policies and propose changes when necessary.

Participatory Democracy: History and Context

Very few authors today argue for a return to Athenian democracy, which, in any case, is simply not feasible for most of the world's nations. In Athens, every citizen (but not every person) had a vote on multiple issues. Sinclair explained that the number of citizens in the Greek city-state was extremely small and certainly nothing close to the population sizes of most societies today.[19] Butler and Ranney highlighted John Stuart Mill, James Ford and Joseph Schumpeter's contention that the dream of direct democracy is only relevant for polities so small that individuals can meet face to face in one place at one time.[20] The question then is not how nations might replace representative governance with Athenian style government, but rather whether principles of participatory democracy can improve the functioning and effectiveness of such regimes. The next section provides an overview of the theory and practice of such constructs.

A Case for Participation and Its Impact

Patemen, Bachrach and Botwinick, Barber, Mitchell, Albert and Hahnel, and Mason have contributed to this study's understanding of the participatory approach.[21] Each of these scholars argued that politics reflects citizens' daily experience and that participatory democracy may occur whenever individuals make decisions with others on behalf of their community.

Kramer argued that because humans are autonomous beings, they should control the policy decisions affecting their lives.[22] This understanding accepts social justice as an end in itself and takes its cues from a particular view of human nature. It also accepts participation as a means by which to work towards social justice, an epistemological claim. Gould supports this argument in *Rethinking Democracy*, noting that human beings have the ability to, and actually do, shape the world in which they reside by means of deliberate action.[23] Writing as long ago as 1905, Zueblin observed the following: "One can be a citizen only by participation and that is not merely in the annual casting of the ballot, but in daily citizenship."[24] In this view, individual or personal and community development are intrinsically tied. Sandel suggested that "we cannot conceive of our personhood without reference to our roles as citizens, and as participants in a common life".[25] This perspective suggests that a high value be placed on the knowledge and experiences of the citizenry and implies an equally strong confidence in the average person's ability to shape society.

Participatory systems privilege deliberation above bargaining within the political process and also encourage citizen involvement. Increased voter engagement also tends to lead to more legitimate results. Several scholars working in Latin America have found that more direct democratic decision methods improve distributive outcomes, which further improve as clientelism is reduced.[26] Selee and Tulchin argued that South American nations reflect a strong social construction of citizenship on the basis of the spaces they witnessed that facilitated vibrant democratic participation. These brought the state closer to the people, which allowed for greater levels of accountability and responsiveness even though these political openings were often limited both in size and duration.[27] Such is possible because of the practices that sustain participatory governance processes to which the Jamaican model also subscribes. Understanding these methods and their limitations is therefore crucial to understanding how participatory governance may be operationalized.

The Processes of Participation

The participatory model suggests that individuals and groups composed of residents from various backgrounds and interests can form a community through dialogue, but this does not always occur. Negotiation among private interests may, as James Madison suggested, produce the public good, but what often happens instead is the "fallacy of composition". In such cases, the sum of negotiated private interests does not produce a suitable public outcome.[28] Something more is needed than the aggregation of private claims for citizens to think and act publicly. Barber's concept of "democratic talk" or speech addresses this concern. Barber argued that a citizenry begins to think and act publicly through dialogue when the members express their shared history and experiences. Democratic talk asks collective questions such as these: What shall we do? How does our society resolve its differences? The community's experiential knowledge then provides the answers. This understanding can be moulded and applied as needed to act in the interest of the common good. Such knowledge is not fixed and is subject to change during the process of deliberation, reflecting the openness and flexibility needed for self-governance.[29] Speech, under the participatory umbrella, stresses listening and active efforts to grasp other viewpoints; participationists know that they must explain their choices in a public language and are therefore constantly open to reflection. This process encourages those engaged in it to become more actively empathetic and open to bridging differences in order to further the interests of their broader community.[30] Mutz argued similarly that the more "talk" occurs among different groups, the greater the likelihood that enmities will break down, friendships will develop and each will become more tolerant of the other's views.[31] The aim of such dialogue is not conformity, but an acceptance and awareness of others' values.[32]

This process assumes willingness among all players to come to the proverbial table and to be open to alternative points of view. A later section of this chapter concerning conditions for participation will explore the role of social capital in enabling engagement, but first the following outlines the formal and informal manifestations of the participatory approach as well as its various outputs.

Participatory Democracy: A Formal Manifestation

The participatory approach assumes that citizens constitute a crucial, valuable and active resource. This premise suggests that state institutions should be designed to reflect and encourage deliberation, and several states and non-states alike have sought to develop measures that might realize this aim. *Participatory Governance in the EU*, for example, traced the EU's attempts to address its democratic deficit by embracing participatory governance. Specifically, the European Union sought to involve interest groups and civil society groups more intensely and in greater numbers in policy discussions to promote more deliberative governance. In an analysis of this initiative, Lindgren concluded that it had not eliminated the European Union's democratic deficit, but had gone a far way in reducing it.[33] The World Bank has likewise supported a move towards more active citizen engagement in governance, and several scholars have supported analogous efforts.[34] Sirianni, for example, advocated for institutional designs which ensure that citizens are put in a position by the state to "co-produce" public goods, mobilizing their own assets, including localized knowledge for problem solving and promoting civic associations.[35] This orientation suggests why the highly successful Chicago Alternative Police Strategy defined its mission as, "Safe Neighborhoods Are Everybody's Business".[36] Putnam argued that the Northern provinces of Italy historically have registered the best political and economic performance in democratic Italy because their civic cultures promoted active citizen commitment and horizontal relations of trust, tolerance and cooperation. Putnam dubbed these characteristics "the civic community".[37] Local knowledge, according to Lindblom and Cohen's *Usable Knowledge: Social Science and Social Problem Solving*, is "knowledge that does not owe its origin, testing, degree of verification, truth, status, or currency to distinctive . . . professional techniques, but rather to common sense causal empiricism, or thoughtful speculation and analysis".[38] Mitchell underscored how crucial the role of local information is to effective environmental governance.[39] Similarly, Borkman studied self-help groups and documented how citizens assisted each other on the basis of the experiential knowledge they possessed. Borkman's analysis highlighted alternatives to bureaucratic organization (the doctor-patient relationship is an example) as citizens assisted each other through "talk" in sharing circles. Local understanding is hard to codify and includes such information as, "so how do I get through Christmas parties without drinking", for example. In her work with occupational therapists, Mattingly found that biomedical discourse allowed these professionals to reason about the body, but stories allowed them to show how they helped patients enjoy a fuller life despite their impairments.[40]

Participation also occurs in the workplace and appears to be a positive factor there as well. Several scholars, including Kramer and Pateman, have proposed that the participatory model be extended to all institutions in society.[41] Rousseau admonished that there can be no substantial political equality without economic equality. In this view, workplace productivity will always be low when the relationship between workers and their overseers is one of domination; that is, institutions and individuals cannot be considered in isolation.[42] With this idea in view, Pateman set out to test John Stuart Mills's claim that participation develops an active character in involved individuals. More specifically, Pateman contended that a sense of political competence or efficacy developed in the workplace may be applied elsewhere, including in national politics. Nonetheless, her primary concern was the workplace, and her study of businesses showed that democratization of industry through job security, which aids in minimizing inequality, does not hinder profit making and participation at several levels, while also serving an educational role.[43]

Several analysts have suggested that democratized workplaces result in increased profits. DuPont Chemical Company, for example, used quality circles, or a team approach, in which "the level of thinking and ultimate performance of supervisor and supervised can be significantly and permanently improved through communication and joint participation in problem solving". DuPont's adoption of this approach resulted in an increase in productivity and improvements in manufacturing, marketing and product distribution. The firm was also able to reduce administrative overhead.[44] In principle, participation may result in the removal of all hierarchy (where it exists as domination), but as Thomas explained, even when such domination removal is not achieved, increased engagement can nonetheless yield more just outcomes.[45] In contrast, Hyman, Thompson and Harley contended that present-day workplace involvement schemes are more rhetoric than substance.[46] Nevertheless, it is important to emphasize that they exist.

Participatory Democracy: An Informal Manifestation

Many scholars have argued that participatory democracy not only serves a moral agenda but also fosters engaged communities. Mason, Olsen and Davis all have embraced a more politically involved citizenry as a positive output of citizen engagement.[47] As Davis explained, the participatory school is aimed at "the education of an entire people to the point where their intellectual, emotional, and moral capacities have reached their full potential, and they are joined freely and actively in genuine community".[48] Crenson argued that neighbourhoods may rightly be regarded as "political societies".[49] John Locke used this term to refer to an agreement by the citizenry "to join and unite into a community for their comfortable, safe, and peaceable living one amongst another, in a secure enjoyment of their properties and a greater security against any that are not of it".[50] For Locke, these groups fill a niche between the anarchy found in the state of nature and the development of formal government. Neighbourhoods assume a political character when they engage in the aggregation and articulation of public sentiment: "The residents who argue about the loudness of a radio – or join together to clean a public alley – are not engaged in merely private business. They are shaping and creating public goods, and for that reason they are performing a kind of political work."[51] Crenson has lamented the fact that neighbourhood politics is often unrecognized in everyday life.[52]

Lessons Learned: The Conditions for Success

Jamaican lawmakers created the PDCs to facilitate more robust citizen participation. The examination of the characteristics and roles of these entities was guided by studies that have investigated examples of other similar thriving and less successful initiatives. Pearce and other scholars, for example, pointed to Porto Alegre, Brazil, as a model for participatory democracy in Latin America. That endeavour benefited from a felicitous confluence of factors. First, Porto Alegre boasts an active civil society, support from political parties for the project with strong linkages between them, a municipality that possesses sufficient resources to sustain the project and a state with similar capacity and political interest in doing so. Second, the community's social indicators are some of the best on the continent; Porto Alegre is a middle-class jurisdiction with high literacy rates.[53] Because only a few areas could meet such lofty criteria, a wide variety of participatory initiatives were surveyed to identify the conditions that have underpinned their success or failure. One such factor is continuing legislative support.

Legislator Support for PDCs

A body of scholarship suggests that legislatures which provide ongoing institutional and infrastructural support for participatory initiatives are more likely to see those efforts succeed than those that do not. Baiocchi's research, for example, echoed Selee and Peruzzotti's findings that participation "work[s] best" when programme designs include civil society as well as political parties as this secures relevance and longevity within the broader political spectrum.[54] For example, Tasso Jereissati and Ciro Gomes, reform governors in the state of Ceará in Brazil between 1986 and 1990, were elected to cut public employee pay in order to, among other things, have additional funds to spend on social services and infrastructure.[55] One of the programmes that benefited from their choice was an award-winning grassroots preventive health programme that led to a 32 per cent decrease in infant mortality in the state in four years, and another was a successful participatory self-housing programme. The effectiveness of these initiatives partly explains why the two reformers generated the highest approval ratings of any governor in Brazil during their tenure.[56]

Sirianni advised that government officials need to train people in how to conduct fair and informed deliberations if the potentially beneficial outcomes of participation are to be fully realized. Following Barber, he argued that not all citizens should be educated to undertake high-capacity tasks, and that some will learn by doing. He also suggested that other less demanding tasks need no training, such as assisting in distributing food to the homeless.[57] Evidence from past initiatives suggests that states would be remiss not to take steps to encourage widespread and diverse forms of citizen engagement.

Opting to engage stakeholders in planning public initiatives offers value for money. Sirianni contended that states can ill afford not to engage in participatory governance. He cited the city of Seattle as an example, where legislators invested US$4.5 million in independent neighbourhood planning groups and hired ten project managers to help build trust among various stakeholders and to vet emerging plans. A subsequent programme evaluation found that without this investment, comprehensive planning would have stalled as a consequence of delay, disruption and legal action, all of which would have resulted in much higher costs for the city, investors and homeowners.[58] This case suggests legislators financially promoting participatory governance reap real financial benefits for the governments they serve. The more supportive an environment, the more likely it appears that the envisioned programme outcomes will materialize. To add to this finding, I examined the level and nature of legislative, for-profit organization and civil society group support for Jamaica's PDCs.

Civil Society and Private Sector Support for PDCs

Civil society groups and for-profit firms must be willing and active participants in the co-production of public goods and the process of citizen engagement for such processes to yield significant public benefits. The authors of *Participatory Development and Empowerment* argued that civil society is expected to promote democratic stability and good governance, as well as encourage the empowerment of those on the margins of society.[59] Gaventa found that nongovernmental groups play several roles in boosting the likelihood of successful participatory initiatives and suggested that their support must be consistent to result in positive outcomes. He contended that such bodies should act as advocates for greater transparency and accountability across the political spectrum, while also serving the needs of society by pressing strategies that might include a shift from confrontational to more conciliatory advocacy approaches.[60] Such involvement does not remove the role and responsibility of the state to support participatory democracy. Instead, it highlights the synergy required among various stakeholders across the political economy to achieve envisioned outcomes for more democratic participation.

Socio-economic Security

Poverty acts as a barrier to individual and group involvement in politics. As Navarro concluded in his study of rubbish recyclers in Porto Alegre, "the combination of the immediate needs for survival and the rigidity of forms of social domination develop a formidable obstacle to enhance spaces of reflection about [their] daily lives".[61] Navarro argued that participatory projects will not survive or succeed unless there is "social emancipation of the poor".[62] This argument has immediate implications for Jamaica and other countries in the region with large numbers of economically impoverished residents. This project examines the structural forces, including economic conditions, shaping Jamaican society and their influence on the work of the PDCs.

Young demonstrated that structural forces are not limited to economic ones. People are often too busy to participate actively in governance. He suggested that most people are not apathetic, but simply otherwise engaged. In his view, this situation is manifest in the limited involvement of otherwise middle-class professors on university boards as well as lower income residents on community councils.[63] Similarly, Stouffer found that most people are too focused on their private needs to spend much time on public concerns. Stouffer asked respondents, "What kind of things do you worry about most?" Of the respondents, 80 per cent answered in terms of personal and family problems, 43 per cent were most worried about economic challenges and 24 per cent pointed to the fear of health issues for themselves or their families.[64] In this study I asked PDC members what motivated them to participate and also discussed with each interviewee the strategies they employed to balance their community involvement with family and other commitments.

Political Culture and History

A country's political culture and history influence the character and possibilities of any participatory process. Leib and He studied China and found that even in that totalitarian nation, there are spaces in which people gather to deliberate in an effort to develop suggestions that can inform policy. They recognized, however, that the goals of the participatory process fit Chinese culture poorly, which has long promoted hierarchy and consensus.[65] Rothschild-Whitt's study similarly revealed that cultures embracing hierarchy as well as non-democratic attitudes and values did not easily adapt to consensual settings.[66] For these reasons, this analysis paid particular attention to the Latin America experience, which was most likely to produce parallels with Jamaica's story, and interrogated the country's culture and political history to understand its influence on present-day participatory governance efforts. The section in this chapter on emancipatory politics explores the role of such activities in carving a space for participatory democracy in Jamaica throughout its evolution. The low levels of social capital in present-day Jamaica, however, may constitute a substantial obstacle to the success of the PDCs, as explored in the next section.

Social Capital and PDCs

Dialogue among various groups is essential to the success of participatory initiatives, according to Sirianni, Chambers, and Martinot and James.[67] Chambers and Martinot and James have observed that the process of engaging different sections of deeply divided societies in dialogue is more unifying than offering those same citizens the opportunity to vote periodically.[68] In contrast, MacKinnon argued that participatory forums are beacons for unproductive meddlers and those eager to boost their egos. He also suggested that those expressing fundamentalist beliefs are unlikely to engage in significant interaction with those not sharing their perspectives. Moreover, MacKinnon argued that meaningful dialogue among citizens with different views is unlikely if they do not already trust each other, and such conversation is also less likely to occur among groups that possess significantly different levels of social influence and power.[69] With these concerns in view, this analysis did not assume the existence of "communities" or citizen capacity to engage in reasoned debate;

instead, the groups were studied to find evidence of the capabilities required to support such interaction and deliberation.

Crenson critiqued the seemingly general acceptance of the existence of "community", noting, "No community can span Donald Trump and New York's homeless."[70] Similarly, Cornwall critiqued Habermas's claim of the possibility of consensus derived from discussions that have occurred under conditions that all at the table are assured an equal say, to make the broader point that assumptions about participatory space often are not manifest in practice. She argued that "entrenched biases [tend to] result in persistent exclusion".[71] Dahl likewise documented that deliberative arenas tend to privilege particular voices and accounts,[72] while Nelson and Wright argued that the term "community" is often invoked by governments, but rarely by citizens.[73] Sirianni and other scholars contended that healthy levels of social trust are therefore necessary if participatory initiatives are to thrive. So important is this element for Sirianni that he urged all governments to invest in building the social capital of their citizenries.[74] Gran, on the other hand, suggested that divisions and distrust within a community could serve actually to bring people into the participatory arena out of concern that their interests not be compromised.[75]

In any case, the "participationist school" of scholars seems largely to overlook how entrenched particular divisions can be in some societies and, in particular, in postcolonial countries, such as Jamaica.[76] Diamond argued that this polarization among groups leads to a diminished capacity for an altruistic understanding among residents and that, in consequence, the overall level of reasonableness of the public conversation declines as well.[77] In light of these arguments, it is difficult not to be concerned about the implications of a 2008 national survey conducted by the University of the West Indies Centre for Leadership and Governance which found that 83.3 per cent of Jamaicans did not trust each other.[78]

In contrast, Muller and Seligson suggested that perhaps too much emphasis is placed on the role of social capital in the sustenance of democracy. They found that Argentina, Portugal and Spain registered substantial increases in their level of democracy from the 1970s to the 1980s despite relatively low interpersonal trust levels of 21 per cent, 28 per cent and 35 per cent, respectively. Similarly, Belgium, France and Italy were able to maintain high levels of stable democracy despite low interpersonal trust levels of 29 per cent, 26 per cent and 27 per cent, respectively.[79] In what may constitute a partial explanation of these findings, Paxton argued that social capital helps to shape democracy and vice versa.[80] It appears that higher trust levels can be a boost to democracy, but they may also be an outcome of its practice. During fieldwork for this study, scholars were asked, in particular, to share their views concerning how Jamaica's social trust levels are influencing the relative success of the nation's PDCs. Having a firm grasp of the importance of social capital and other conditions to the success of the participatory experiment may facilitate the identification and design of appropriate changes in Jamaica's existing policies and programmes.

The Analytical Approach and Jamaica

Tilly offered a useful outline of the potential utility of examining conditions to ensure democratization happens successfully in a society. He contended that "for democratization to develop in any regime, changes must occur in three areas: trust networks, categorical inequality, and autonomous power centers".[81] "Trust networks" refers to the need to eliminate clientelist relationships, and "categorical inequality" implied societies treating different ethnic and religious groups differentially, thereby shaping their life chances accordingly. By "autonomous power centres", he meant military-controlled regimes and similar entities.[82] Several Latin American cases, however, have raised questions about these and other possible preconditions for deepening democracy. The population of Mexico, for example, had direct governance thrust upon it, and El Bosque, Chile, did not eliminate clientelist networks prior to the introduction of participatory governance. Yet, both initiatives resulted in positive steps away from existing anti-democratic and patronage-dominated relationships.[83]

Karl studied several similar scenarios in *Dilemmas of Democratization in Latin America* and pointed to what she took to be a fundamental paradox evident across Latin American democracies.[84] Karl cited Brazil as an example. That nation's route to democracy emerged through a pact among elites, including the military, which ensured room for future bargaining. Uruguay, on the other hand, had no such history of compromise between military and civilian authorities, and at no point did its armed services submit fully to elected officials' control or to diminished prerogatives.[85] Prevailing economic conditions sometimes may also be paradoxical in that times of need, as well as times of plenty, may provide ideal conditions for compromise, depending upon other social factors at play. Over time, elites may come to appreciate aspects of a more open government and choose not to suppress, but to entertain, calls from below for deepening democracy. They also, just as easily, could choose not to do so. Instead of focusing on creating a specific set of conditions, Karl suggested that "democracy [be viewed as] an ongoing process of renewal".[86] With this in mind, this project's predictions will be modest. Its principal contribution lies in offering a rich description of the participatory experience in the PDCs as they operate today.

Emancipatory Politics and Jamaica's History

De Certeau and Scott documented how subalterns often engage in what Scott refers to as "everyday forms of resistance" in pursuit of self-determination. These include foot-dragging, dissimulation, desertion, false compliance, pilfering, feigned ignorance, slander, arson and sabotage.[87] The Jamaican population's historic embrace of tactics geared towards autonomy and the recent introduction of formal participatory governance structures by the state could serve similar purposes. Benjamin, Davis, Brown and other historians have documented how subalterns in Jamaica and across the globe have used the tools at their disposal to combat oppression.[88] Few scenarios could exemplify oppression more self-evidently than slavery and genocide. White Europeans brought approximately 850,000 Africans to Jamaica as slaves to provide labour for their sugar plantations. This number does not include those born in captivity. Africans were not the first to face the violence necessary to maintain white power on the island of Jamaica. Brown has estimated that between sixty thousand and several hundred thousand Taino (indigenous inhabitants) witnessed Columbus's arrival in Jamaica in 1494, yet none were present in 1655 when Britain captured the island from Spain.[89] Shortly thereafter, British planters began reaping the benefits that came with being at the apex of the profitable sociopolitical powerhouse that was the sugar plantation.[90] Slaves remained the majority populace throughout the period of slavery, reaching 94 per cent of the population in 1774.[91] The Jamaican census of 1808 listed 350,000 persons as enslaved.[92] Planters maintained that situation against the continuing resistance of slaves by means of a system of immense and ongoing violence.

Davis explained that flight was a common form of opposition practised by slaves, and their frequent recourse to attempted escape is even more impressive when one considers the horrendous punishment administered if caught. The price of unsuccessful efforts to get away often included branding or the severing of a limb.[93] Continuing attempts to escape slavery, despite the risks involved, provide testimony to individuals' rejection of their condition.[94] Slave owners often dismissed another slave tactic, feigning illness to protest work conditions, as indolence and idleness. Nevertheless, such efforts resulted in real economic costs to growers and there was little the enslaver could do to prevent such actions without risking further breaks in production.[95] The result in practice was that enslaved individuals were able to negotiate many essential attributes of their daily routines.

White control over the black body was not always up for negotiation. Many individuals preferred to die rather than be enslaved and opted to commit suicide. This phenomenon denied whites a return on "the most significant investment of the slave owner".[96] Many people captured in Africa chose to jump into the ocean and drown while undertaking the voyage to the Americas, suggesting that the resistance to white oppression took many forms and occurred at every stage of the enslavement process.

Davis documented that Jamaica had several armed insurrections during the period from 1670 to 1831. Frederick Douglass, on his lecture tours for the abolitionist cause, was always asked why there were so few revolts. His response neatly captured the situation; he observed that slave rebellions were almost always suicidal.[97] The marvel is that they nonetheless happened. The December 1831 Jamaican insurrection stands out because it lasted six weeks and resulted in approximately £154,000 in property damage. Whites killed two thousand enslaved persons in suppressing the revolt. The brutality of the planter's tactics in this incident and the size and long-lived character of this revolt helped usher in Emancipation soon thereafter.[98]

As a practical matter, for the blacks of Jamaica, emancipation from slavery meant they were now free to endure poor wages, then twenty-five cents a day in British territories. Renowned historian Eric Williams described the shift from slavery in Jamaica as "a change from the discipline of the cart whips to the discipline of starvation".[99] Keeping black workers unemployed or employed at very low wages proved an effective method of maintaining the status quo in Jamaica. Whites instituted a successful disciplinary technique in the form of ensuring high land prices that were accompanied by equally inflated tax payments. The general population responded by becoming ever more sophisticated in its forms of resistance.[100] The nation's majority black population illegally occupied vacant lands or purchased small plots to grow bananas. In 1924, Jamaica's director of agriculture contended that the country's banana industry has been "built up by the genius and courage and industry, and capacity of the people. . . . [I]t is the most democratic agricultural industry to be found in the West Indies. . . . [I]t is a fact that the small man in Jamaica is the largest producer in this trade and that it is principally due to him that the banana industry has been built up to what it is today."[101]

In 1936, the Jamaica Commission on Unemployment reported that where peasant cultivation prevailed, there was little extreme hardship.[102] The Jamaican majority's history of engaging in emancipatory political activities prompted the search for "hidden transcripts" or clever tactics aimed at securing self-determination among the PDCs examined in this study. Jamaica's majority has long had to discern ways to survive and circumvent an otherwise oppressive political and economic system through discipline, hard work and shrewdness.

Emancipatory Politics and Jamaica's Culture

In her book *Anansi's Journey: A Story of Jamaican Cultural Resistance*, Marshall neatly captured how emancipatory political action "Anansi tactics" became entwined in Jamaica's culture. Anansi was a mythical "trickster" figure often portrayed as a spider. Originating in West African folklore, Anansi stories were adapted to suit the Jamaican plantation reality. As Levine explained, animal trickster tales "were not clever tales of wish-fulfilment through which slaves could escape the imperatives of their world. They could also be painfully realistic stories which taught the art of surviving and even triumphing in the face of a harsh environment."[103] Anansi stories contain examples of preying on the weak and doing generally whatever it takes to advance one's cause. Marshall situated the debate concerning the utility of such lessons in present-day Jamaica by contending that Anansi narratives are ambiguous for a reason; they require listeners to ponder their values: "Through enabling a reflection on one's moral, philosophical and political outlook and providing scope for a critique of one's socio-political situation, Anansi tales can encourage the use of intelligent means to survive disempowerment."[104]

Former prime minister Edward Seaga (he served from 1980 to 1989) also accepted the presence of Anansi tactics in everyday Jamaican life. When asked at a lecture at Oxford University in 2003 about the possibility that Anansi was now contributing negatively to Jamaica's cultural identity, Seaga declared the following, in line with Gaventa's views on agency and participatory space: "People need to carve a space for themselves, if they have no education, they use their wits and brains for other things. They need to carve a space of their own, something which belongs to them, and using Anansi tactics is the only way they can get it."[105]

Even more importantly, he went further to acknowledge that the use of such tactics is not restricted to the poor. The former prime minister explained that while those who want to eliminate Anansi from Jamaica's culture are from the upper classes and, "they have privileges and rights, and they don't need to carve themselves a little space; they have space enough – [although] you find that they too use Anansi tactics to get what they want".[106]

Emancipatory politics is accepted across the spectrum of Jamaican society. As such, political elites and citizens from the lowest economic brackets alike can be seen adopting Anansi strategies. One notable difference, however, is that for those on the lower end of the socio-economic ladder in the country, the quest for justice often occurs in the streets by way of roadblocks and demonstrations. As Johnson described, "the street has become the locus of collective struggle and expression for many urban poor. This 'public space par excellence' is where the poor assemble, make friends, earn a living, spend their leisure time and express their discontent."[107] In the same vein, Bernal, McBain and Danielson demonstrated that the threat of withdrawal of political support by Jamaica's poor has prompted the World Bank to delay repeatedly imposing its harshest financial requirements.[108] Politics engages all on the field of play. The use of Anansi tactics sketched here has not automatically resulted in a reversal of the hierarchical socio-economic order.[109] Nonetheless, the existence of such efforts suggests that the general citizenry is willing to confront the highly unequal socio-economic reality they face. One result of that continuing resistance has been governmental provision of more formal spaces to engage in governance (as signified by the PDCs). This turn suggested that to be "thick", the examination of the PDCs had to include an assessment of the application of emancipatory political action/Anansi tactics among the stakeholders studied.

Jamaica's Formal Participatory Space

The introduction of new formal avenues for popular participation through local government reform in Jamaica might very well be little more than a placatory smokescreen. Schoburgh argued that the critical premise of local government in Jamaica has not changed with the advent of the PDCs; these remain nothing more than an extension of the central government.[110] Jamaica's National Advisory Council on Local Government Reform was frank in its 2009 report, which succinctly categorized the extent to which the state's focus on governance at the local level has changed the order of politics in Jamaica: "Notwithstanding the powers granted to local government by law, central government continues to shape the pattern of local government administrative organization and in many cases determine how its functions are carried out."[111] In her analysis of why the Jamaican state embraced PDCs as a central element of local government reform, Schoburgh concluded that legislators did so as a legitimating device.[112] The next section expands on this assessment.

Jamaica's Participatory History

Jamaica enjoys the oldest system of local governments in the Western Hemisphere,[113] although those entities were not at first meant to benefit the general population: "The system [local government] was first established in Jamaica in 1664 on the original Elizabethan parochial model of Vestry and Justices after the English conquest. Unlike in West Africa and India . . . Jamaica's adoption of these imported institutions could be looked upon as a qualified constitutional success."[114]

The Morant Bay Rebellion led to the brief abolition of local government in 1866, but elected local representation was restored in 1886 through the creation of parochial boards. The nation's governing class, however, remained small and dominated by planters working for the benefit of their perceived interests.[115] The country's political leaders dissolved local governments again in the 1980s. In 1984, under the leadership of Edward Seaga, the Jamaica Labour Party (JLP) centralized most of the functions previously enjoyed by local authorities. He argued that the country could not afford the local tier of government. Similar arguments had underpinned the Democratic Labour Party's elimination of local governments in Barbados in 1968.[116] The People's National Party (PNP) in Jamaica campaigned for the restoration of parish-level governance institutions in the country's 1989 general elections, a stance that partly explained its victory over the JLP that year.[117] Jamaica's citizens wanted to play a role in helping to govern the nation at the grassroots level.

The PNP supported both formal and informal participatory programmes directed at both governance and the workforce as early as the 1960s. The party knew from its history and from opinion surveys that substantial numbers of citizens supported such an aspiration.[118] The party, for example, supported local literacy programmes manned by volunteers.[119] In addition, the PNP supported the creation of the National Volunteers Organization, which began operations in June 1965, with a mission of "harnessing and exploiting the skills and talents of those persons who want to help in the development of their country by giving service on a voluntary basis". The National Volunteers Organization benefited from leadership training, and its projects involved residents providing clothes, toys and furniture to those in need.[120] In the 1970s, the PNP introduced "workers participation" to the private sector. This arrangement allowed for limited employee input into management decisions, a situation that had never existed before. Carlene Edie declared that workers gained a voice through trade unions and that their organizing principles evolved to include "participative management, shared ownership and worker representation at high levels of business policy formulation".[121] These initiatives continue today, largely due to external (foreign) financing.

Financial assistance from international financial institutions initially enabled and continues to support Jamaica's shift towards a more participatory approach to governance.[122] The state was able to launch the Parish Infrastructure Development Project under the leadership of the Local Government Reform Unit in 1994 in part because of a US$20 million grant from the World Bank and US$600,000 grant from Japan. The World Bank's International Development Fund also supplied US$200,000 to support non-governmental partners in efforts to establish a participatory model of local governance, to document best practices in locally initiated development and to develop training materials to promote citizen engagement. The United Nations Development Programme also provided a grant of US$500,000 to facilitate the Preparatory Assistance Programme to help local authorities prepare implement the Parish Infrastructure Development Project. About US$21.3 million in total was spent on the reform programme.[123]

Horace Levy, a research fellow at the Institute of Criminal Justice and Security at the University of the West Indies, Mona campus, offered a summary of Jamaica's evolving engagement with participatory democracy initiatives by highlighting three distinct stages:

> Each [had] initial success followed by a setback. In stage one there was the heady success of Jamaica Welfare, as starting in 1937 it built scores of community councils but was followed by the Hundred Villages failure of the 1960s. Stage two was the revived Community Councils of the 1970s with plans of linkage to Parish Councils, followed in the next decade by a defoliation of the Parish Councils themselves. The 1990s and 2000s, stage three, brought the formation of Parish Development Committees linked to re-strengthened Parish Councils, and the Jamaica Labour Party finally signing on to the process; but the process itself has stagnated, thanks to the power-hugging of the two main political parties and the weak acquiescence of civil society.[124]

No official government report I have been able to locate concurs with his assessment that the present manifestation of decentralized governance structures intended to encourage citizen participation has stagnated, yet those documents do acknowledge areas requiring improvement. Direct observations undertaken for this study can help readers gauge whether the nation's participatory objectives are more rhetoric than substance, as Gaventa argued is too often the reality for many participatory initiatives.[125]

What We Know: Parish Development Committees

Insight into the operations of PDCs for this analysis is limited primarily to government reports, which reveal that the most recent parish development structure was the brainchild of members of the PNP and that it was launched in 1999. PDCs are successors to the Parish Advisory Committees that the government created in January 1995 as part of the nation's local governance reform process. The PDC was a natural outgrowth of that effort, based on Ministry Paper 8/93 (February 1993), which suggested that "a strong and vibrant system of Local Government is essential to attaining a society in which all citizens enjoy real opportunities to fully and directly participate in and contribute to the management and development of their local communities, and by extension, of the nation".[126]

Ten years later, in a fresh iteration of reform, the state issued Ministry Paper 7/03 (February 2003) that instructed local authorities to "create space for the participation and representation of civil society in all Local Government Structures".[127] As cabinet secretary Carlton Davis observed at the time, "Public sector reform is not a matter of choice, but a matter of necessity and survival."[128] Put differently, citizen demands and the nature of Jamaica's governance challenges combined to elicit this political response.[129] This argument is developed further in chapter 4.

Ultimately, any participatory model's legitimacy must be derived from the Jamaican people. PDC authority to exist and function arise from the collective will and decisions of the citizens they serve. Their government-sanctioned charters charge the PDCs to develop programming with the guidance of the SDC. The state expects PDCs to operate as the principal mechanism for facilitating the participation of civil society in local governance and sustainable development processes. In other words, PDC initiatives should complement the work of local authorities, and both should adhere to the national government's principles of good governance.[130] Engagement is one such element, and it involves "a political system in which all people are able to participate in and influence government policy and practice".[131]

In a 2008 report, Keith Miller, a consultant on local government reform to the national government, sketched how participation could work in practice and outlined its anticipated outcomes. Miller's analysis stressed particular elements crucial for PDC success. For the PDCs to function effectively he contended, they must "be inclusive, non-political, non-sectarian and multi-sectoral". The consultant saw these attributes as serving as a corrective to the entrenched political divisions in the country.[132] Miller's report offered recommendations concerning what the PDCs should address going forward, including building social capital among the citizenry, strengthening residents' affinity to their communities, promoting good citizenship, engaging in campaigns for needed shifts in values and attitudes, and providing a pool of professionals/experts to support local development initiatives. He contended that the subvention from the local government department to the PDCs was both inadequate and not particularly secure. Miller also observed that many PDC efforts to the date of his report had been supported by members' personal funds, which he argued was unacceptable for the roles the PDCs are expected to play. Miller contended that government aid should be both formalized and routinized. In addition to receiving public funds, Miller suggested that PDCs be expected to solicit support from local and overseas donors.[133] Osei contended similarly in 2002 that the entire local government reform effort had fallen short of a necessary comprehensiveness.[134] Meanwhile, Miller's report listed several challenges confronting the PDCs that might hinder realization of his recommendations:

1   Not all PDCs are clear on their roles and responsibilities.
2. There is little clarity within and among PDCs concerning their operations, including how leaders are elected.
3. Members of the existing Parish Advisory Committees were not asked to join the new PDCs when these were created and were not formally dissolved or thanked for their prior voluntary service.
4. Agencies expected to be partners in the process were not aware of their roles.
5. The PDCs do not have legal status, which has hampered their activities.[135]

Miller's report did not treat specific PDCs, nor am I aware of the extent of existing groups' (PDCs) impacts or specifically which parishes were then most affected by the challenges he outlined. The role of the PDC on paper seems to conflict with that of the parish council, "Developing communities is what [the parish councillor's] job is all about [and that such] is the standard by which your success as a local government leader will be judged!"[136] This situation led me to be attentive during interviews to the possibility that local authorities might have met the PDCs with scepticism (at least initially), rather than embracing them as partners, based on what appears to be their overlapping aims.

Reports from the SDC underscore the PNP-led administration's continued support for the participatory experiment. This backing is expressed in no small part through the SDC's mandate. The organization's commitment to development saw it engaging in strengthening the participatory governance framework to ensure that all PDCs, DACs and CDCs are given necessary support to address their mandates, including training and access to funding. Since the mid-1990s the SDC has pursued an integrated community development process model that aims to secure national development outcomes. A strategic goal of the SDC is to "improve local governance by building and strengthening Community Service Organisations (CSOs), including Community-Based Organisations, Community Development Committees (CDCs), Development Area Committees (DACs), and Parish Development Committees (PDCs), to engage in dialogue, decisions, and actions that promote development". The SDC aims to deliver "strong and vibrant Parish Development Committees . . . [which] can advocate on behalf of civil society as well as to support the local authority". No definition of what "strong and vibrant" entails appeared in the SDC documents, but it declared 85 per cent of formally established PDCs "active" in 2012.[137] A 2010 assessment by the National Association of Parish

Development Committees (NAPDEC) of all PDCs defined "active" as PDCs that held "regular executive meetings, which were planned and implemented by the members, during the six-month period prior to the assessment".[138]

With this as its evaluative criterion, the 2010 NAPDEC assessment found that eleven PDCs were active, two partially active, and one was inactive. Almost all PDCs indicated some level of support from members of their community, expressed as time, expertise and labour support. Only five PDC leaders could answer "yes", however, to the question of whether they received monetary support from members or the community.[139] Similarly the assessment found that only five PDCs had held an election in 2009, with many citing a lack of funds to do so.[140] This fact immediately raises the issue of how democratic these organizations are. The 2010 report further indicated that twelve of the fourteen PDCs have vision and mission statements while an impressive thirteen had clear objectives, yet not all these documents could be readily produced for review. Of parish council secretary managers, thirteen are PDC members, and twelve mayors were found to be PDC members as well. The report noted, however, that the relationship between PDCs and local authorities "still need(s) work".[141] The majority of PDCs (64 per cent, or nine of fourteen) declared that they kept a minutes book or file and a constitution, but the NAPDEC report's authors identified only one executive member of one PDC who actually possessed a copy of a relevant charter. Moreover, PDC constitutional provisions were often not realized. Just under half of the organizations are registered as legal entities, of any type, which hampers their ability to engage in formal transactions on behalf of their member.[142] With the stress laid on developing partnerships with other local governance entities[143] in every description of PDCs reviewed, surprisingly, only four of the PDCs in the 2010 study indicated having undertaken a complete stakeholder analysis, with several NAPDEC study respondents going further to question the importance and purpose of such a process. Seven, or half, of the PDCs treated in the report and responding could offer a formal menu or list of issues they were seeking to address, while the remaining representatives seemed unclear about the question. In consequence, the report's authors recommended an ongoing training strategy for all PDCs to "build the 'knowledge base' of their leadership".[144]

The authors of the 2010 PDC assessment shared the limitations of their effort. First, they noted that the data collected was immediately outdated and partially inaccurate as no timelines were attached to the questionnaire they administered. The research team did follow up to verify the information collected, but their document also suffered from additional concerns, including PDC members coming to their focus group meetings ill-prepared. The PDCs uniformly suffered from a lack of information management systems as well, making it difficult for those interviewed to provide timely and accurate information to the evaluation team. Overall, as the authors of the report put it, "the main challenge faced during the assessment was the desire of PDC representatives, understandably, to portray a positive image of their organization, which obscured the difficulties the PDCs are facing".[145] The investigation addressed the lack of state financial support for the PDCs, but as was the case with other government reports reviewed, the report did not mention if this was across the board, nor did the authors review the nuances in needs among different groups. To build on the findings of the NAPDEC report, the interviews and observations conducted with stakeholders for this analysis were framed in a way to analyse the resource and other challenges PDCs face today.

In addition, none of the state reports on the PDCs identified the values participants held or what particular development issues they considered important. Gaventa stressed that actors within participatory spaces not only interact but also constantly shift perspectives as they relate to each other, with consequences for the character and outcomes of their engagement for governance.[146] Consequently, knowledge of PDC member values and priorities is important and offers insights into how PDC members are interpreting their mandate and what aspects of development are of greatest interest and focus as they undertake their work. This study has sought to address this gap. It appears that many of the assumptions of participatory theory, such as the strength of dialogue or the inclusive nature of communities, have been accepted without qualification as part of the design of Jamaica's participatory model. This study explores the extent to which these assumptions have been realized in practice and the impact of such efforts on the realization of PDC goals.

Conclusion

This chapter has defined participatory democracy and described variants in its practice. The literature presented offered insights into the conditions (institutional, infrastructural and superstructural) that are required to support participatory initiatives. Together, these constitute the analytical criteria by which the character of Jamaica's PDCs will be examined:

- The assumptions built into the programme's design and their manifestation in practice
- The aims of the PDC as articulated by its stakeholders
- The role of Jamaica's culture and history in shaping the workings of PDCs
- The extent to which the PDCs facilitate dialogue concerning local governance concerns among various groups

- The degree to which citizens want to and are able to participate and if they have a say in determining the activities pursued by PDCs
- The nature of and level of support that Jamaica's legislators have offered to the initiative and the factors that appear to influence their backing
- The types and extent of the strategies employed by stakeholders to overcome challenges to accomplishing PDC goals.

Ultimately, the analysis for this study was based on "analytical categories and conceptual schemes" derived from the literature. A full discussion of the findings appears in chapters 3 and 4.

3.

The People and the Paradigm
of the PDC Process

This chapter examines how stakeholders involved in Jamaica's participatory process interpret the state's expectations. It captures how this understanding is manifest in actions. This study explores the mechanics of the PDC experiment's design as well as the perceived outcomes of their activities in order to identify whether and how the citizenry is engaged and empowered by their involvement with them. This section also describes the people who drive the committee process. Specifically, what beliefs and norms guide members and what motivates them to keep going? How do these values and the actions that result from them contribute to output from the PDCs? This knowledge will facilitate a deeper understanding of the participatory process and shed additional light on factors that influence the relative success or failure of the nation's participatory democratic experiment.

The Participatory Paradigm in Jamaica

The Jamaican government, led by the PNP, conceived and developed PDCs in 1999 to give the nation's citizens a more direct voice in their governance. While each PDC authors its own constitution and member selection process, most have an annual general meeting (AGM) at which individuals are nominated and elected for PDC posts by those in attendance. An elected chairperson heads each PDC, and the structure of each was similar across the cases examined. In addition to the chair, other elected offices often included a vice chairperson, a public relations officer and a treasurer. Larger bodies have deputies for each of these positions. Other posts include the chairpersons of the DACs in the parish. The other members of the team are invited representatives of agencies vital to parish development. These include the Ministers' Fraternal,[1] the National Youth Service, the National Training Agency, the parish's chamber of commerce, the Jamaica Constabulary Force, a representative from the parish council and members of Parliament for the parish. During the study, I did not encounter an elected official at a monthly PDC meeting. A few interviewees indicated that, at best, there is only one member of Parliament in attendance at any PDC meeting (VT032).

The presence of elected officials at meetings notwithstanding, the state has declared that PDCs are necessary to "spearhead plans and initiatives for the orderly, balanced and sustainable development of the parish as a whole, and major towns in particular, and for boosting economic activity and local wealth creation within the parish".[2] In creating the PDCs, the state conceded that citizens at the turn of the millennium felt alienated from governmental "decision-making processes", creating a situation in which citizens "receive very little information about the activities in their parish until implementation is well underway".[3] Officials also acknowledged that their aim for these groups was much more than to create entities to assist in sharing information. Instead, successful PDC implementation hinged on creating an entity with transformative potential: PDCs should engage communities in "programmes and projects which foster community empowerment".[4] Outside of the guidelines analysed in chapter 2, each PDC has free rein in its selection of projects and its choices are informed by the demands of its constituents. This has led to each PDC having a different programme mix and different aims. The following section offers a more complex accounting for the emergence of the PDCs and uses interview responses to explore how stakeholders view these organizations.

The Advent of PDCs: A Complicated History

It is not clear from the literature why this path (the creation of PDCs) was selected above another, but the interviews revealed a more nuanced argument than the "it's in their [the population's] best interest" claim by the Office of the Prime Minister. In this section, I argue that the reasons for the creation of the PDCs and for the entire participatory structure are rather more complicated than the official version suggests. In essence, a web of emancipatory political action, including advocacy by a share of the citizenry and by the Bretton Woods institutions, created an actant underpinning the move to develop Jamaica's participatory democratic experiment.[5] While these claimants did not demand a PDC structure per se, they did advocate for more citizen engagement in Jamaican governance and for efforts to secure that result. For instance, prior to the advent of the PDCs, the government faced several large-scale popular street demonstrations calling for policy and programmatic shifts to support citizen needs more effectively.

Using roadblocks and various other actions, protesters made it clear that they wanted a greater say in matters affecting their lives (VT086; VT126).[6] The 1999 gas riot in Jamaica was particularly memorable. It reflected popular discontent with a state-proposed tax increase on fuel that would likely have led to an increase in the cost of all goods and services. Business and elected leaders alike agreed that the unrest indicated to the government that it could not continue to conduct "business as usual" (VT057).[7] For example, the former prime minister, P.J. Patterson (who served from 1992 to 2006), said, "The new more informed Jamaican, is more demanding than ever to be involved in a meaningful way in shaping his or her destiny."[8]

The same riots pushed two members of Parliament to propose a community-centred employment programme called "Lift Up Jamaica".[9] A former parliamentarian explained why the legislature responded to popular demonstrations with the Lift Up Jamaica initiative: "The PNP recognized that it was disengaged from its political force on the ground, meaning that the smallest of people [ordinary Jamaicans] felt that things were not coming to them" (VT057). Schoburgh, a leading scholar on Jamaica's local government, has argued that there has been an "upsurge of citizen activism in certain localities for more voice in the management of local affairs. [The roots of which lay] in factors such as rapid urbanization of certain local jurisdictions . . . a more educated population and increased level of ownership of residences in localities that increase the level of psychosocial attachment of residents to geographic spaces."[10]

A political scientist I interviewed saw the government's move towards a more participatory governance model as connected to a longer historical trajectory. He argued that the PDCs served as a response to the failure of the authoritarian and state-centric colonial project during which the people were not consulted on matters pertaining to their welfare (VT039).

The creation of the PDCs also facilitated receipt of foreign assistance that would not otherwise be available to the country. As one legislator explained, "with respect to getting support from the NGOs and even funding agencies and so on . . . [PDCs] would be better able to access funding because of the fact that it would be non-political and all of that" (VT086). Many other elected officials and PDC members shared their perception that non-governmental organizations (NGOs) are often able to access international funds that are otherwise off limits to elected representatives, which is an advantage for PDCs relative to central and local government agencies.

International pressure also encouraged creation of the PDCs. As one PDC administrator observed, "I think the government set up the PDCs because they were forced to. Like everything else that happens in this country or most other things, they find themselves in a situation where the overseas agencies are saying, if you don't do this, we are not going to give you any more money" (VT056).

As she explained, that situation emerged when the Jamaican government agreed to the United Nations Agenda 21 plan (a set of guidelines aimed at attaining that body's Millennium Development Goals), and thereby obliged itself to act accordingly. This interviewee also noted that "having signed on to implement it [Agenda 21], . . . they [the government] came up with their local Agenda 21, and [out of] the local Agenda 21, [they] gave birth to the PDCs" (VT056). If her insights are correct, it would suggest that emancipatory political action in Jamaica in recent years was pursued not only by the citizenry but also, in this instance, by the state.

The creation of the PDCs suggests an effort to improve governance by allowing residents to have a say in policy choices and direction beyond selecting a representative to Parliament every five years or to the parish council every three years. As viewed through arguments offered by Barber and other democratic theorists, the participatory experiment in Jamaica may be considered a supplement to representative democracy and also an improvement on that model.[11] A Jamaican political scientist explained that the concept underpinning the PDCs was about "bringing people into the decision-making process; it is about participation, it is about capacity building, it is about community development, it is about decentralization" (VT039). The PDCs simply represent "a better form of governance" (VT042), one Ministry of Local Government and Community Development official said.

As envisioned, PDCs were supposed to be geared towards improving the welfare of community members (VT042). The actual character of their activities is another matter as several stakeholders stated that they believed the PDCs were "created to fail" (VT059; VT012). By this, they seemed to mean that there was no real effort on the part of the state's representatives to ensure the experiment's success. Each of these respondents pointed to how underfunded the PDCs are as evidence of this intention. This perception ties into the observation by the administrator quoted previously (VT056) that the PDCs were a reaction to outside stimuli rather than representing a self-initiated attempt to improve governance. Irrespective of how much weight one accords to these specific factors, it seems clear that a confluence of local and external demands spurred the PDC experiment. Whatever the reasons for their creation, the PDCs constitute another formal channel by which citizens may participate in governance.

The PDC Today: Defining the Participatory Space

The formal reports from the state on how many PDCs are in operation do not match stakeholder accounts. According to government reports, 73 per cent of all PDCs originally created remain in operation today.[12] Many interviewed stakeholders were sceptical of that figure, suggesting that the actual number of functioning groups is much smaller. Stakeholders contended that the surviving organizations' include some that are thriving when judged against their aims.

The following section discusses how those interviewed stakeholders inter-preted the state's expectations of the PDCs and captures how their perspective manifests itself in actions within Jamaica's participatory space. A discussion of the experiment's design as well as examples of the outcomes of PDC activity to date follows that discussion.

PDC Aims: The State's Perspective

Jamaica's PDCs formally embody the definition of participatory democ-racy outlined in chapter 2 in that they uniformly seek to engage citizens in pursuit of the public interest.[13] As de Tocqueville reasoned, inclusive commu-nity participation offers opportunities for individuals to develop democratic habits such as "deciding, electing, consulting, [and] deliberating".[14] This supports Miller's contention that PDCs seek to bring communities together and mobilize local assets, including the incorporation of localized knowledge for problem-solving.[15] In so doing, and to the extent the vision for PDCs is realized, Jamaican society may be said to be moving away from the privatiza-tion and expert primacy embedded in the neoliberal vision of democracy.[16] Government reports concerning the PDCs show that they serve parishes or are situated within a "defined geographical area in which the citizens share common ownership of resources and facilities and regard themselves as having common objectives, interest and needs".[17] This design ensured that each PDC had a narrow and pragmatic geographic focus, which is an orientation that facilitates efficiency.

By legislative design, the PDCs are loosely connected to the Ministry of Local Government and Community Development. The ministry supports their efforts to work closely with local governments by providing partial budgetary support and paying the salary of an office administrator. This financial contri-bution is made available at the state's discretion and usually is provided as a single payment to NAPDEC. Thereafter, allocations are distributed to its active members. An agency of the ministry, the SDC, offers capacity building and provides operating guidance, especially as it pertains to the start-up of a PDC in a parish. As such, the PDCs are partially autonomous organizations that enjoy a degree of independence in charting their specific programmatic course.

The PDC: Semi-Autonomous by Design

This relative autonomy might be a mixed blessing, as in order to facilitate this relative independence, the state considers PDCs to be non-governmental enti-ties. In consequence, the PDCs do not directly report to any state agency, but instead to NAPDEC, an umbrella group that comprises the chairpersons of all the PDCs across the country. Apart from the Portmore Citizens Advisory

Council (PCAC),[18] the PDCs have no government-sanctioned legal standing, leaving most to adopt a formal status on their own. With no prescribed model that each must follow, some PDCs have registered as NGOs or benevolent societies under the Friendly Societies Act (VT038).[19] One ministry official spoke candidly about his frustration with the state's inaction regarding the PDCs' legal status. He spoke fluidly throughout the interview when addressing how valuable the groups are to local government reform, but stuttered when expressing how legal status would support them: "I would not say demand, but, but, but to give the local authority no option, but to include the PDC in the discussions that affect the parish" (VT052). This statement is quite similar to that of a few other interviewees who suggested that the government had intended for PDCs to have significant autonomy over their affairs and play a pivotal role in governance.

PDC Aims and Functions: Stakeholder Perspectives

PDCs are free to do what they think is in the best interests of their parish. As mentioned, even when the legislature provided recommendations for their roles, such as building "social capital . . . strengthening the affinity to one's community, and promoting good citizenship and engaging in campaigns for values and attitudes", they were generally vague.[20] For this reason, no two PDCs are exactly alike in organizational structure or focus. The specific programmatic objectives of each PDC are met through dialogue with its citizenry to identify local needs. The PDCs draw on the resources of their companion parish councils and also use local volunteers to pursue their aims. Each PDC creates its specific constitution, and the common denominator appears to be an acceptance of the state's proposed four-tiered participatory organization structure. This arrangement locates PDCs at the apex, followed by the DACs, then the CDCs and, finally, community-based organizations.

Interviews with stakeholders revealed that the great majority understood the core functions of the PDC as the Jamaican Parliament had outlined them. Almost all interviewees were asked to explain the aims of the PDCs. One senior SDC executive explained in detail what PDCs are and what is expected of them:

> It is a part of the whole local government reform process. The parish development committee, in fact, represents the highest point of civil society participation and the structure you have what is called the participatory governance framework, which starts with the community-based organization. . . . At each part of that structure, the idea is that you need to have the regular citizens; persons without any political (at least demonstrated) political interest, being able to represent themselves and represent their community as well. At the lowest level, you have the community-based organizations. This can be anything, if there is any interest group, citizens association,

youth group and sports clubs. And then now the idea for the citizen involvement side is that these community organizations must now be federated into community development committees, as you know the structure. So a community development committee is a grouping of community-based organizations in a particular geographic location, and the same goes for what you call development area committees, which would be the groupings of the CDCs in another geographic location. So you would find, for example, that where you have a number of communities that are closely related or aligned and that there is a central business district there, then that central business district becomes a developmental area, so you understand that structure. So the parish development committee is simply a coming together of all development area committees within a parish. So the idea is that the PDCs must draw representation, must be comprised of persons from the lower organizations. So the idea then, is that the parish development committee [should] be that body that would parallel the local authorities, that is, the parish council. Parallel does not necessarily mean act as a watchdog. Parallel also means support, being included in subcommittees of the parish councils, attend parish council meetings, support ideas [and] bring representation. . . . A parish development committee by virtue of its composition also gives space for the councillors to be apart, for the members of Parliament [within the parish] to be apart, for businesses to be apart, so it is broad based that all stakeholders within a parish must be able to sit [and] identify germane issues. (VT030)

This interviewee argued that the PDC "supports" the role of the locally elected parish councillors. A virtually identical response was given when I asked the same question of a senior ministry official. He noted that PDCs were created with a view to formalizing and organizing an active citizen's organization that would partner with the elected and administrative arms of all the local authorities to devise operating plans, strategic plans and a vision for the parish (VT038).

The response I received from PDC members concerning their PDC's role was less scripted. Some members simply reduced their organization's functions to catch phrases, such as "we lobby", but there was no mistaking the view among them that their organizations also were chartered to give the citizenry a voice and to act as best they could to assist with any issues presented to them. This is elaborated on next, but there was some confusion.

There was some bewilderment about the relationship of the PDCs to the state, as one office administrator observed, "I am hearing that the PDC is an NGO, and NGO is non-government, and I don't think governments give NGOs a mandate, so if you get the mandate from the government, then the PDC then falls under the Ministry of Local Government" (VT059). As mentioned in chapter 2, there seems to be an overlap of duties between the role of PDCs and the role of parish councils in promoting development, but most stakeholders expressed a collaborative outlook to address this reality. The non-governmental title ascribed to the PDCs seems to reinforce the state's claim that they have operational autonomy. In fact, however, as with the administrator quoted here, they are actually quasi-governmental organizations because of their birth at the behest of the state, financial dependence on the national government and subjection to public accountability claims.

PDC Aims and Values: A Fluid and Shifting Definition

Gaventa argued that organizational efforts to be more inclusive are often more rhetoric than substance.[21] With the members of each PDC determining its aims and values, this study explored the extent to which the PDCs investigated were able to be inclusive, and the forces that prevented them from achieving that goal. The vast majority of the PDC members interviewed eschewed partisan politics and emphasized their interest in improving Jamaica's political system by minimizing divisions across society. Members overwhelmingly recognize and are strong vocal proponents of the unifying principles underpinning participatory democracy. For all members and stakeholders interviewed, this implied in practice that PDCs must be inclusive and non-partisan (VT029). Two stakeholders even described the PDCs as serving as watchdogs over local parish council activities (VT086; VT064). This view was tenable because the PDCs typically enjoy a non-voting seat at local government meetings. For example, the PCAC has the authority to request an audit of its local parish council's finances when its leaders have reason to believe there are financial issues meriting closer consideration. Most group members interviewed, however, did not use the term "watchdog". Perhaps that stance was strategic so as not to appear antagonistic to their local elected representatives.[22]

PDC members tend to stress the economic outcomes of their work above the intrinsic benefits to the country. One member outlined the PDC's responsibilities as involving both community participation and tangible development (VT076). This perspective does not deny the multiple needs of the population, but stipulates that economic needs are highest on the list of issues requiring citizen attention. A 2010 national poll found similarly that only crime had a higher priority than economic improvement among the citizenry.[23] PDC members are keenly aware of the public's priorities. One focus group respondent described his PDC's aims this way: "We know what we want to do to create employment and create wealth" (VT054). Bread-and-butter issues and community development were paramount for a majority of PDC members. One chairman was very specific on this topic in the interview. He outlined his vision for increasing agricultural output by increasing the rearing of rabbits, and he shared plans to expand on the parish's harbour and to boost tourism through new attractions (VT054). A past PDC chairman recalled at length the plans he had to boost education levels and entrepreneurial activities through hosting job and trade fairs. According to these interviewees, these and other similar activities would be accomplished through partnerships with community groups and individuals. The former PDC chairperson acknowledged that the "PDC does not bring the solution", but instead is involved in "bringing together the persons to have discussions towards solutions" (VT067). These approaches highlight one of the PDC's key mandates: providing opportunities aimed at empowering members of the community in ways that allow them to advance their welfare.

The Praxis of Tactics: The Application of Aims

PDC Duty: Embracing the Parish Model(s)

This section addresses what an effective PDC looks like, and who is doing the PDC work. Effectiveness, according to several of stakeholders, involves having a participatory structure in place and meeting targets determined by the PDC's leadership. When asked what an ideal PDC would look like, the responses tracked closely the aims outlined earlier: they should meet and produce reports and attend committees of parish councils (VT038). In addition, members believe that PDCs should have "developed their own plans or programmes, maybe with or without the local authority" (VT038). With regard to the work of the PDCs, most members agreed with the sentiment offered by this interviewee, "year in year out, there are regular elections [for posts within the PDC leadership]; there is recycling of the executive" (VT038). Importantly, the interviewees overwhelmingly pointed to PDCs they considered to be meeting these basic operating responsibilities effectively.

Stakeholders were asked to describe an ideal PDC and list one whose activities they knew came closest to this ideal. Their responses were remarkably similar. One legislator did not hesitate to list the Manchester PDC as close to the ideal and noted, "Portland is not that far behind, and then you have Clarendon after that" (VT107). Most interviewees had a similar short list, reflecting less than half of the PDCs across the country. A legislator said, "I think Manchester is well on its way; St Elizabeth [and] St Catherine to a lesser extent" (VT 086). The NAPDEC representative indicated that a "strong, effective PDC looks like Clarendon, looks like somewhere in Manchester and St Elizabeth" (VT029). The primary reason these individuals cited for selecting these PDCs revolved around their ability to attract funding and to produce tangible developmental projects.

There is a reason more PDCs were not mentioned. According to a senior Ministry of Local Government and Community Development official, only half are operational, which is counter to the official government report[24] (VT030). A former member of Parliament indicated that she felt only Manchester was in operation (VT126). Such is not the case, based on observations as well as discussions with knowledgeable officials, including individuals at NAPDEC, SDC and the Ministry of Local Government and Community Development. Most PDC members accept the fact, however, that few citizens know of their work, and a high percentage of interviewees said that they only came to know of the PDC on which they served when they received an invitation to join it. In short, these organizations may be unintentionally closed spaces that run the risk, as Gaventa warned, of making decisions without the input of the larger population, whatever their formal mandate.[25] To that extent, the PDCs have a way to go before they can truly be regarded as participatory organizations.

PDC Duty: Formally Represent the Citizenry at State Meetings

For the most part, representing the citizenry in the PDCs examined involves attending various legislator-convened meetings on their behalf. PDCs send representatives, at the invitation of their local parish council, to sit on that body's various subcommittees. This includes groups that focus on budget and construction approval. At one meeting, I observed members engaged in playful banter as they sought to secure the best parish council subcommittees on which to sit. In the end, all the volunteers walked away, more or less pleased with their choices, although the chairman had earmarked a particular spot for himself in advance of the options offered to the rest of the group. At no meeting I attended was there a report of what had transpired at a parish council meeting. Several interviewees explained that such subcommittee gatherings are rarely held, or they have never been made aware of when they were held.

PDCs meet monthly and members often refer to these gatherings as management meetings. The core component of PDC work occurs during these sessions. The particulars of those efforts depend on the dynamics of each parish. Members of PDC 2 indicated during interviews that they have a representative serving on the local public accounts committee as well as on other parish council committees, all of which typically meet monthly (VT058).[26] Monthly PDC meetings routinely employ formal procedures, such as those set out in *Robert's Rules of Order*. A typical gathering will involve the chairperson calling the meeting to order followed by consideration of the agenda, which usually involves reading, correcting and accepting the prior gathering's minutes. This action is followed by discussion of new business, after which, the chair adjourns the group, following a formal request and second to do so. Members stated that they often vote on issues, but in the meetings I observed, participants appeared to operate on the basis of an unwritten rule of seeking consensus.

PDC Duties: Hear Views and Gain Consensus

"We aim always for consensus" is how one former chairman described the meeting process (VT076). During four months of observing four PDCs, no issue, except for elections, involved a vote. There was never a need to do so, as all present were generally on the same page regarding matters arising and the way forward. An idea to capitalize on a particular market demand during the 2012 independence and Olympic celebrations at PDC 2, for example, was not only accepted but also eagerly embraced with a committee formed to realize the concept at that very meeting. Dissent among members of each of the four PDCs in question was rare. It was very common instead for the groups to provide a general show of support for ideas and accomplishments. I watched as a report of a particular achievement from a DAC chairman, for example, drew praise. Likewise, a request to support a particular activity by that same leader led to a few follow-up questions and the programme's entry into member note-pads or cellular phones.

In line with best practices for participatory initiatives, there were notice-able attempts by members of two of the four PDCs to soften the hierarchies built into the experiment's design. Almost all the participants I met were intro-duced to me with their very distinct titles, from chairman to vice chairman to public relations officer. Nonetheless, the two more established PDCs (PDC 1 and PDC 2) held their monthly meetings in a circle or around an oval confer-ence table. At one meeting of PDC 1 in particular, the group maintained a circular seating pattern despite a scheduling conflict that required it to gather in a smaller room. It was difficult with this PDC, upon walking in, to deter-mine quickly who was serving as chairperson based on the seating arrange-ment. The DAC meeting I attended was not held in a circle, despite there being more than enough space in the church auditorium to permit that option. The fourth group (PDC 3) followed a similar format, in which executive members occupied a head table, and all others sat in rows facing them. Both the DAC group and PDC 3 organized their gatherings in a way that placed hierarchy on display, with the chairman flanked by administrative persons, vice chairper-sons, public relations officers and office administrator. Meeting attendees sat in neat rows aligned to face the chairperson, who guided the proceedings. Despite the seating arrangement, members actively participated, including those in the back. Participants simply pivoted in their seats as needed to engage colleagues as they spoke. The optics aside, this design did not seem to create notable communication challenges for participants.

PDC Duty: Construct and Maintain Community Networks

PDC members serve as a liaison on behalf of the general citizenry between international and government agencies. PDCs encourage citizens to attend forums where pertinent public information is disseminated. A PDC staff member offered an example where an agency geared towards "public health . . . usually come[s] through us [the PDC] . . . we do the mobilizing, the sensitizing and get the people out" (VT 059). This role arises from the PDC's mandate to advance community welfare.

Members of all four PDCs explained during interviews that they aspire to convene AGMs to obtain direct feedback from the wider community and to gain insight into new frontiers and issues to pursue. I witnessed one such gathering in which a new PDC executive was also elected. The meeting began with thirteen people participating and ended with twenty-five engaged.[27] I also witnessed plans being developed for two other such gatherings, which did not occur until after my observation period ended. The most recent NAPDEC report suggested that the ideal scenario is to ensure that the entire parish population has the opportunity to meet and discuss pertinent issues quarterly, but such frequent gatherings rarely happen due to financial and other constraints involved in advertising such events to all citizens.[28]

PDC Duty: Respond to Citizen Demands

During many visits to PDC offices while in Jamaica and considerable time spent in several conducting interviews with staff, I did not see many citizens walk in to discuss matters nor observe many incoming telephone calls. As discussed earlier, members realize that the majority of the citizenry is not aware of the PDCs, and so the absence of a flurry of activity at PDC offices was not surprising. In fact, some citizens do call on the PDCs as means to attain particular ends. A member of PDC 1 and a member of PDC 3 addressed the roles their organizations play by noting that they serve as a community directory (VT087; VT019). Most PDC members interviewed suggested that their organization should be "in the know" about everything from project funding opportunities to which state agencies are best suited to address a particular community need. One member expressed this sentiment: "they (PDCs) are a body that guides you to getting development done" (VT019). On the matter of function, most PDC stakeholders declared in some way during interviews that their organizations serve as lobby groups that seek to influence elected representatives to rank policy/programme choices in particular ways (VT033; VT112; VT019; VT058).

Although the CDCs or DACs undertake much of the community-oriented work, many issues do filter up to the PDCs. The presence of DAC chairpersons as members of PDCs suggests that local concerns receive PDC attention and consideration. For example, at one gathering, I observed one DAC's request for support from its sister organizations and witnessed the PDC give consideration to information concerning ongoing activities in a particular area. Many issues reach the PDCs in this way as well as through their general meetings and phone calls to their offices. This array of "pipelines" results in PDCs being asked to address diverse issues. One PDC office administrator summarized the range of concerns brought to her group's attention:

> Most of the issues that came out had to do with infrastructure, schools . . . you have persons talking about the high light bill, the frequent cutting off of the light and these things, and the cutting off of equipment . . .; anything that affects the public on a whole, so we call in OUR [Office of Utilities Regulation], and they come in and also the police civilian oversight authority when it had to do with police shooting persons. And at a time a schoolas [youth of high school age] from my scheme was shot in the back, a schoolas, and that was when we had to get them in for a meeting because of the abuse and the relationship with the police. (VT059)

Ordinary citizens, according to several stakeholders, do try to arrange meetings with the authorities about these issues, but usually to no avail. The PDCs serve as their recourse instead.

When pressed for specifics concerning how PDCs actually assist residents, most interviewees' responses were similar to this one: "You set up the meeting with the relevant people . . . we have a community general stakeholder meeting, and we get the relevant persons. Say we have an issue with light, so at a general stakeholder meeting, you will have four reps from OUR [Office of Utilities Regulation], police, it depends on what the issue is, and they have to be there" (VT059).

These gatherings are usually held in the relevant parish's capital or in the community from which the request emerged. The rationale for doing this was clear, according to one respondent: "The PDC from my understanding, and how I am viewing it, is supposed to be the channel through which the citizenry have a voice" (VT059).

Residents from all social classes who find navigating Jamaica's public sector bureaucracy challenging, often call on PDCs to help them negotiate it, according to interviewees across all the PDCs investigated. On receiving such a request from citizens, PDCs then lobby the legislator/bureau on their behalf (VT030; VT112; VT019). Interviewees provided a range of examples of such efforts, including crime-related concerns and water supply disruptions (VT029; VT067). A manager for one PDC observed that his organization often advises residents to engage in self-reliance. His parish has a low water table and therefore often receives complaints about water shortages, and he often counsels citizens to press for the use of community funds and talents to construct additional water storage tanks that would assist all affected (VT056).

As seen in the history of emancipatory politics, positive change, in any direction, can be a slow iterative process. The authors of *Slow Democracy* capture in their text's title the typical pace of participatory initiative implementation.[29] The process through which citizen needs are articulated to PDCs and thereafter shared with public authorities for consideration and action is generally a slow one. At one PDC meeting I attended, a member suggested that the PDC capitalize on a particular market demand across the parish. Participating members unanimously embraced the suggestion and immediately organized a committee to operationalize the idea. Subsequent gatherings in which I participated, however, made no reference to the plans, and the period for which the idea was applicable quickly faded, as did memory of the notion itself. However, that same PDC acted quickly to intervene in a case of alleged police brutality that threatened to lead to social unrest. In general, members of the PDCs studied calibrated their responses according to the perceived urgency of resident claims and concerns.

PDC Duty: Define Success and Its Variants

Despite their frequent role as intermediaries between citizens and their government, clear-cut "wins" for the PDCs investigated were infrequent. Success and failure were each complicated in character. Many members of one PDC pointed to the completion of a road as a success story. However, it took multiple factors at play, rather than PDC actions alone, to explain that particular result; that is, the interviews revealed that several actors perceived their efforts as directly responsible for the outcome. That fact made it clear that multiple stakeholders had contributed in some way to the result. One PDC member noted, for instance, that he led consultations with the community from which calls for a particular road infrastructure were formalized (VT012; VT014), while an SDC representative explained that plans for the roadway were drafted at the home of the member of Parliament representing the area (VT010). She further explained that the leap from a sketch at the member's home to the completed project was only possible because the legislator knew that he had the support of the community as evidenced by discussions within the PDC (VT010). There was no mention of the citizens who made direct complaints to the media or to an elected representative, or the significance of having a member of Parliament with access to adequate funding. It was clear, however, that all were interconnected, and the entire network of actors played roles in this successful outcome (a needed road). In interviews with some of the actors, each took particular pride in this project and in the role they played in bringing it to fruition.

With similar satisfaction as that evinced above, a PDC administrator told another story concerning a successful businesswoman in the parish who had issues with the presence of an illegal massage parlour in her affluent community. In her interview, the manager described how this businesswoman had turned to the PDC for help and how the PDC had assisted her:

> She [the business woman] says she has been writing the parish council for years, and a councillor . . . referred her to the PDC. . . . She says she has been going to the parish council on and off [before] she came to the PDC. It [the massage parlour] was beside her [home]. She wrote another letter to the parish council and copied it to the PDC, [and] the PDC attends council . . . so, every month, we usually have to send a report to council. . . . Usually it's any executive [of the PDC], sometimes, . . . most times I go. . . . I put that in my report, and then I get a report from them. Then the mayor, now, he sent somebody there from the council because frankly she was getting a runaround from the planning unit, so he sent somebody there, and every meeting I went, we would bring it up. I think what happened, she says, it's like the police was to serve them the notice [message to the massage parlour to leave], so they insisted on the police, but what she is saying, that some of the police were patronizing . . . so eventually we were just on it, on it, on it, till they had to close it. (VT087)

In this case, aggrieved citizens, as well as the PDC, used constant lobbying or advocacy to press the government to act, and, in the end, both groups could celebrate the accomplishment of a specific goal.

The representatives of every PDC studied could point to tangible results of their work. One PDC member, based in a parish with a high crime rate, noted the role her group had played in "getting the three warring factions in Star Meadows[30] to come together" (VT058). This allowed other social groups to enter the community to offer social programmes. The interviewee went on to discuss how representatives from the PDC serve the community as mediators of conflict, even among social agencies (VT058). During the focus group interview with PDC 4, a member shared how educational needs across a particular community were met through a partnership with their DAC and a government training agency (VT054). Such actions sometimes lead to external validation for the PDC's role in accomplishing specific tasks. One PDC chairman cited almost five years of efforts which received many prizes, including one for community self-reliance initiatives and another for "best community" (VT

076). The projects included construction of a post office, a local clinic and a library. An archival search of the local newspapers revealed several references to PDC's lobbying the state or engaging in community outreach.[31] Every PDC effort does not, however, result in victory.

PDC Duty: Define Failure and Its Variants

PDC aims are not always attained. In one particular meeting I attended, a representative from the Jamaica Public Service appeared. PDC members invited that individual to field residents' concerns regarding their service. The company in question had been a magnet for protests across the country because of what many considered its unfair billing practices. Well aware of the issues she would face, the representative came prepared and was the consummate professional, from the Blackberry cellular telephone on her waist to the tailored suit she wore. She quickly demonstrated command both of the English language and of the room. She clarified for the audience members how the firm determined their bills and astutely backed every claim she offered with practical examples. Those in attendance left the meeting persuaded that the company was not seeking to target any of them unfairly. Instead, their own choices actually played a large role in determining their costs. These might include, for example, purchasing flat-screen televisions that look good and are save space, but consume more energy. Likewise, refrigerator and light bulb selections similarly shape consumers' power bills. When pressed to explain why certain areas experience frequent power outages, the representative offered to pass the question on to someone in her firm who could address it. She seemed genuinely concerned about the issues raised and judicious in recording citizen complaints. She was not aware, for example, that the toll-free line her company offered only worked for landline telephones, a fact that had led some in the audience to expend money wastefully while on hold while seeking to secure services via their cell phones. She said she would look into it. My sense of the gathering was that the group left feeling that their voices had at least been heard.

Stakeholders sometimes weigh in on the "success/failure" debate concerning the relative effectiveness of the PDCs. An administrator shared an incident in which a frustrated citizen had confronted her about the PDC's seeming inability to serve as a site of "radical possibility"[32] because it was not "delivering" on its promise to help. The manager reported that the resident had commented, "*Mi tiad fi come a* [I am tired of coming to the] PDC, cause how long mi road no fix." The administrator observed that "she [the frustrated citizen] is thinking if she comes to the PDC, she can get her road fixed, but we have been effective in some ways" (VT 087). What stood out for the PDC official were the unreasonable expectations of this citizen who believed that the PDC should not only advocate for her but also ensure that the road was repaired. After some consideration, I believe the citizen's forcefulness was partly a tactic aimed at pushing the PDC to explore all possibilities to attain her desired result. Indeed, her approach had been successful, at least in ensuring that the issue was considered germane by the PDC's leadership, as the administrator not only remembered the incident but also could quote the person verbatim. The undated exchange had a clear impact on the administrator, even though she believed the citizen expected too much from the PDC. A former PDC member and DAC chairman recounted how his group's best efforts to lobby the local parish council had thus far failed to redress a specific community concern:

> I have been president for my area for over twelve years, and we had a situation where a property owner had a property almost in the middle of our community, and I have taken it to parish council. We have sat with them in negotiating, we have petitioned the owners to develop the area or get rid of the forestation. [The issue was raised at the] PDC at monthly meetings . . . and that is many years ago because I have told you about that forum from 2007, and, at that forum, I also made mention and today is 2012. If you should come here right now, you would see the forestation remains the same. The owner died, and we don't know what is next. The parish council has the information; they know about it, they sent somebody to look at it, and right now it is still an eyesore in this community. (VT 068)

According to this interviewee, representatives from the PDC ensured that the authorities were made aware of the issue yet has not attained an acceptable result or even a declaration from the government concerning whether the complaint had any legal foothold, despite several years of petitioning. As with several other interviews across the PDCs, I left this conversation struck by the immense frustration and sense of failure PDC members felt when a particular desired outcome was not achieved.

Advocacy often involves PDC members writing letters to relevant public agency personnel or constantly raising issues at parish council meetings. Members of the PCAC went so far as to take the government to court concerning the state's decision to convert a well-used thoroughfare into a toll road. The case continued by means of a long and expensive legal process until ultimately, the Privy Council, the nation's highest court, considered it. The PCAC lost its legal battle, but government officials learned that when consultation with the citizenry is forgone when making decisions, the ramifications of that choice can be disruptive and costly. This is a lesson Sirianni presented cogently when contending that broad consultation prior to action leads to better results for all stakeholders. Sirianni cited as an example the city of Seattle, which since the early 1990s, decided to invest in independent neighbourhood planning groups and project managers for emerging plans. This investment has paid dividends in the form of fewer delays, disruptions and legal actions; all of which would ultimately cost the city more than the present consultation process.[33]

PDC Duty: Accept Success and Failure

Most stakeholders asserted that they could identify success when they saw it. When asked what accomplishment looks like, the answers were varied and sometimes went beyond specific community concerns to include long-term development aims. This is what a senior ministry official declared: "Manchester [that is, the process was led by the Manchester PDC] . . . developed a full thirty-year strategic plan for the parish post bauxite, urban and regional development. It looked at agriculture, it looked at climate change, it looked at potential economic value, housing, water provision, the whole works" (VT038). The plan is only available in print, but it is used nonetheless by some elected representatives who cite the findings as proof of support for policy preferences. The production of a comprehensive parish plan is essential for any group tasked with promoting development. Ideally, all parishes should have one, but very few do.

The ministry officials interviewed generally appeared dissatisfied with the work being done by the PDCs. As one ministry official said, "I would certainly want to see more assertiveness from the level of those PDCs. I don't think, and the local authorities themselves I don't think, they have been as assertive. They have done a lot but in terms of trying to shape the thing, I think they have not been as forceful" (VT041). NAPDEC officials expressed related sentiments, and even some PDC representatives argued in interviews that their groups had a way to go before they reflected their ideal view of their PDC's possible functions. Indeed, only one PDC's (PDC 1) members consistently self-identified as meeting their entity's aims. That group has a large budget and significant funds courtesy of overseas donors, allowing it to have a secretariat, a manager, consultants and ongoing income-generating ventures.

The overall interview responses pertaining to the perceived successes/failures of the PDCs show that the benefits of pulling the community together through maximizing local resources and expertise remain largely untapped by PDC members.[34] In addition, the very presence of the group doing the work of a watchdog body tends to force representatives to act cautiously. A good example of the invisible benefits of capitalizing on community consensus and "slow democracy", is the outcome of the Portmore toll road issue. Residents of Portmore mounted attempts to have the courts stop the government's conversion of a popular thoroughfare into a fee-only access road.

The interviewees did not view this effort as a successful campaign; in fact, it was recalled as a devastating loss because the government won in court and maintained the right to convert the road in question (VT073). Such represented the worst possible outcome for the aggrieved residents. My view of that process, however, is that it developed a community cognizant of how to unite and mobilize for a common purpose. Most PDC members accepted and reported the visible signs of their success, for example, concerning police brutality, about which residents still have complaints, but report a noticeable reduction in its occurrence (VT080). Democratization is a slow process of social learning typically characterized by incremental change towards social justice attained through dialogue. This "slow democracy" among residents and legislators also pulls the community together around mutual concerns, a benefit impossible to quantify. The takeaway from PDC efforts in this domain is similar to the conclusion reached by Selee and Tulchin in their survey of participatory democracy across Latin America. They noted that success may be said to be occurring as long as there are efforts afoot to deepen democracy and explained that as long as a space is created for democratic participation or a project brings the government closer to the people, no matter how limited those steps, they represent movement in the right direction.[35] PDCs are catalysts in these processes.

Profile of Participants: Who Am I, and Why Am I Here?

Much of what the PDCs have achieved is attributable to the determination of their members. The literature on democracy and participation does not typically offer a profile of those involved in such initiatives. *Slow Democracy, Investing in Democracy*, and *Participatory Planning in the Caribbean* represent an exception to that general rule.[36] There is, however, no such accounting for the PDCs of Jamaica, and this section aims to help fill that gap. By focusing on the "who" of the process, the study could explore how members became involved in their PDCs, as well as identify their values, personalities and motivations. All the interviewees provided valuable insight into the dynamics of the participatory process while also offering puzzle pieces useful in creating a bigger picture understanding of what describes a surviving or thriving PDC within Jamaica's political space.

PDC Composition

Members in every focus group conducted for this study argued that most citizens are apathetic, but they were equally confident that there are a select few individuals always available and willing to serve. This was expected, as Navarro and other scholars have argued that such is often characteristic of participatory engagement.[37] I witnessed that when someone ends their involvement with a PDC, another member acts in their place until replaced, by way of majority vote, at the next general meeting. Succession planning is crucial to the future prospects of any organization, yet there was little evidence of formal succession planning in the PDCs examined. I suspected that such planning as occurred was undertaken informally, with a NAPDEC official confirming my view by noting that there are a faithful few who are informally expected to assume leadership responsibility when a chairperson demits office and that such had been his experience (VT029).

Migration is another factor that affects an individual's availability for a leadership role. Smith argued that rural to urban migration is a longstanding strategy among Jamaicans to improve their economic options, and while the numbers of citizens so engaged may have changed since the 1960s, the tactic has not.[38] Members from both rural parish PDCs in the study explained in interviews that they expect frequent leadership turnovers. As one interviewee expressed, "[this parish] is a rural parish, and the urban drift is one of our realities" (VT052). Across the board, members rally, as needed, to fill vacancies as they emerge.

Invited members, including agency and private sector representatives, were frequently absent from PDC meetings, which led to the conclusion that they were not as committed as the other members to the PDC's agenda. When they did show up, many were often late, and then spent a significant amount of time on their cell phones while the PDC meeting was in session. They were also the most reluctant to volunteer for PDC duties. These members likely had other priorities. The need for sufficient time to devote to the experiment helps to explain why so many PDC leaders are retirees (such was the case for two of the four PDCs studied) with sufficient time to invest in the participatory experiment. A SDC parish manager explained that the business community, in particular, was often not present because they have more pressing matters with to handle (VT081). A senior SDC official opined that a firm's aims rarely intersect with the communal needs that drive the PDCs (VT124). However, there has been a confluence of interest when the business community has sought a PDC's assistance to minimize violent turf battles among gangs within their jurisdictions. These conflicts, if not resolved, would otherwise hurt firms' profit margins (VT124). According to PDC members interviewed, there is limited input from the larger community of citizens concerning the undertakings of PDCs. Chapter 4 will explore the reasons for this apparent apathy. The next section examines how PDC structure and composition affect their effectiveness and chance of thriving.

PDCs: Small and Homogeneous, but Not Conflict-Free

Most PDCs are small and relatively cohesive. As an "invited space" in which various state agencies and community representatives meet, the creators of the PDCs envisioned them as heterogeneous in character. Nevertheless, the everyday management of the groups investigated fell to a small, largely homogeneous, volunteer group. Rothschild-Whitt argued that diversity within groups tends to attract conflict, and hence small like-minded entities are better situated for consensual engagement.[39] It was hard to spot overt antagonism among the members of the PDCs investigated; I witnessed only one hostile disagreement. In the main, all participants seemed to agree on everything, which leads to the danger of groupthink.[40] On the other hand, the prevailing compositional homogeneity of the PDCs seemed to spare the groups serious internal conflicts.

This is not to say that there is an absence of disagreement among PDC members. The interviews suggested that squabbles do occur from time to time, and two former members of one PDC were willing to speak to me concerning them. One mentioned that his chairman needed to leave, as his autocratic leadership style and poor management skills did not facilitate the emergence of new ideas. This interviewee argued that he had conveyed this view to the chairman directly and publicly. He added that he was perturbed about the loss of potential foreign funding because the individual in question was slow to act and seemingly more concerned with retaining his leadership role than with the PDC's development. According to him, the chairman was "a dinosaur" and "more to me a liability than an asset" (VT032). He added that, for the most part, he believed the leader was well intentioned, and he commended his past service to the organization. Indeed, by the interview's close, this individual had scaled back his earlier criticism considerably. He reasoned that the PDC would benefit from additional youthful insight, and he added that such would complement the wisdom of the chairman and in no way should be construed as a threat to him (VT032).

One PDC chairman said that leadership struggles had occurred at the CDC level, but in so stating, he also noted that he has had only limited experience with the CDCs. He noted, however, "power struggles can become very apparent very quickly as to who is running things . . . and things can often break down . . . and then you have this faction that faction, and each one thinks they should be the head of it" (VT111).

Other interviewees spoke of conflicts so severe that they led to contentious meetings and leadership change. I witnessed a few eyes roll when a person took too long on the floor, and I observed a member going on the record with her disgust with the continued absence of another member, leaving her to act in that person's stead. These were largely passive and non-confrontational steps, but perhaps just as effective as direct confrontation might have been. My presence perhaps prevented overt episodes of public disgruntlement with leaders, and the rather short summer agenda left PDCs little worth arguing about in any case.

PDC Values: Principles versus Practice

Participatory democracy implies a diversity of views.[41] The vast majority of PDC members interviewed rejected partisanship and embraced inclusivity as a core value. The website of the Kingston and St Andrew Parish Development Committee, for example, states the organization "embodies a governance mechanism which facilitates both social and financial inclusion through a participatory process that fully incorporates the views of all stakeholders in the democratic process".[42] PDCs, the apogee of Jamaica's formal participatory structure, are, however, dominated by middle-class individuals. The leaders of the PDCs across the fourteen parishes during this study were almost always retired or semi-retired men. Indeed, only one woman was serving as a PDC chairperson during the summer of 2012. The members of PDCs are a relatively homogeneous group in their socio-economic status. They are typically successful at their various careers, and many are considered titans in their particular fields. They do have diverse backgrounds, including hoteliers, large-scale farmers, teachers, lawyers, civil servants, doctors and pastors. The over-representation of the professional classes reflects something of a departure from the advertised mantra of inclusivity. Less easy to observe, but shared in many interviews, is the frequent PDC departure from their claims to be non-political. Chapter 4 will address the challenges involved in attracting a broader spectrum of members and avoiding partisan political influences. The following section discusses the values the PDCs purport to embrace, including being transparent, accountable and inclusive, and the extent to which these exist in practice as evidenced in this study.[43]

PDCs and the Question of Transparency and Accountability

PDC members uniformly embraced principles of accountability and transparency in their interviews, recognizing that these are crucial for meeting standards of good governance. A few PDC representatives spoke to successful financial audits as proof of meeting governmental and public expectations. Those PDCs registered as benevolent associations are subject to annual financial audits, as mandated by the terms of their membership, which might explain why the NAPDEC representative was dismissive of the question concerning how the PDCs ensure transparency and accountability to the general public. That individual explained "the little money that we get . . . we have to hand our annual report in, we are audited enough boss man, we are audited by the government auditors" (VT029). An SDC parish manager remarked that the person who handles that area's PDC finances is "an auditor . . . [the] books [are] well put together" (VT081). I also witnessed member scrutiny of accounting statements provided to the group at one monthly PDC meeting (PDC 2). At that gathering, however, the conversation concerned not how funds were being spent, but the general absence of resources for expenditure.

The PDCs are not laws unto themselves, so to speak, as they are expected to create and then be guided by a constitution. Efforts to see a copy of one of these constitutions proved futile across the board. Indeed, the most recent government study of the PDCs found that even where such a charter was available, its provisions were not always followed.[44] I once witnessed a PDC member questioning how a meeting should finish, to which the chairman explained that he "calls each meeting to an end". This claim was never questioned, which speaks either to how much confidence the individual had in the chairperson or to how little members value the formal rules, as meeting procedures seemed to matter little to stakeholders. Conversely, the most passionate discussions, across all the PDC meetings observed, were those that addressed the more substantive goals of the organizations. I left these meetings with the impression that members did indeed give precedence to fundamental issues.

If the PDCs are not meeting the needs of the population, very few citizens would know of that fact because, as acknowledged by most of the stakeholders interviewed, most Jamaicans are not aware of the PDCs or their functions. Of the four PDCs studied in detail, three had a functioning secretariat with a listed telephone number and someone available during business hours to answer calls. The fourth did not have such means for citizens to contact the organization. This group had restarted operations in the previous year after being dormant for a period and opted not to use office space and communication services provided by the SDC. My contact with that PDC occurred by calling the relevant parish council and obtaining a personal cell phone number for a PDC representative. I did not receive the contact information until I explained that I was conducting research on the group. I left that experience contemplating whether the average citizen would be given the same access.

The observations in this study showed that responsibility for accomplishing the goals of the PDC rests primarily with the PDC members and, to a lesser extent, the Ministry of Local Government and Community Development, the NAPDEC and the SDC. The PDC representatives hold each other accountable by posing questions to the chairperson and each other at their group meetings. Attendees, sometimes including SDC representatives, also review reports they are provided carefully. The single election I witnessed had members nominated on the spot and those present voting by the raising of their hands. In one extreme case, representatives from the Electoral Office of Jamaica oversaw an election. Parish government representatives and a member of Parliament also attended this particular contest as witnesses. When I asked about the need for such high levels of oversight, the SDC officer who described the incident in an interview and who had helped coordinate the process, explained the importance of not only being transparent but also of giving the appearance of transparency to all onlookers (VT053). No other PDC has gone to such lengths, apparently because there was no similar demand in their parishes.

The PDC Has "No Colour" (No Political Affiliation)

PDC members across the board openly declared that they were non-political in their interviews. In almost all the conversations, members expressed their dismay with the present poor economic situation in Jamaica and the negative effects of policy enacted for partisan gain. Almost all stakeholders declared that the PDC model should be non-political, in that member partisan preferences should remain personal, and the body should avoid the divisive actions that remain a lingering feature of Jamaica's social and political life. The PNP's internal review cited partisan activity as a major obstacle to democracy.[45] A few of the legislators were vocal proponents of the PDCs being non-political, stating that "it [the PDC] has to be non-political now to work; it has to serve the interest of the majority" (VT088). Another interviewee described the organization as "a more independent account to representation [in] those areas that the community would want to have going forward without necessarily putting a colour to the programme [colour referring to the colours of a political party]" (VT086). Chapter 4 will address the assumptions embedded in the PDC design in detail. Notwithstanding, the architects of Jamaica's participatory structure appear to have assumed that the well-documented partisan political culture of Jamaica could accommodate their request that these groups, including PDCs, should be non-political. As expected, no PDC member confessed to being a political activist, as such an admission would run counter to the PDC's embraced norm of non-partisanship. One member during a focus group discussion casually mentioned her connection to electoral politics as she addressed a separate issue (VT054). I discovered that some PDC members were also active partisans through interviews with civil servants, former members of Parliament and former PDC representatives. These individuals were interviewed individually, allowing them to share such information without fear that their identities would be divulged.

When the matter of partisanship was raised in the focus groups, the response was always the same: members claimed the ability to overcome personal political inclinations in the interest of the parish. No obvious partisan political decision was made during my observation period, but a few interviewees suggested they do occur. Specialized recruitment of older distinguished members with a long history of service to the community might constitute a tactic employed by a few PDCs to try to minimize the presence of partisan individuals. A 2012 study suggested this might be a necessary strategy considering participation by the average citizens in their parish councils typically involves patronage of some sort.[46] With this ongoing situation, PDCs face a democratic dilemma because of their efforts to be apolitical. One chairman explained that the degree to which access to the PDCs becomes more democratic corresponds with an increased risk that the PDCs will be usurped by higher numbers of partisan activists (VT111). The chairman explained how these advocates could decide simply to form the majority at an AGM and vote for their candidate of choice (VT111). The dilemma extends further when one considers the extent to which the political culture in a particular parish embraces partisan politics. In order to secure support, including financial aid, PDCs might find themselves embracing a particular political party (VT099). An interview with a ministry official suggested that the line can be blurred in instances where PDC members covertly support a party to secure the benefits that come with that alignment, while striving to hold to their non-political mantra (VT038). In essence, this strategy places members in the position of engaging in national politics clothed in emancipatory political garb for the purpose of securing means to reach its established goals.

Gender and Age in the PDC: A Complex Societal Gift

Based on observations and interviews, some ground needs to be covered before women attain parity with men in terms of their roles with the PDCs. As noted previously, women are nearly absent as chairpersons and fill predominantly stereotypical roles within the organizations. Webster argued that there have been advances towards gender equity in Jamaica,[47] but according to Hotchkiss and Moore, when employed in the formal sector, women routinely receive lower remuneration for comparable posts than their male counterparts in the nation.[48] A 2010 study by the International Development Bank showed that women in Jamaica received those lower salaries despite being more educated on average than their male peers.[49] Nettles argued that, in Guyana, gendered societal norms, such as the disproportionate role played by women in the home, influence the scope and nature of their participation in civic life.[50] Women contributed in notable ways to the PDCs studied in this analysis, but the stereotypical roles they generally played could not be ignored. For example, all the office administrators hired by the PDCs studied were women, but it became clear that whatever their job titles, they carried a significant portion of the PDC's responsibilities on their shoulders. In fact, if anything were to get done, the input of the PDC office administrator was critical, if not paramount. One chairman continually called on his PDC's administrator to clarify questions from the audience during monthly meetings, which is indicative of how much of the actual work of the body falls on her shoulders. Her seat was immediately to his right for that purpose. In between answering questions, she was constantly attending to her cell phone, too, as the arrangements and overall success of this meeting were her responsibility. In another parish, the office administrator conceptualized a youth programme for a population she felt was underserved due to partisan politics. The emancipatory tactic she employed involved using the PDC to secure funding as well as volunteer instructors. Her strategy facilitated operationalization of the project. This and other emancipatory actions by women seemed to be crucial to the survival and thriving of the participatory experiment in the PDCs they served.

The complete picture in terms of workload, responsibilities and opportunities to drive the PDC's agenda was often masked by traditional titles. This analysis fits with bridge leadership theory, as advanced by Robnett, which has sought to complicate how analysts regard organizational relationships by moving away from simple linear hierarchies.[51] She was clear that the women profiled in her study were forced to create their own leadership roles "not because they lack leadership experience, but rather because of the social construct of exclusion".[51] The women of the PDCs similarly have used the opportunities within the space provided to carve out for themselves various and shifting roles, including leadership roles, by connecting stakeholders, funders and the community to their PDCs and to each other. These efforts indicate high levels of efficacy among these women. That point was driven home when one office administrator told me that my next correspondence should be addressed to her and went on to note that many make the mistake of contacting the chairman first. Her point, politely made, was that if I wanted anything done, she would make it happen. This proved to be so not only for her PDC, but also across the PDCs studied. In each case, key female employees were critical to PDC operations and success. One chairman spoke of his PDC's administrator as the PDC's connection with the community, and he described another woman volunteer, who had assisted the organization for seven years, as the entity's "anchor" (VT111). The chairman noted, "She has a real passion for the PDC, to help the people, and I really praise God for her because if it was not for her, we would be between a rock and a hard place" (VT111).

The interviews revealed that gender-based challenges were subtly imposed but continually challenged. Nevertheless, gender had an impact on whose opinions carried the most weight. For example, a young woman represented a DAC chairperson at the PDC 1 focus group I conducted. She exuded confidence but was soft-spoken, and while trying to answer my questions was sharply asked by an older member to speak up. In my estimation, the elder could have asked more discreetly, as she had done earlier with an older male member, who she thought was taking up too much talk time (VT018). This young woman did not speak much during the meetings. This case is especially poignant as this occurred at the PDC meeting that reflected the least overt hierarchy, with members seated in a circle, and which had exhibited limited exercise of centralized authority by the executive during meetings. The case suggests that such ordering affected the youth, as well. The observation notes of PDC 1 included that a young man was often the object of the group's jokes. Meanwhile, older members shared no such fate. These cases are particularly significant, as they suggest that subtle ordering might be more pronounced elsewhere. It was in at least one meeting I observed.

At the DAC gathering I observed, no woman had a place on the platform (VT055). At this meeting, a chairman raised his voice at a middle-aged woman, telling her that she was wrong about an issue. She mumbled her disapproval, and her reserved smile indicated to this observer that she was not insulted enough to leave, but displeased enough to complain under her breath. It is hard to decipher whether the chair's action was in fact gender-based, but there was no comparable action concerning men present at that meeting. There was also no other contentious issue. However, this was not the rule, as most members generally agreed on issues and engaged in discussions interjected often with humour or requests for clarity. Later I learned that not all members followed through on signing a letter as agreed at the meeting, which would have addressed the contentious issue in question. This tells me that disagreements are dealt with perhaps by inaction and left for a later date instead of during gatherings, which might lead to disruptions. Mumblings under the breath facilitate a smooth meeting but still send a message that such censuring was not appreciated.

It is no secret that "grey-haired men" generally lead these groups, as one SDC official described the leadership of the PDC (VT030). One Jamaican academic argued that this behaviour is typical and would be in evidence at a council meeting in Blacksburg where I attend school too [such is not the case]. She suggested that there are practical reasons for this situation, as older persons are more likely than their younger cohorts to have the available time, financial resources and levels of expertise to commit to the PDCs (VT110). For these reasons, PDC gatherings reflect an undeclared but accepted older, middle-class space.

PDCs and Class: Where Norms Meet Pragmatism

The leadership core of the PDC is composed of older, middle-class individuals according to my observations and interviews. The general membership of the PDCs is also disproportionately composed of middle-class individuals, including teachers, lawyers, doctors and pastors. It was clear that this was a space for older, educated professionals. The lack of diversity with regard to class is particularly salient as it partly reflects the value system that determines one's positions on the issues faced by the PDC.[52] In this environment, other positions are then easily neglected. It is in situations like these that the needs and concerns of some members are overlooked within spaces that should be committed to inclusiveness. Nathan noted that the norms of a space can make those who are not holders or subscribers of those values uncomfortable and therefore voluntarily stay away.[53] This might partially explain the absence of those outside of a particular class and age range from the PDC.

Gaventa identified scenarios where invisible power is present: "Invisible power shapes the psychological and ideological boundaries of participation. Significant problems and issues are not only kept from the decision-making table, but also from the minds and consciousness of the different players involved. . . . By influencing how individuals think about their place in the world, this level of power shapes people's beliefs, sense of self and acceptance of the status quo."[54]

From the cars in the parking lot, to the titles of the members introduced, to the formality of the dress shirt, to the service club pins on lapels – these, where witnessed, served as props in a performance on the middle-class stage that is the PDC meetings I observed.

The activities at one PDC meeting involved devising sustainable community development project ideas and then writing them on issued sheets of paper that were to be posted on the wall later. The organizers knew that all would be literate, but, even so, education and comfort levels varied. I remember one woman leaning over to me and asking, "Mr PhD, which sentence sounds better?" She was being playful, yet had a real problem. She was working with a colleague, but between them, they could not agree on the wording of a sentence and did not want to post their work up on the wall with a grammatical error. Reflecting on the incident revealed how hard this seemingly innocent exercise would be with a less educated group. For some in the group, it was mildly disconcerting. Further, it is possible that the dress code and the credentials of the members present could serve to intimidate anyone not fitting into a similar mould. One interviewee suggested that someone from the lower socio-economic bracket might simply not be comfortable in the setting (VT052). Most stakeholders interviewed noted that those less well represented in PDCs still have access to the participatory structure at the lower levels or through civil society groups and other persons/institutions connected to the PDCs. Town hall meetings and advertised general assemblies are expected to bring the entire spectrum of the citizenry to the participatory table. My observations, however, confirmed what a few stakeholders were willing to admit in private – this occurs less in practice than theory might suggest it should.

A few PDC discussions I witnessed were undergirded by an implicit acceptance of "right" values that the rest of society would do well to emulate, at least according to the views of those who held those values dear (VT109). The extent of the attachment to such values may serve to restrict deliberation. When middle-class groups lay claim to the "right" values, it is hard to see how dialogue (outside of the dominant epistemic frame) can occur. The participationist construct of "community" must then be more thoroughly examined. As stated earlier, observations in meetings show almost no competing views on societal values. There was, therefore, no need for members to understand or accept a multiplicity of values. Consider the following statement from a member:

> As for me, coming up in a community so to speak – youngest had to be urged to speak up – and where persons now refer *wha gwaan, dawg* [what's happening, friend], and you know all these little things that were . . . outside the norm so to speak . . . to show them that you can be a good person and still be a light, you don't have to stick to the *negative side of things* to be seen. . . . Even so, I am one who wants to be seen, on the other hand, as out of the norm because nowadays everything negative seems to be classed as normal, but we are all called to be leaders, and I want to be that leader. To say that you know *you can be good* and still rise above all the odds despite the setting or the economic status or the, you know, the social development. You know the social part of it seems to be deteriorating, and I want to grasp and to maintain and to show persons that come, what may, you can stand for *what is good and what is right morally and advance*. (VT019; emphasis added)

Here, the speaker's behaviour is not only positive, but allegedly above the behaviour of other members of the community, "a light" to counter the darkness of those who historically are the "others", and considered backward and unenlightened. It might not be a coincidence that he says, "a community", as opposed to "my community", indicating a separation on the basis of beliefs and practices. Instead of a multiplicity of views, PDC members in this setting agreed, through nods of approval as the speaker made the quoted remarks, that there is the correct way and the way yet to be corrected. The value system he embraces in terms of dress and speech are arguably Eurocentric imports by way of Jamaica's colonial experiences, yet other values seemed more reminiscent of the Protestant work ethic as espoused by most Jamaican churches. PDC member efforts to offer a "corrective" is embraced and celebrated broadly as a moral and religious obligation.

In *Political Disagreement*, the authors make the case that there is usually more variety of thought than meets the eye, even among seemingly homogenous bodies.[55] My four-month sojourn in Jamaica did not reveal much diversity. In fact, when the opportunity arose to challenge what seemed to be a habitus of thought among PDC members regarding the economically disadvantaged, it was never challenged.[56] Interviews with stakeholders suggested the same, that there can be no compromise in terms of embracing the values shared by the general population.

In their interviews, a few PDC stakeholders expressed willingness or recounted past efforts to re-evaluate their long-held assumptions. Bailey, Branche and Henry-Lee's study of one participatory engagement effort across low-income communities in Kingston, Jamaica, showed such to be the case. As one participant the authors interviewed explained: "Before I started working with UWI [the University of the West Indies], I thought the people of Drewsland were violent, ignorant, and the people of Southside were even below them. I now see that we are all the same."[57] A PDC chairman I interviewed noted: "Well, I have been involved in community development and my willingness to work with community members: for bringing out the full development of their communities, for clarifying their vision of community development and also to motivate them in their mission to make community development a possibility" (VT076).

This attitude indicates some degree of maturity and a transcending of the group in terms of clarity of roles and openness to accept other views in the community and not just PDC member perspectives. Even with the willingness to legitimize the views of other community members, there still seems to be a separation through the use of "they", which is especially difficult for someone at the helm of a parish-wide participatory network. The response, however, also suggests room for optimism in that members can appreciate the broader community's views over time. This experienced volunteer and recently elected chairman described what he does differently now and why: "We are in poverty, and to move that poverty away from us, we have to give a helping hand" (VT054). Most members indicated that they volunteered to serve because they wanted to aid their communities, but few, as in this instance, indicated doing so more as an assistant on the ground and less like a saviour from above. Such is the nature of empathy, which is crucial for attaining envisioned desired social justice outcomes.[58] Not all values are created equal, however, in that there are functional and legitimate reasons to reject certain values, especially if they do not fit the mission of the PDC.

The Emancipatory Values Dynamic

All the members in the focus groups rejected values that promote short-term unsustainable gains. This rejection of "competing" value systems runs in accordance with the approach of the PDC, as embraced by their members, to promote sustainable development for all. The members are aware that the promotion of illegal activity is detrimental in the long run to all Jamaicans. In so doing, the PDC offers a corrective to the negative forms of Anansi tactics where "everything goes" and where one gets ahead using "any means necessary", even to the detriment of the wider society and one's own future. Pilfering was useful to erode the economic system during slavery, but now it deters investment, leaving those at the lower end of the socio-economic ladder disproportionately affected. The Jamaican political scientist interviewed for this project explained that the mindsets of many members of the economically disadvantaged class need to be reset to accept a participationist and communal approach to social justice as opposed to an individualist view:

> In his mind, he is rebelling against the "Babylon system", a system of injustice that cause that man to have so much land and him not to have any, but at the end of picking that man's orange and having a bellyful of it, what happens? How does he get to be a member of a cooperative that grows oranges? He has never been taught, he has never really thought about it, so communities have to have ways of empowering people that way. (VT039)

This view supports those offered by the PDC members who seek to create a sustainable economy in Jamaica by empowering the poor through changing the perception among them that engaging the informal sector is the only route forward. They seek to empower the citizenry through education about sustainable channels for economic advancement, lobbying for those alternatives as well as taking the lead in their creation. It is not touted, but the PDCs are involved in promoting values that aim to support sustainable development.

Inclusivity versus Efficiency

Dryzek and Beck contended that an inclusive democracy is essential for public life.[59] Efforts to ensure the survival of the PDCs, volunteer and underfunded entities, demanded creativity. Interviews conducted with past and present PDC members captured various strategic efforts to identify persons already possessing the skills needed for the survival of PDCs, as opposed to any or all citizens who might be interested in serving. This strategic recruiting allowed for the emersion of PDCs and aided in their survival as more efficient and homogenous groups with fewer conflicts.[60]

In *Slow Democracy*, Clark and Teachout observed that the architects of participatory initiatives must embrace inefficiency and conflict. This is the cost of matching the participatory process with the moral imperative that all be offered opportunities to engage and reap the benefits of their involvement. As discussed earlier, the downside to exclusion is very expensive and ranges from higher litigation costs to social unrest. In any case, I observed that efficiency is accorded high priority within the ranks of the PDCs. Hence, members of the professional class are sought out to serve. When stakeholders were asked to share the profile of an ideal candidate, on several occasions, the response would be "people like you" (VT086; VT032). These individuals only knew that I was pursuing a PhD, but that seemed to be enough. One PDC member linked one's professional status with being relevant to the PDC and saw this attribute as superior to enjoying popular support within the community:

> A citizen association, for example, could send somebody because he is popular in the citizen association, right, and he is very vociferous in his association, but there are some topics . . . when you really need to discuss it, that individual could be found wanting. But we are hoping that in the mix of expertise that we do have on any particular subject, there should be enough knowledge to come to a logical workable conclusion. An example, how could somebody ask, for example, how this month you [are] paying more light bill than last month, and so on? Those are no-brainer questions . . . right . . . but when you have persons with business skills, and so on, they would pick that up immediately, so they would not ask that no-brainer question. . . . I don't know if you get what I mean? (VT073)

This individual showed little patience for people who are not as educated as he and implied that the absence of formal education suggests low intelligence. If such a view expressed in an interview setting were to find its way into a meeting, it would certainly discourage those who do not "fit" from continuing. One former PDC member saw benefits in diversity, but diversity for this individual meant incorporating a blend of older and younger professionals (VT032). He explained, "Nine out of ten times, you find it in younger persons, people like yourselves [the interviewer] who [are] sometimes more exposed in terms of technology and so on and so forth, you know, and at the same time, somebody like you, past experience like myself . . . can help. . . . So there is always a need to mix the present with the past" (VT032). These responses suggest a strong preference for educated professionals for PDC membership.

This of course is counter to what is expected of the participatory model; the promotion of broad "local knowledge" defined as "knowledge that does not owe its origin, testing, degree of verification, truth, status, or currency to distinctive . . . professional techniques, but rather to common sense causal empiricism, or thoughtful speculation and analysis".[61] Such a mantra expects all citizens to have a role in "co-producing" the public good.[62] After all, as Zueblin stressed, "One can be a citizen only by participation . . . in daily citizenship."[63] Interviewees never gave the impression that the views they expressed were meant to be disparaging, but more so a practical response to assemble the most "competent" team for the job at hand. This version of capacity speaks also to the superstructural issues facing the country where many citizens simply view elected officials as incompetent. The idea among the PDC members interviewed seemed to be to infuse competent individuals into a parallel structure. Similarly, ministry officials speak of raising the "quality" of those who serve on the parish councils through higher pay to suggest that higher education might attract better qualified/competent candidates, all in an attempt to improve the present situation (VT038). If this professionalization of the experiment goes unchallenged, the class-specific make-up of the PDC will be its central, if not defining, feature for some time to come.

Stakeholder Networks and Emancipatory Actions

Fewer than half of the members interviewed were active volunteers who served in community associations, neighbourhood watches and related organizations that had been incorporated by CDCs and DACs. This connection carried them (often through elections) to the PDC. The majority of PDC members interviewed, however, revealed that their presence at the PDCs had been forged primarily by the activism of their local SDC and then by members seeking them out – with a particular profile in mind. One of the mandates of the SDCs is to energize the participatory framework, including PDCs. Specific factors appear to mediate the success of these efforts, including the passion of the team pressing the initiative and the demographic and economic composition of the parish itself. These factors help to explain the extent to which the structure emerges and is sustained in one parish and not in another. An SDC representative described his team's input this way:

> We engaged the key stakeholders in the parish and sensitized them to the organization's aim and objectives, and, from that, we have persons who buy into it. Then we put a skill body in place . . . for about six months, then, after that, we go into an election of officers, but the same committee was given a specific task to put together, like the constitution and to carry out wide sensitization meetings across the parish, to ensure that people are aware to get their input at various levels. (VT081)

This invitation method laid the foundation for the composition and perhaps survival of the overall experiment. The account of this past PDC chairperson of how he became part of the PDC on which he served is very similar to that of many of those interviewed: "I am a community worker; I work within communities from youth clubs all the way up. I got involved because once the SDC officer wanted to get a group [unclear] the DAC and invited me to the meeting, and the next time we met, they elected me as the president for the DAC" (VT037). This chairperson said that he has been a volunteer for the past forty years, an attribute that matches the established profile of individuals PDCs are looking for. Interviews with members revealed that they joined their PDC already possessing leadership skills and understanding the fundaments of managing volunteers due to decades of such service and engagement.

The interviews suggested that these steps were undertaken strategically to ensure a firm foundation for the new experiment. Entering with decades of voluntary experience meant less training requests of the SDC and an increased likelihood of skills transfer to other members. During my fieldwork, I witnessed urgent appeals by SDC members to their broader membership to help in expanding the reach of the PDCs, specifically by creating DACs and CDCs. This indicates an effort to bring the broader population into the process, which, if successful, implies development of a more representative mix of members over time. When the involved individuals were asked about other experiences they have had with volunteerism, in every case, the members shared extensive experience, often with many voluntary organizations. The interviewees had served or currently serve on boards of schools, churches, banks, the Red Cross, in civil society organizations, Kiwanis and the chamber of commerce, to name a few. All these factors make them perfect candidates to help lead a struggling new experiment. The point is that PDC members are some of the most politically efficacious and empowered in the country and are the least in need of learning democracy in the de Tocquevillian sense. It appears that the formula for determining who joins includes recruiting individuals who feel a call to serve, possess the competences necessary to do so and actually receive an invitation to participate. In true tactical fashion, these steps can sometimes be truncated (though not often) if targeted individuals do not have adequate finances to fund the expenses of their participation.

The PDCs for the most part actively seek leaders and to some extent members who are influential and have sufficiently deep pockets to help support their operations financially. One former chairman stated so candidly, whereas others sometimes only reluctantly admitted that one must have a motor vehicle and enough personal funds to serve effectively (VT099). Almost every member interviewed noted that they have had to fund PDC activities out of pocket and could recount sizeable expenses involved in attending related events and meetings in other parishes. Recruiters are without a doubt aware of the nature of PDC responsibilities and cost of volunteer service, and that fact informs their efforts to attract financially independent individuals to participate. The insufficient funding of the experiment serves as an actant here in this formulation; with a broad cross-section of the populace simply not able fiscally to participate even if they wish to do so.

The impression given by one interviewee in particular is that PDC chairpersons are often expected to be more than financially independent, as well as elite, in the society. Again, this is functional. The member explained, "The PDC is a parish body, and if the leader doesn't have a profile, it might impact negatively on the group. You can't just use any and anybody because the leader must be able to attract other key players to get on board" (VT081). That is, choosing a leader goes beyond job competence to consideration of whether that person can appeal to other possible players; be someone who commands the respect of the community as well as political leaders; and who has enough social standing and funds not only to pay for their own petrol to get to meetings but also to help the organization financially as well. Finding the right leaders plays a vital role in ensuring the survival of the experiment.

The PDC: Not All Need Apply

The PDC's mission requires members who are committed to social justice, intrinsically motivated to serve and possess skills beneficial to the experiment. Every person serving on the PDC is expected to contribute in some way; they should be able to design and manage a community project, as well as be versed in best practices in regard to fiduciary and programmatic accountability and transparency. They are expected to fulfil their duties with limited or no oversight or prodding. In short, members need to be not only skilled but also highly motivated.

The complexity of who PDC members are and what they do overlaps. Competence in one area, tied with a passion for service, sometimes manifests as a calling, especially when reinforced as the right thing to do by church and family. Most respondents listed several capacities and attributes as necessary for service including possessing communication skills and being generally resourceful. Some standout comments included "a commitment to enhance community development" (VT054) and being a "critical thinker" (VT032). One PDC participant provided a specific example of this necessary inventiveness: taking advantage of a telecommunication provider's free text message promotion by using it to send reminders to members of meeting times (VT019).

Most PDC members brought the knowledge and skills necessary for their roles with them when they became involved. This comment embodies much of what I heard from multiple interviewees:

I have had training that was very helpful and very facilitating in getting me to understand some of the concepts and some of the needs and aspirations of people. I did a
first degree in urban studies, which looked at various issues as society emerged. . . .
My master's degree . . . [focused] on planning policy and development, and I actually worked abroad in that area for many years, and I was also head of a voluntary
nongovernmental organization. . . . The whole thing came out of a work in progress
always evolving to a different level and always seeing opportunities for clarifying the
vision and putting it into action. (VT076)

This same former PDC chairman described his former team:

Over the years, we have had very interesting people who share the similar vision.
I know one of them, at the time we started, he was the principal of a community
college and very much having community development at heart. I have worked with
people who are very qualified in environmental concerns, people who are very qualified and showed expertise in social development, cultural development, spiritual
development, and, as a result, as a team, we were always able to look at the development of the whole person, not just building things, but we look at the educational,
the emotional, the spiritual, environmental, economic and social. All the areas that
impact on people's lives in the community. (VT076)

This interview suggested that not only specific skills, but particular qualities
are needed to serve on PDCs. There is little light between what you can do and
who you are and that fact makes the character of a potential PDC member very
important. Interviewees across all the PDCs studied suggested that participation demands a particular type of character, one which embodies resilience,
confidence and social conscious. In addition, "you have to be willing to listen to
them [members of the community] to find out exactly what they would like in
their communities" (VT029). Another member expressed that you must "love
people", highlighting the empathetic orientation needed to do the job (VT058).

This blend of skills and character traits seemed particularly important in the
selection of a chairman. The administrator for one parish, during one focus
group, used my question about skills needed to advise the PDC members
present on whom they should elect as the next chair, to outline the skills and
characteristics essential for the post and to emphasize that these were especially significant for these leaders:

We need people who can do projects, persons who can raise funds, some business
person, it's a whole skill set – I am going to send it back to you guys - it's the roles
and structure . . . we need somebody maybe in [unintelligible] somebody who is in
private sector, who can go out there and garner support for the PDC, not maybe
somebody on a nine to five job, who don't have any time, somebody who is doing
their private business but your time is more your own, you can set your time, that

sort of thing. So that is the prerequisite for this chairman we are looking for and that is one of the reason[s] why the meeting . . . it has to [be kept] by September but that is one of the reason[s] we did not rush into it and because this person want it, we say oh right you are the chairman. (VT087)

Apparently, finding the "right" individual means considering the election date as fluid so as to ensure sufficient time to identify a candidate who meets the established criteria. This statement dovetails with that by a former chairman who described how much time leaders must devote to PDC work and suggested that it is best if the PDC is staffed by retirees: "as a pensioner . . . I had the time, and I think that one needs to have the time to go about and do what was . . . it does not fit readily into [what one does with] an occupational job" (VT099). This fusion of skill, character and availability is only useful if members are sufficiently resilient to take on the challenges implicit in it.

A few stakeholders during interviews expressed in some way the need to be determined in order to serve successfully. A former member of Parliament described one PDC chairperson as having the "stick-to-it-ness" needed to rise above the challenges. She particularly lauded his outspokenness, courage and tenacity as essential for working in inner-city environs (VT057). One civil society actor who educates inner-city youth explained why bravery is needed to work with and within inner-city communities. She was awakened once at gunpoint and told to leave the community. She did not leave until sometime later, when her house was firebombed. Over time, it became clear that her good deeds had matured to the point where she was officially a threat to the status quo (VT078).

There were a few cases mentioned in interviews and meetings I observed of persons believing that community leaders, such as those working in the PDCs and at different levels of the participatory process, are benefiting financially from their work. This, these individuals felt, made them a target for unscrupulous individuals. The deciding moment for one particular community worker facing such an allegation/assumption occurred when it was rumoured that the personal motor vehicle she purchased was a gift from a politician: "Jennifer[64] had to get out in the middle of the street one day and shout and carry on at the top of her voice" to show resolve that the rumour was false and needed to be quenched (VT057). The former member of Parliament in question in retelling the story made it clear that she had no role in the purchase of the vehicle in question (VT057).

The PDCs recruitment checklist is broad, as it must meet the objectives and demands of the participatory experiment. This is paramount because failure to act accordingly might negatively affect the experiment's survival. This is particularly crucial for a new PDC as a few stakeholders related that early in the participatory experiment, members possessing immediately useful skills were accorded higher priority for recruitment. These capacities, such as the ability to apply for a grant, are often not possessed by the majority in the community. The following example was given: "Here is where money is. Environmental Foundation of Jamaica has money, but many of the community leadership don't have the capacity to write those programmes, don't have the accounting capabilities, they need to build out that kind of community management skill base, and the PDC needs to take the lead in doing that" (VT057). The tactic of engaging people with skills most suited for community interaction might best be understood through examining the opportunity cost of doing otherwise. Finite resources mean there is limited space for a learning curve.

A former member of Parliament offered an example of such a lesson when she relayed the story of a warder in her constituency who managed a particular community centre. As part of his management style, he always kept the keys to the facility with him. This ultimately stifled community usage of the building: "There was a clear transformation when a person with community development experience and who is employed by a local foundation took over" (VT057). This approach, she explained, was one of openness and inclusion and not of a disciplined guardian, which resulted in centre use increasing exponentially (VT057). These examples from the interviews revealed that the prior experience of stakeholders had prompted them to select experienced persons with track records of successful community engagement for PDC service. The participatory process in Jamaica still has an uneven reliance on technocrats and, as such, perhaps falls short of Borkman's conceptualization of self-help.[65] Members, however, strategically incorporate needed skills for a particular result and a continuing opportunity, and the potential for the transfer of skill sets to other PDC members as well as the rest of the community does exist.

The Takeaway

Generally, there was a high level of expressed and demonstrated efficacy, but when interviewees were pressed, they also shared skills and insights they had gained through participation with the PDC. A few PDC members mentioned, for example, that they acquired new capacities through training workshops offered by the SDC, and those experiences in general had equipped them more fully to write effective grant proposals and to understand and appreciate governance procedures and community needs. One member, who started a community organization before joining the PDC in which she is now engaged, explained how she learned of state funds available for community needs:

> It was a meeting that I was invited to at the SDC office . . . somebody mentioned the funding the MP gets annually, and I did not know about it. When the MP was at our meeting a few weeks ago . . . a lot of persons [were made aware] . . . that this fund was

available so that they could get help for their children to go to school. They had no idea that these things were available. (VT019)

Another noted that there is "a lot of wealth and knowledge that you gain as you go along. Sometimes you meet people of . . . industry and commerce, social, academia . . . who have knowledge in the areas in which you learn from them" (VT064). A young teacher noted an improvement in his confidence levels and an expanded network since engaging the participatory experiment. In a focus group, he explained, without hesitation, that his volunteer work gained him entry into his present profession (VT019). He did not mention the PDC specifically, but the analogy was clear as the question concerned what individuals had gained from their PDC experience. The analytic point to stress is that much of the learning is not obtained simply from prior expertise but also through engagement:

> So it is a learning experience, cause while we may not be at the front and . . . might be a little bit different than the urban centre, the next door neighbour might have different experience so when you go in there and walk on the ground and talk to these people, you learn from them, what are the barriers in there. . . . It is always an experience, it is always a rewarding experience. (VT054)

What the PDC member described is an example of effective communication where "each individual understands the message being transmitted by the other individual"; persuasive communication involves a change of perspective by one party.[66] Effective communication is essential to attaining Barber's idea of democratic discourse. Only through dialogue, Barber argued, can private needs be transformed into communal concerns.[67] This example shows, however, that willingness on all sides of the conversation must be present for such to occur.

Staff Standards

PDCs recruit their paid office staff members with criteria quite similar to those for members. PDC employees are expected to support the survival and thriving of the PDC experiment too. The interviews conducted with PDC staff members revealed a high level of commitment to community development and history of and passion for volunteerism. This is not surprising as the SDC uses similar standards to identify both PDC members and office staff. The profile of PDC staff, as with their members, is beholden to the vision and activism of the SDC in particular, but also to the current members of a particular PDC. Staff member educational levels vary, but most arrive as experienced community organizers and volunteers. One administrator I met had a degree directly related to community development, but what was common in every case among many administrators was a direct connection to the SDC. This is how one manager explained her journey to a PDC. Her trajectory was similar to that of most other staff members I interviewed:

> Initially, I was active in my community, and so I was invited by a SDC representative to participate in some facilitation training that they were doing . . . and then from the training, I was offered a position to do data collection. I didn't take it, but then after they said they wanted to do the profile now, and they wanted organizers, and because I had done the training, I decided to come in and see what it was all about, and I have been here since. (VT056)

PDC office staff members are expected to reflect the qualities of the PDC members as reflected in their passion for service, history of volunteering and pragmatic management skills. A chairman described the PDC office administrator's role this way: "the administrator must have a vision for the PDC and be a volunteer". He added the following to the criteria: "a good organizer who can put it together, and you need some people who can go to the ground and relate to the people . . . have organization skills as well because you are going to have to go out there and keep the CDCs together" (VT111).

This statement suggests that the ideal person must be able to provide a bridging function with the average citizen, which is not an easy feat. Each day, they take on these roles and functions, as they are often the first and only line of contact with the citizenry. These individuals are paid less than their private sector counterparts, but they stay because their commitment to the process lies not with a pay cheque, but with the passion they have for improving their communities.

One administrator, who mentioned several times that she had not been paid in months, explained that she has volunteerism and helping others in her blood, which is why she sticks around. Another administrator could not help but laugh as she described how she became part of the team and her "pay cheque": "When I got involved . . . I was doing some . . . research at SDC, and the parish manager . . . said that she felt that I was the sort of person that could make an impact, so I actually came in as a volunteer, still a volunteer, although I get a little thing [pay cheque]. What I get can't pay me for what I do for the PDC; it is still 90 per cent volunteer for me" (VT087).

This does not mean that all are as committed, but most with whom I interacted were indeed devoted to their work. As one chairman explained of that parish's administrator, "she has been working with us for a couple of years full-time as the PDC administrator, then she went off to get a job, but she still worked with us two afternoons a week" (VT111). In another example, a PDC chairperson explained that sometimes there is no money to pay the staff, and I followed up by asking how such situations are addressed. With a sombre voice, the reply was, "Then we have a conversation" (VT067). This indicates that the individuals involved are willing to push through despite the absence of a pay cheque and also underscores the need for strategic hiring if one is cognizant of this reality. Also crucial to retention efforts and therefore the survival of the experiment is the presence of members who are motivated to serve. It is clear that the tactic of identifying and selecting committed volunteers has paid off in relatively low staff attrition, despite ongoing difficulties.

The PDC and the Question of What Motivates Participation

What motivates an individual to join and stay with a PDC? There is more to the picture than explained thus far. Members are not manipulated into participation, and there is no easy way to delineate their varied motivations for engagement. Members were given the opportunity to share their reasons for joining and continuing with their PDC. These responses provided insight into the motivations of the PDC members interviewed. One chairman noted that for him, joining the development PDC was a strategic matter:

> Well I was invited to be a part of the PDC many, many, years ago; I worked with an organization which is an environmental and development organization . . . as such, we facilitate empowerment of community members to make better decisions among themselves. We had started these councils . . . and their roles would be very similar to the role of the PDC, so we thought rather than having overlapping organizations with the same persons or doing the same thing, why not, um, make it a part of the PDC because we have other concerns, we have other [groups] looking at safe schools, industrial pollution etc., so we thought that merging the citizen association with the PDC made more sense. (VT067)

It is plausible as well that what is not said is that joining the PDC came with some government financial support. All civil society groups I interviewed noted that identifying funding was a major challenge.

Most PDC members emphasized a passion for helping others through voluntary service as the chief motivating factor underpinning their participation. As one volunteer put it, "volunteerism is a bug" that latches on to you (VT058). His statement was followed by nods of agreement and a chorus of "true" from other members of the focus group in which he was participating. This explains why many accepted the invitation to serve and fight through the frustrations that arise with their service, as well as contribute their time, finances and other resources to the effort.

A few members also saw themselves as particularly suited to serve and therefore felt compelled to do so. One PDC chairman described his move from assisting youth clubs and citizens associations to the PDC, for example, as "a natural progression" (VT054). Another observed, "I love that aspect of life; I live to help other people, anyway I can, I love to assist" (VT087). The PDC offered an avenue to channel these passions and competencies. Evidencing an interesting mix of perceived personal and professional responsibility, another interviewee mentioned that they viewed service through the PDC as an extension of their professional obligations, "being a part of the teacher's association, you are called to service, so that is a part of the professional responsibility when you develop schools. In order to develop the schools, you have to develop the community from which the children benefit" (VT054).

Not all scholars see such voluntary efforts as those profiled here as evidence of selflessness. Linden, Hodgson, and Moyo and Ferguson examined the aid industry and concluded, along the lines of the neoclassical paradigm, that offered services are often more suited to the needs of the giver than to those of the recipients.[68] This reality can be found in practice in those cases when NGOs, in particular, have been created to fill personal needs such as boosting self-esteem and actualization among donors and volunteers. There is also a redemptive element to founding such initiatives. The Nobel Prize provides an example of an individual founding an important philanthropy to help offset the effects of the sources of those riches, in this case, explosives.[69] Such arguments, however, seemed not to fit the PDC volunteers I interviewed, as most had endured tremendous emotional and financial sacrifice to keep the concept of the PDC alive. This does not discount, however, that they may have personally gained from serving.

Etzioni has offered another interpretation of the issue of volunteer motives. He contended that people make decisions based on emotions and value judgements, and this can and often is an effective formula for making decisions. He explained further that human beings make decisions within a collective and not as individuals, as assumed by the neoclassical paradigm. Individual choices still exist, according to Etzioni, but within the context of relationships within communities. It is only in such communities, he argued, that one can find the necessary "psychic and social support that . . . is required to sustain decisions free of pressures from the authorities, demagogues, or the mass media".[70] This does not negate self-interest as a factor in human choices, but it does offer a more complex accounting for actions involving several motivations as opposed to a singular explanation. Members must navigate an implicit tension between their personal interests and those of the community they serve. One PDC member captured this dynamic well: "It is simple for me; if you are living in a space . . . in a community, if you mean that community any good, and you want to see change, you have to be involved! There is no two ways about it; you must be involved" (VT058). A few PDC members sought to point out the dangers of not engaging in the process of developing their community and addressed the fear of the alternative to the structure, noting, "the dons [informal community leaders] are the ones who fill that vacuum" (VT107). The vacuum often means individuals finding themselves with limited opportunity for employment or positive engagement, which leads them towards antisocial behaviour. This was not an alternative these PDC members were willing to accept.

PDC membership aids the community as well as participants. Representatives across all the PDCs I examined spoke freely about the personal benefits of service. Most members could point to some benefit of participation, including skills acquired through engagement, as mentioned previously. In addition, many benefited from the opportunity to expand their networks of friendships and business contacts. One administrator used as an example a growing relationship she forged through the PDC with a senator (VT087). Reflecting on that interview, I concluded that such a relationship should serve the purposes of the PDC as well. The "I and We" paradigm suggests members participate both because of the opportunity to network and to ensure that issues that are important to them get addressed. There are also other factors that seem to go unrecognized among participants, including religious beliefs. These were often mentioned in interviews but not overtly stated as a motivator for participation.

Religion and Altruism

From interviews and observing meetings, religion, particularly the Christian ethos, clearly plays a strong role in motivating participation for many PDC members. As mentioned earlier, the PDC is composed predominantly of middle-class individuals. Historically, class status in Jamaica has involved professing the Christian faith. Educated, middle-class individuals went to church while those of lower status groups professed Rastafarianism or some other faith.[71] Christian prayer in schools and at the start of all state ceremonies daily symbolizes and solidifies this fact. The scope of the religious contribution to engagement and democratization is debatable, but there is no doubt that it guides many PDC member world views.

A senior SDC official underscored the importance of religion by stopping me sharply when I began a focus group session with one PDC. This gathering was to occur as the first session of a period of pre-planned PDC meetings. I called the group to order and began explaining the focus group process, only to be reprimanded by the leader who reminded me that prayer starts every session. I had to step aside quickly for that invocation before I began. My field notes immediately had a new category of enquiry: religion. I started paying attention after that to references to faith in my interviews, including the nature of the devotions and opening prayers before each meeting I attended. The

Christian principle of being your "brother's keeper" has been passed down through socialization channels, including the family unit, and is manifest in the present day in the form of voluntary service through the PDC and other related organizations. A DAC chairman's statement was particularly helpful in outlining the robust nature of socialization and, in particular, the religious norms of service to others:

> With me, it is a family thing; it goes back . . . about five, six generations back, we have always been serving. Even if I ran away from it, cause technically I ran away from it, cause it reached a stage where I say, look here, man, this community work thing, I going have to get rid of it, and I was away from it for about like fifteen years, and I am drawn right back into it. You understand? For successive generations, we have had like teachers, pastors, for example, my dad is a parson, my aunt is a parson . . . people have always been coming for help, advice, anybody gets sick in the area. When I was nineteen, this fellow, his daughter was very sick, and his wife ran with her to our house and just threw her in my hand like this and ran screaming out! Poor me at nineteen years old, I did not know what the heck I should do more than get some, um, what you call the thing smelling salts and put against her nose. *Likkle after that mi si har walking. Percy*[72] *she all right? Mi seh yeah man si har here* [Shortly after I saw her walking. Percy is she ok? I said yes, here she is]. You understand? So our family has always been serving; so I guess it's a pull you know. (VT019)

A few others provided similar stories of growing up with Christian parents who spent their lives in service trying to improve the well-being of the community and who provided them examples thereby. These individuals sought to serve not only through religious organizations but also via other civil society organizations. The director of one such organization recalled how her father would invite the poor home after church for dinner, which meant the little they had was now divided among more individuals. She retained the jovial mood she was in as she explained how later in life, she came to understand the lesson and now tries to help the needy in Jamaica's poorest communities. Such norms might help to explain why many join and remain committed to the PDCs, providing the stability needed for the PDCs' survival.

Leaving the PDC

Ending tenure with a PDC is rare. Members tend to leave only when they are constitutionally required to demit office or if the balance of responsibilities that they face shifts significantly. In true emancipatory fashion, we see a shift from one organization to the other when members perceive that the reasons for joining do not seem to be satisfied through their involvement (VT109). Past chairmen tend to stay on as advisers. One member explained that he still plans to serve the PDC as a mentor even though he is retiring from all his obligations. When former members were asked why they had left a PDC, two members noted that they voluntarily withdrew to run for public office. They each observed that keeping their posts in their past PDCs would have been contrary to the norms of the organization. Seeking elected office shows an additional level of competence, if not confidence, gained in part through participation in the PDCs. Neither individual was successful in their bid, but their efforts suggest that PDC service could become a gateway into representational politics in the future. Legislators supportive of participatory democracy have been shown to be effective advocates when in office. The election of legislators philosophically aligned and experienced in participatory democracy should bode well for the future of the experiment.[73] There are also factors at play that make ongoing PDC service a sometimes onerous responsibility. All members across all the PDCs examined indicated high levels of frustration with PDC work, and many were employed by private ventures that competed for their time. One former PDC chairman coming to the end of his term observed that he was looking forward to leaving as his business had begun to suffer because of the amount of time he had been devoting to PDC activities: "I tell you something, I run a business, and I spend more time in [the PDC] and government work than in my business" (VT073). All other members complain about the time spent away from family, yet it appears that only term limits[74] and extraordinary circumstances cause one to leave.

Conclusion

For those involved in PDC activities, a complex blend of passion for the cause, fear of the alternative and personal and professional growth keeps them at the table. The degree and mix to which these factors are met for individual members explains the continued effort to push ahead and sacrifice. Sacrifice in this sense is defined as reduced time with family and business, as well as financial expense in personally bankrolling a share of PDC operations. This loss comes at all levels, in that office staff remain connected to the enterprise even when they are not paid on time with chairmen providing bridge funding to pay bills to keep projects and staff afloat. Keeping the organization in business requires a blend of motivated and dedicated members with the skills necessary to secure survival. The absence of these would put severe strain on any PDC. That said, members possessing these capacities are strategically sought, which gives PDCs a fighting chance of overcoming the challenges they confront while seeking to improve and advance the welfare of the population they serve. These trials and the strategies PDCs employ to overcome them are discussed in the next chapter.

4.

Rowing against the Tide of Assumptions
Testing the Limits of Survival and Creativity

Vignette 4.1	
Me:	Would everyone agree that resources are number one [referring to the list of challenges facing the PDC]?
Focus group:	[Chorus of "yes".]
Me:	Number two?
Focus group:	Cooperation, commitment [chorus and many nods of approval].
Me:	I think we are talking about the same things, right? Getting people to come to meetings and participate?
Focus group:	[Chorus of "yes" responses follows.] (VT019)

The government made several assumptions when it created the PDCs, the first of which is that there would be sufficient funds available for the experiment's maintenance. A decade later, all the PDC leaders with whom I spoke referenced insufficient funding as a key challenge. The government also assumed that if it built a participatory space, the citizenry would come. The response in vignette 4.1 was echoed by most PDC members and stakeholders associated with the four groups studied. Almost all of these interviewees suggested that they view citizen apathy as a grave concern. The third assumption of the experiment's design was that participatory democracy would help bring together a society experiencing an epidemic of distrust[1] undergirded by what scholars have highlighted as the nation's entrenched partisan political culture.[2] The latter challenge was typically not shared forthrightly by my interviewees, but instead was often mentioned in restrained and guarded language and usually only during individual conversations. These individuals pointed to what many of them referred to as "politics" as a threat to the sustainability of the participatory experiment. "Politics" here for the respondents broadly included a lack of support by elected officials because a particular PDC was not "properly politically aligned" (partisan support for the party in power) or as the infiltration by political activists of PDCs to secure proper alignment. When successful, partisan infiltration has generally led to

PDCs being distrusted by their citizenries. If not addressed effectively, these challenges increase the likelihood of the experiment's failure.

This chapter explores the assumptions built into the design of the participatory experiment in Jamaica and explains the ways in which these expectations have not materialized, but instead continue to pose challenges to the success of the PDCs. The strategies PDCs have employed to circumvent or ameliorate these ongoing trials are also highlighted and assessed. It is perhaps most straightforward to begin with the core of the participatory process, its participants. Note that Parliament consulted little with the population prior to passage of the law creating the PDCs. This fact suggests that the programme's designers assumed that not only did the citizens want participatory democracy in this form but also that they were able to engage fully in such an effort (VT126).

Assumption 1: The Citizenry Wants to and Is Able to Participate

Ackee lub fat, ocra lub salt.
(Every man to his taste.)

In the interviews, the overwhelming majority of stakeholders cited citizen apathy as a major challenge to the success of the participatory experiment. This finding echoes a national survey which revealed that only 11.5 per cent of Jamaicans reported even attending a local government meeting in the past twelve months.[3] During a telephone conversation as I sought to secure an interview, a PDC chairman stated frankly that "voluntarism is dead". The chair was referencing the volunteers needed to conduct the business of the PDC. The most obvious question is why this is the case and how it squares with the reality (as discussed in chapter 3) that most of the citizenry are not even aware of the PDC as a formal channel for participation in governance. This section surveys the health of voluntarism in relation to the participatory structure of which the PDCs are a part. It also assesses the measures in place to improve on that condition. The interviews revealed that the extent of volunteerism in any area is a reflection of a host of factors, including the financial and physical ability to do so, the availability and accessibility of structures for participation and the other options available to the citizenry to satisfy the needs expected to be met through participation.

Is Voluntarism Dead?

I often used the chairman's observation that "voluntarism is dead" in interviews to raise the topic. This is how many responded: "It's not dead, but I would say it is on the verge of dying for most persons . . . we still have persons volunteering. It is not dead, but if we are not careful, it might just reach there, but it is not dead" (VT066). Another opined, "It is not dead, but it is diminishing" (VT060). These answers may appear alarming, but they nonetheless reflect the lived experiences of the stakeholders.

Attendance at the PDC meetings I observed was sparse and irregular. Most PDC members stated in the interviews that such is the case at all levels of the participatory process, including CDC meetings, DAC meetings and general stakeholder meetings, which theoretically should involve all citizens in the parish. In a focus group interview with PDC 4, a member stated that at the CDC level, the meetings average "sometimes five, sometimes forty [people]" (VT054). Meetings are usually held after business hours, although I witnessed a general stakeholders meeting, in which the PDC executive was elected, at midday and during the workweek, which automatically barred most working people from attending. The participation numbers represent a serious dilemma, as input by "the people" provides the foundation on which the process is built.

A few members explained during interviews, and my observations confirmed, that absentees rob the body of its functional elements. In particular, absenteeism deprives members of the ability to harness citizen's knowledge, which contributes to community consciousness and ultimately empowerment.[4] Consider as well on a more basic level that individuals at the participatory table serve the function of achieving constitutionally required quorums for a meeting to be held. The first PDC meeting I was scheduled to observe was cancelled for lack of a quorum. In an interview, a PDC chairman explained that low participation levels sometimes hamper PDC elections. As he said, "I was supposed to have been in office for one year, and it rolled over into two years, because we were having some problems with support in terms of persons coming out and supporting the meetings and coming to the AGM to have a proper quorum for persons to vote" (VT066). Low participation has immediate and long-term implications for the PDCs daily functioning and effectiveness. This is even more troubling when/since the absentees are disproportionately individuals from the youth and those of the economically disadvantaged. The reasons for this are explored in this section.

Empirical studies in North America support the claim that people rank their private concerns over public concerns, even for those not in dire financial straits.[5] Such ordering suggests that consistent and engaged participation might always be undertaken by a select few. Young argued that people are simply too busy to engage in governance activities as mentioned earlier. Lane offered a similar verdict. His study of residents in the eastern United States revealed that the majority of respondents were more concerned with earning and other aspects of daily life than with issues pertaining to governance.[6] According to the *Jamaica Survey of Living Conditions*, the percentage of the country's population living in poverty has increased in recent years, from 12.3 per cent in 2008 to 16.5 per cent in 2009 and 19.9 per cent in 2012, meaning that one in five Jamaicans lives in poverty.[7] When there is a daily struggle to subsist, logic explains why citizens would rank ensuring food and other necessities higher than participation in governance. As basic needs become satisfied, there is more likelihood that citizens will find time to engage the state in line with the expectations of the participatory model. For many Jamaicans, their socio-economic reality restricts formal civic engagement and that absence negatively affects the mission of the PDCs.

Dahl highlighted the role of culture in understanding why political apathy is strong in present-day America. He cited consumerism as the principal culprit. His argument has implications for Jamaica as well.[8] As Thomas pointed out, the island's culture is influenced by America's consumerist orientation.[9] Thomas highlighted the importance, however, of a dialectical reading of the relationship between the two nations in that the cultural transfer is not one sided, and many Jamaicans expressed their agency through consumption. She cited Miller's finding that Trinidadians were not passive consumers, but consistently creolized what they consumed.[10] Similarly, Jamaican youth were found to be selecting American brands, but at the same time defining trends. Thomas refers to this as "radical consumerism".[11] To the extent to which Dahl is correct, that politics would be secondary for most citizens to acquiring goods, the apathy that PDC stakeholders describe within Jamaica's formal participatory space is to be expected. Jamaican culture, in this case, ranks private consumption over communal concerns, which implies that a cultural shift might be needed before improved levels of participation are recognized. Several interviewees mentioned that the island's youth are in urgent need of such a shift in their personal orientations.

Many stakeholders singled out Jamaica's youth as particularly politically apathetic. From the interviews, it is clear that this belief is part of an "us" versus "them" dichotomy in which members of the PDCs come to see themselves as fundamentally different from those outside their organizations, which, in many ways, might be an empirically sound perception. Consider this claim: "I think the younger generation has not been trained; these attributes and values have not been filtered down from my generation and the generation before" (VT060). This stakeholder accepts some culpability for present-day values but still argues that the problem is limited to the youth of Jamaica. This assertion obviously makes it harder for the PDC to reach the younger populace to the extent they are approaching them in this negative way.

Very pointed in the "us" versus "them" scenario is the claim that civic or public values were not just absent among the young but also among most of

Jamaica's citizens. The majority of stakeholders explained that individuals were not very concerned with the welfare of their communities. They mentioned, for example, that "some of the people . . . will participate, but some will not because it is a volunteer service" or "most people don't do volunteering unless they are getting a salary" (VT105). The implication is that too many Jamaicans are simply self-serving or too absorbed in their daily lives. To further the point, let me expand on the focus group discussion presented at the start of the chapter:

Vignette 4.2	
Me:	I think we are talking about the same things, right? Getting people to come to meetings and participating?
Focus group:	[Chorus of "yes" responses follows.]
Me:	Why is this the case? Don't they have the drive that you have?
Focus group participant:	They are just not motivated; a lot of times they are not interested in giving. They want to know what they can get. (VT019)

The reason given for the suggested absenteeism/lack of involvement in vignette 4.2 is selfishness on the part of the larger community. This individual also implied that the quality of caring is not found in the "others" of the community. Based on these interviews, PDCs must undertake significant efforts in partnership with the government to demonstrate to the general population the importance of citizens engaging in matters of public concern.

The Poor and Participation

The poor in Jamaica have historically been sidelined from the formal political process. As one member of Parliament explained, "Jamaica has suffered from a centralized government system, and this is the typical behaviour of a centralized government system where it is not the person at the lower end that is contacted or mobilized; they come after" (VT042). Any top-down approach to engaging citizens in governance contributes to the extension of this relationship. This is what some have referred to as "Astroturf", as opposed to a truly bottom-up grassroots movement.

Some PDC members do recognize the factors underpinning the dearth of citizen engagement they lament. These individuals expressed in interviews their recognition that the role of one's economic standing determined the extent to which engagement with the PDCs was possible. The participatory governance literature has documented the impact of finances on participation. The Jamaican situation is no different. Isaac and Heller suggested that efforts to improve the lot of many marginalized groups underscored the success of the Kerala participatory experiment.[12] Lane as well as Campbell, Gurin and Miller very early realized that public activity is generally the remit of the middle and upper classes.[13] Jacobs took a different view, suggesting that democracy is not always harmed by income inequality and arguing instead that group diversity actually promotes democratic vivacity.[14] Locke noted that there would be no need for a political society if there were no distinct and competing interests. Crenson concluded that economic equity might aid the participatory process and that social integration should be promoted.[15] The examples of surviving models show, however, that economic equity is not a necessary precondition for participatory democracy.[16] It appears the PDCs might not be able to rely on economic improvement or a more cohesive society, both of which would contribute positively to greater levels of citizen engagement in matters of governance, but should instead pursue initiatives and activities that would aid in nurturing those particular goals.

The role of economics in driving participation in Jamaica is clear. Many of the nation's poorest stakeholders have concluded that active participation is a luxury they cannot afford (VT066). This is the frank explanation for the absence of the general population at PDC gatherings. One stakeholder explained during an interview, "you can't go tell a hungry man about concepts of governance when him a try mek a hustling on the road [he is trying to make a living in the informal sector], right?" (VT038). Likewise, Crenson's study revealed a clear disconnect in community participation with the poorest residents, in particular, showing a lack of interest in neighbourhood rejuvenation as many of them were struggling to keep their homes.[17] Judging by the complaints among PDC stakeholders in interviews, Jamaica offers a similar experience with impoverished residents seemingly engaging in a cost-benefit analysis, and often concluding that extensive and formal participation is not a worthwhile investment. In other words, financial constraints appear to inhibit the attendance of people at PDC and general stakeholder meetings. A stakeholder explained that the transportation cost alone to the town centre for a meeting is too much for some citizens (VT056). Individuals therefore are not likely to participate if they do not see the tangible value in participating or do not possess the financial ability to or have access to the meeting venue. The extent to which these scenarios exist compromises the participatory process, as the views of these citizens will remain absent from deliberations. These interview responses pertaining to this issue compelled me to dig further to grapple with how social class shaped participation in the study sample. I subsequently presented almost all interviewees with a hypothetical scenario of a handcart man, who symbolizes the economically disadvantaged in society needing help to navigate the bureaucracy of the state. I asked stakeholders if the handcart man is likely to know of or even see the PDC as an advocate.

The Handcart Man

Empty bag cyaa stan' up.
(A hungry man cannot work.)

In 2005 a popular song in Jamaica addressed how a handcart vendor and a woman from a higher-income family found love. The lyrics simply noted common knowledge, that being a handcart man is synonymous with membership among the economically disadvantaged.[18] This awareness allowed me to be comfortable asking the following hypothetical question: Does the handcart man, facing problems in the farmers' market with the authorities, know that the PDC can assist him? No interviewee had a problem responding to this query. Stakeholders quickly knew the issue I was getting at, which was the extent to which poor residents know of and actually engage with the participatory structure's various organizations, including, especially, PDCs. Two issues emerged which will be expanded on in this section. First, those living in poverty find consistent formal participation in the PDC beyond their capacity, and, second, some PDC members appear to be "othering" the poor and de facto limiting their participation in any case.

In recent years, Dahl developed a particularly pessimistic outlook on America's democratic future based on the glaring (and growing) economic divide in the country. He saw inequality as an obstacle to democracy's justice aims. He explained how the "cumulative advantages in power, influence and authority of the more privileged strata may become so great that even if less privileged Americans compose a majority of the citizens, they are unable and perhaps unwilling to make the effort it would require to overcome the forces of inequality arrayed against them".[19] One such manifestation as it pertains to the Jamaican political space it seems are the views of a share of present PDC members concerning the poor.

Many who responded to my query suggested the handcart man was in the wrong, although the situation stipulated simply that he was having problems with the authorities and did not suggest which party was right: "First of all, remember that you have various zoning areas in town centres, and if he wants to park at an area that is not for that, you would have to advise him that you have to abide by the rules and regulations that are set down by the town planners, but if that is not the case, then you make representation on his behalf" (VT054).

This was a hypothetical scenario, and the response could have easily been one where it is assumed that the handcart man was in the right. Nevertheless, the respondent here was clear, that if only the vendor was not in the wrong, help would be forthcoming. Maybe I was reading too much into it. After all, an investigation is the responsible thing to do. When several other interviewees made a similar claim, it became clear that there is an established profile of "those" who are economically disadvantaged. Take, for example, this response: "Somehow the governance structure of the country assumes that people know the law, but I think that our civics has been left out over the last thirty years has not been taught . . . in school or being enforced . . . so one of the fundamental things that we want to do when we are doing our organizational structure, is to begin to educate our members" (VT054). The implication of this interviewee's observation is that it is likely that the handcart man erred. In this view, this was not because he was a bad person per se, but because he was unaware of the rules – a failure of the education system. In this member's view, the solution involves the PDC playing the role of educating and aiding the affected individual. The upshot of this example, however, is that any misconception of a group has the potential to alienate and limit dialogue to the detriment of the experiment.

Stakeholders did note that one is not totally alienated due to one's economic status, as there is often the limited relay of issues from the poor through stakeholders to the PDC for resolution. This is done via direct contact with a PDC member or through civil society actors with connections to the PDC. The handcart man, I was consistently told, is never more than a few "web" connections away from the PDC. This of course depends on the existence of a PDC secretariat as well as active and accessible DACs and CDCs that complete the web of government and civil society actors and serve as connectors to citizens. Fewer connections reduce the likelihood of the handcart man's issues getting to the PDC. Some networks are, therefore, more effective than others. The first-hand account and input of the individual is potentially lost within such a scenario. After hearing statements from other members of a focus group who noted that the handcart man is not likely even to know of the participatory structure, one member objected and noted that, in his development area, the participatory framework is so engrained that he [the handcart man] is very likely see the PDC as advocates:

> We are so known in our community that a man knows who we are, you know. . . . The police were enforcing the other day for persons to move off the street and into the market . . . this guy; it was evening time, and he feels he should not go into the market, and [the handcart man] and the police got in a tussle, and, in the end result, somebody came and call. The police wanted to arrest him so before we reach anywhere else persons interact with us first. We are the first person to get the complaint. (VT058)

This recollection explains the possibilities that exist when participatory facilitating agents function as planned and incorporate many civil society actors. One member pointed out how important the church, specifically the Ministers'

Fraternal, is to a parish in connecting PDCs to their larger communities. Churches dispense much more than Biblical teachings to tie various sections of the society together. Hence, religion or better, religious organizations as social institutions, serve as actants. One SDC representative, however, emphasized the role of the individual as opposed to the strength of the participatory structure. He responded to my question by observing that they "who have raw meat seek fire" (VT081). He sought here to point out that if a sufficient need arises, people will find entities, including the PDCs, to assist them. The multiplicity of choices as determined by accessibility and fit, in terms of the aims of particular groups, directly affects the numbers involved in formal participatory organizations.

The Poor Can Be Choosers

The poorest residents, a few interviews revealed, use many creative channels to address their needs. Crenson outlined how impoverished individuals, having recognized that community organizations were not adequately representing their interests, took matters into their "own hands" and engaged in extensive self-help schemes.[20] The low numbers at formal PDC meetings mask the extent to which the majority of the citizens in Jamaica participate in governance by carving "claimed spaces" for participation.[21] These include directly addressing relevant members of Parliament or civil society organizations, engaging in protests and roadblocks, making calls to daytime talk shows and passing their requests to the PDCs (VT033).[22]

A few stakeholders suggested that many economically disadvantaged citizens are also knowledgeable of which body is best suited to deal with particular problems. Such individuals are largely absent from PDC management, but they do engage the PDCs or their local government when such action accords with their perceived needs. As one PDC member declared, "Well, depending on what his issues are, because there are some things that affect him that would come right under a parish council. If he has a problem with his roadway right away [right of way], if he has a problem with his garbage collection, if he has been affected by how we carry out our enforcement, those issues come directly to the parish council" (VT084). This interviewee's insight suggests that the marginalized are not just grabbing at straws, but are strategic in terms of where they go for help. Direct contact with a parish councillor might mean a speedier route to redress, and, as discussed in chapter 3, the citizenry often strategically uses alternatives as well as parallel channels to boost their chances of success with a particular issue.

The handcart men are sometimes better organized than the PDCs, which they predate (as an organized group) in some cases. Interviewees noted the existence of vendor's associations, of which handcart men are a part: "At the council, there is a committee that deals with the issues relating to the market. I know that because the license vendors have come down, we have had meetings with them to discuss what they are supposed to do . . . I like to call it the handcart franchise" (VT088).

Participation Does Occur

Who have raw meat seek fire.
(When in need, one will seek help.)

Polsby cited the community referenda as evidence that citizens more often mobilize to oppose an issue than to support one.[23] I referenced earlier the situation in Portmore where opposition to state-applied toll charges brought the community together.[24] Interviews conducted with stakeholders revealed that most citizens were willing to participate when they believed the issues in play were germane to their perceived interests. That is to say, residents will engage, as I contended above, when the value of the issue surpasses the value of the money/time they will expend in addressing it. An unspoken but calculated incorporation of opportunity versus cost determined which course of action citizens will take. One scholar explained the logic of this using her personal experience: "A couple years [ago] . . . there was something that I needed, and I remember writing to my member of Congress the first time in my life because I needed help with a government agency. . . . I think that's very natural to not bother till you need something; it is not ideal but very rational" (VT110).

This observation expands on Young's claim that people are too busy to participate in governance. He maintained that people do engage, but on their own terms and in their own time, based on the value they place on the outcome because they are busy.[25]

Abers noted that scholars often gloss over the reasons ordinary people participate. She argued that "deliberative processes are most successful, when initiated, at least, by self-interest". This view is based partly on her study of Porto Alegre where she found that "people are not drawn into the process because they wish to deliberate, but because they wish to get infrastructure for their neighbourhoods to improve their lives".[26] The designers of the successful Porto Alegre programme ensured communities had to mobilize in order to garner the votes that determined the neighbourhoods that would receive first benefits. Kerala in India had a similar experience, in which one person from every household participated, and projects were targeted especially to the poor.[27] On the other hand, Brazil's watershed PDC attracted limited participation, as the general population was not keen on its environmental focus. The project recorded it highest levels of engagement in areas suffering from critical pollution levels. Abers concluded that any experiment desiring to reach a major share of a community's residents must incorporate a design that channels self-interest. The demonstration effect takes over as others are attracted to outcomes. She argued that, over time, "competitive participation" starts the learning process, which continues as individuals gain the capacity to reason and debate within the group.[28] In this view, self-interest provides the necessary adjustments to the calculus that would cause a citizen to engage in governance as opposed to becoming involved in some other activity.

A few of the stakeholders expressed in their interview that when a PDC promotes projects that people want, it attracts and keep members. Maslow found that buy-in happens when locally initiated projects reflect the needs and desires of a community's citizens.[29] When practised, this approach has borne fruit in the Jamaican PDC experiment. Here is how one mayor put it: "When they have activities, people will come out . . . they did a GSAT [Grade Six Achievement Test] class, people are participating; they did a mother and child project, people are there, you know . . . so people come out" (VT088). These exceptions to the "unengaged rule" suggest that a programme's focus does affect participation numbers. Designers of participatory projects are therefore wise to seek citizen input prior to implementation. Doing otherwise might result in low participation numbers that adversely influence the likelihood of success.

As is the case with engaging projects the community wants, having supportive legislators, according to several key stakeholders, is crucial to attaining a thriving participatory initiative. One former member of Parliament recalled a meeting she had with a community where there was not enough room to contain the turnout (VT057). Another former member of Parliament suggested that effective leadership influences participation levels:

> Councillors and the MPs, they have to be willing to go out and make this happen. When I was a MP . . . I never missed citizen association meetings, even if it was to show my face for ten minutes, I even had them work to prepare a development plan, and students of UTECH [University of Technology] worked with them, and we had a document, but the politics of [he pauses], but anyway, we are talking about the PDC. (VT107)

Clearly, supportive legislators can contribute greatly to pulling people into the process despite structural issues, including poverty, which act as a barrier to participation for many.

Attracting Citizens to Deliberating Tables

Members of the PDCs I interviewed reported seeking consistently to address the issue of low citizen participation. Members listed, in interviews, the strategies employed to achieve this, and a few offered strategies that they would not consider, for example, providing remuneration for participating. According to these interviewees, the PDC should not "adopt a policy of this kind where we begin to compensate because once you open that door" (VT041). The implication of these comments was that, cognizant of Jamaica's economic reality, compensation would attract the greedy or needy elements and ultimately degrade democracy to another form of consumer transaction. It is clear that a fundamental condition underpinning the success of the participatory experiment is the economic realities the citizenry confront.

Spreading the Word: Using Old and New Methods

PDC members across all groups studied employ various strategies to ensure that the citizenry knows about the participatory process, especially when meetings are held. A tried and true tactic is to make use of each PDC participant's personal network to get people to the table. This grid constitutes a web of friends and associates within the community. Members reach out using "word of mouth" or by sending a "text to all members" (VT054). One stakeholder with significant experience working in different communities noted that "when you go to a Sethemba[30] [CDC] meeting, first of all you get a text message telling you that there is a meeting. It takes place on a scheduled day, and all the entities that operate programmes within the community are . . . invited to the meeting to provide an update" (VT036). In addition to texts, some PDCs have used town criers and flyers in some cases to advertise meetings. The worrisome participation numbers for the PDCs would likely be still lower if these strategies were not employed.

Offering "Sweeteners" to Boost Participation

A few PDC stakeholders related in interviews that they use "sweeteners" to engage citizens in the participatory process. Many active PDC representatives stated that they recognized the need to keep members involved and that easily completed projects give those engaged a sense of efficacy and accomplishment. Small "completable" projects might not offer a significant contribution to the development agenda, but they support PDC recruitment and retention. Such efforts give those participating a sense that engagement has value and leads to tangible results. This result shifts the scales in the citizen's opportunity cost calculation when deciding whether to participate. One member explained, "people will pay up if there are projects that they will benefit from, if you understand what I am saying" (VT088). The more affluent can afford to wait for long-term outcomes, but people on the margins might need to see an immediate pay-off for their involvement. When asked to explain its success, one of the leaders of one of the PDCs most successful at engaging citizens (PDC 1) argued that it resulted from the specific mix of strategic and functional activities its members have pursued (VT076).

Emancipatory tactics involve using every possible incentive to get people to engage. A former member of Parliament expanded on the strategy of using specific types of initiatives to attract participation by referencing other sweeteners: "It [participatory democracy] needs sweeteners; there has to be things going on, people need to see stuff you understand . . . [the community of] Amani[31] put in place a sport outreach programme where they were tying the community together and cut the barriers . . . so what they use is dominoes, basketball, netball [and] six-a-side football" (VT057).

Another member of Parliament echoed this approach and yet another SDC representative also cited such activities as essential to getting the citizenry involved in governance: "the bottom-up approach is important because you have to start with the community persons" (VT010). This necessary mobilization involves organizing "through various phases. We go through sports right now. We have the SDC 20/20 cricket [competition] going on right, so we get the males, and once you have the cricket team going then the community gravitate around the team, and we use those matches to share sometimes what is happening" (VT010).

Participation "needs encouragement" (VT092). In line with offering sweeteners, at least one scholar and community development activist contended that the work people do in communities needs to be acknowledged formally (VT092). That step motivates those serving to keep going and increases the perceived value of participation for those still on the sidelines. According to Maslow, self-esteem and self-actualization are vital for all humans.[32] This point struck me at the end of an interview with a civil society actor who shared her satisfaction over her selection for an award acknowledging her community service. I then asked if she believed that such honours are necessary to encourage resident involvement, to which she replied affirmatively (VT078). The scholar who noted that participation needed specific encouragement explained that his views on the value of formal recognition for contributors to governance were forged during his on-the-ground experience vetting applicants for the Michael Manley Foundation Award for Community Self-Reliance (VT092). By his account, formal recognition of contributions to the community seems to spur further participation. PDC leaders, however, need always to reflect on both the quality and quantity of citizen engagement that their recruitment efforts attract. Based on the interview data on this topic, it was evident that a few PDC members had come to embrace the idea of the appropriateness of a small yet committed group doing the brunt of the work.

Challenging Assumptions

Another way to put this point is to argue that the PDC stakeholders have real-ized and accepted that an overabundance of participants is not a necessity or an absolute positive. A few members I interviewed also recognized that not all citizens are competent to serve as managers of PDCs, but they could contribute in other ways. This acceptance is pragmatic in that it allows PDC participants to avoid those who may be unprepared or incompetent and the ills that would otherwise attend their engagement. That is, current PDC members strategically search for competent candidates that they deem immediately desirable and useful to attain their goals. MacKinnon emphasized this point by observing that "if participatory democracy should die, the first to give the lethal blows will be the vocal participators who cannot or will not participate effectively".[33] Current PDC members appear to have adopted the view that engagement will generally involve a small number of people who strive to do what they can with what they have while working persistently for even slight improvements in the number of those engaged. While this assumption may be understandable and perhaps defensible, some PDC member views might benefit from higher salience, but they presently go unrecognized, for example, the way many PDC members view the general public.

Unchallenged Assumptions

I did not witness any effort to change the "us" versus "them" culture that perme-ates the organizations I examined because this orientation, to a marked degree, remains invisible to its adherents. PDC participants appear to mature in their views as their interaction with "others" occurs. More experienced stakeholders shared their belief that it is not simply the case that some people do not care, but that they cannot afford to engage. Their interaction with citizens had resulted in empathy that allowed them to see the community's situation through the eyes of others.[34] Greater levels of interaction among PDC leaders and a broad cross-section of citizens could assist the experiment by lowering communica-tion barriers and increasing shared understanding.

To return to a previous analogy, the handcart is a symbol of Jamaican resourcefulness in addressing challenges. This group's creativity, ingenuity and use of available resources literally to make and operate their small businesses serve as an appropriate metaphor for how the general citizenry addresses chal-lenges. Handcart operators skilfully recycle resources to attain desired outcomes. Ideally, to be broadly accepted and fully used, PDCs should undertake a similar effort. That is, the citizenry is not as apathetic as many PDC members think. Instead, the reality is more complex. Individuals are engaged, but just not in the ways that lawmakers envisioned or many members and stakeholders would like. They cannot attend long strategy sessions because many cannot afford the transportation costs to do so or do not have the time available. Many also may not feel comfortable in the formal PDC space. Instead, according to one stakeholder, many participate less directly by monitoring information on PDC activities via their churches (VT057). They also participate strategically by using several other channels of access to government, which do not include the PDC, such as going directly to their member of Parliament. In short, citizens participate, but they do so on their own terms. PDC leaders are aware that "there is a minority of people who attend any organized meeting", so what is crucial is that "the access [remains] there", which depends greatly on available funding (VT052).

Assumption 2: Sufficient, Reliable and Available Resources Would Be Available to the Experiment

Pudden cyaa bake widout fiah.
(You need the right tools for the job.)

A review of documents pertaining to the PDCs, as well as discussions with stakeholders who include former members of Parliament, revealed that a major assumption of the structure's designers was that there would be sufficient funds available to keep the experiment going; however, this has turned out not to be the case. This section discusses how underfunded the initiative is as well as highlights efforts by stakeholders to circumvent and curtail the most negative impacts of that fact. Almost all the PDC members interviewed cited resource limitations as a major obstacle to achieving their organization's goals. At the AGM I attended, the NAPDEC representative made it clear that PDCs should accept the fact that government support will never be enough or consistently available, and they should therefore aim to be financially self-reliant. Ministry officials also endorsed this argument made at the gathering.

The Ever-Tenuous Experiment

Most members and stakeholders interviewed declared openly what the state's 2008 enquiry into the status of the PDCs had highlighted, that current government funding is both unreliable and insufficient.[35] NAPDEC determined that for the experiment to survive, the state's contribution should be at least J$15–17 million annually (VT029). The financial situation of one body was brought to light in one management meeting that I observed during which PDC members spent much more time debating how little money there was to spend and why than on how to expend it. A NAPDEC official lamented, "The government give us J$50,000 a month; *mussi* [must be only] the secretary that can pay for" (VT029). The official went on to note that the absence of sufficient funds has been "our greatest problem, both for NAPDEC and for the PDCs" (VT029).[36] This leader argued further:

> The government promised us twelve million a year, not for the entire parish, for the entire island. . . . Now you can imagine, NAPDEC has to be going right through the entire island, it is a lot of traveling yet they end up getting four or five million, maybe six million for the year? For the year! . . . If you want people to go into pocket and take out money, you are going to be in problem – not sustainable. (VT029)

Limited financial resources ensure that the nation's participatory experiment remains tenuous and also influences the PDC's daily operations: "What you do to a great extent is determined by what you have, not only in terms of manpower resources but financial resources" (VT032). This interviewee offered a list of several needs, including "their own secretariat funding to assist their offices, and that is a challenge. The PDC needs their little office and their little staff and so on to assist them and so on, you know, a stipend to keep going, so that is a challenge" (VT086). Another PDC member mentioned specifically how lack of funds affects participation: "When you have someone volunteering, and you ask them to go into Kingston to attend a meeting on your behalf, and you can't even give them gas to put in their vehicle . . . that's one of the other challenges and then it comes back to the funding" (VT056).

As is the case with attending PDC meetings, almost everything has to be funded out of pocket by members, with the state taking responsibility for the salary of the office administrator only. One member outlined the challenges of maintaining an office under such conditions:

> I can't tell you the dollar figure, but I think we need to have funding. I think right now if the computer goes down, and you have no money, you have to decide to use your personal computer? Do you work with a partner to use their computer? That is not, that makes no sense . . . and we know funding is an issue, but to be constantly worried about how she [the administrator] is going to get paid, that is a little bit diffi-cult for people to work in a situation like that, you know, and it is not like they are getting any big salaries. (VT067)

Another member added to this list, observing that even the simplest tools are not available due to funding restrictions: "If somebody gets burnt out in the community, there needs to be a pool of funds there that people can draw down on you know. When the young persons are there on the corner, and you don't have [a] football to give them. Things like that do have an impact, so you do need the cash to roll out effective programmes" (VT036). The result is not only weaker PDCs, but also an increased potential for even more participatory erosion as existing members become frustrated.

The Frustration Index

A high dissatisfaction level among PDC members explains the lack of passion I observed at some meetings. Staff members expressed a special exasperation when discussing the fact that they often are not paid in a timely way for their work. One PDC employee was very compelling in recounting the many months she went without pay. Her otherwise impeccable English changed to Jamaican Creole as she was unable to maintain her composure as she discussed how close she came to tendering her resignation. As she explained, "The last eight months and *me nu get nu pay* [I have not been paid], and I was a bit like is this a deliberate act for me to get flustered and walk off the job? . . . Yes, I went to that level; I think I reached that level" (VT059).

Members across all the PDCs studied expressed frustrations ranging from citizens' lack of engagement to insufficient funds to their inability to carry out the organization's mandate effectively. It is likely that these concerns partly explain the slow pace with which some matters are carried out, if done at all. Clearly, the extent to which these issues continue to go unaddressed will continue to sap the productive energy of PDC members and employees and hamper their potential effectiveness.

Empty State Coffers

The sense I obtained in my interviews was that government leaders do not view the PDCs as a priority. That said, many PDC members conceded that the economic realities of the country play a role in funding decisions. Members are cognizant of this, and some advocate caution in making financial requests of the government. One participant noted in an interview that "nationally, funds are less than [it was] the year before" (VT073). To expect sufficient funds from a highly indebted state is to dwell in the world of fantasy, a senior ministry staff member declared before suggesting that the PDC he was addressing ranks its needs and addresses the most significant first. He explained that the PDC must "start where you are and [with] what you can afford and do the best with it" (VT041). Basically, *tun dem han and mek fashion* (use the resources that they have). I found that most PDCs have already adopted this stance as their operating creed. I left with the impression that most members were disappointed with the state's financial contribution to the initiative but also accepting of it as a consequence of the government's dire fiscal straits.

I concluded that stakeholders' forceful and repeated mention of the government's undeniable financial situation represented a strategy on their part to highlight both the concern and the need for increased and consistent state support. The PDCs do not see their requests as exorbitant, as they are seeking to meet basic organizational needs. Sufficient funds to pay the electric bill and for equipment maintenance are basic and essential to operationalizing any initiative.

Funding Solutions: *Tun Dem Han and Mek Fashion*

The PDCs' success depends in good measure on the resources PDCs can garner to offset the government's insufficient contribution. Funding determines the group's ability to survive and thrive, and, as mentioned, the amount of subsidy they received from the government does not fully cover the needs of any of the groups studied. This situation contradicts the stipulations of participatory democracy theorists, including Sirianni, who have advocated for adequate state funding of such efforts.[37] As a stop-gap solution to this persisting reality, members have supplemented PDC budgets with personal financial contributions as well as fundraising efforts, both locally and overseas. Speaking matter-of-factly, a ministry representative endorsed such action: "Eddie Seaga said that it takes cash to care, he is some ways right. . . . If you can organize and attract international funding and capacity and technical assistance, take it" (VT038). NAPDEC in particular has been adamant that finding non-governmental sources of funding is not only advisable but also absolutely necessary to ensure the survival of the nation's participatory experiment.

Cost and Benefits: The Pursuit of International Grants

Some PDCs have vigorously pursued international grants as a way of supplementing their budgets. Reflecting on a particular entity, one PDC member noted that securing sufficient international funds was at the heart of the organization's success. The individual argued, that the PDC has two years' worth of salary for its employees already available (VT032). It is able to do this "because they factor all of that in the money that they [get] from the EU and other international bodies" (VT032). A few members believe that the survival of the PDCs rests with how much external funding they can secure. The majority of PDC members expressed interest in obtaining local or international grant money, but securing such funds is especially challenging. Even experienced individuals expressed dismay at engaging in the process. As one stakeholder observed, one has to, "ensure that your paper trail is in place for any NGO funding" (VT057). The process was described as "burdensome": "You have to have three quotes for things, and it takes a lot of work" (VT057). I engaged local officials from funding agencies, who also contended that the process is challenging and that drafting a competitive grant application is a skill that few individuals possess. Members try to recruit for this particular capacity, and NAPDEC offers some assistance in grant writing. However, the NAPDEC representative I interviewed noted that the PDCs most in need of the service do not use it (VT029). I left the interview believing that PDCs that do not pursue additional funding are either not particularly active or have significant capacity constraints.

Cost and Benefits: The Pursuit of Local Donations

The interviewees argued that pursuing support from local businesses produces uneven results, which are often shaped by forces outside the control of the PDC. This makes events planning problematic. One case in point was a successful project in 2011 that benefited from sponsorship by members of the local business community, but funding from those firms declined significantly for the programme in 2012. This reduction arose from a switch by businesses to more visible national projects linked to Jamaica's fiftieth year of independence celebrations. As the office administrator relating the history explained, the business community was engaged in some strategic activity of its own to attain "bigger recognition". That fact reduced this manager's list of sponsors for the PDC event significantly compared to the previous year (VT059).

Depending on the SDC and parish council for resources is not feasible for PDCs either as a long-term strategy because these entities are also chronically underfunded, although they can sometimes assist. For example, one PDC leader reported that they did not have funds for needed equipment: "We did not have funds to pay, and they [SDC] . . . gave us a computer and printer and so on" (VT034). Other PDCs depend on the generosity of their local parish council to keep the stationery cabinets full and the lights on. I also observed two offices that used National Youth Service volunteers partially to offset a continuing lack of funding for staff.

Several stakeholders argued that PDC dependence on parish councils is particularly problematic, as doing so begs the question of where allegiances lie. As one long time PDC member observed concerning this issue: "I am telling them that once you cry to the parish council, it becomes political; it must be non-political or appear to be non-political" (VT029). Co-optation is a possible result in this scenario when a strong partisan public authority with resources is paired with a group desperate for the same. The role of "politics" will be discussed further later in this chapter, but it is important to note here that the relationship must not be permitted to be lopsided on a continuous basis. As shown earlier, Anansi strategies can circumvent or curtail co-optation of the PDC by elected representatives to some degree, but such efforts, however clever, have limits. Nonetheless, as Crenson explained, past efforts to co-opt local PDCs suggests that these bodies are politically relevant and perceived as worth such steps.[38]

Dependence on government agencies has led to conflict and frustration among PDC members in the past. All agencies seek to show utility in an age of shrinking resources, which means that offering aid comes at a price some PDCs are finding hard to pay. One office administrator expressed her discomfort with the relationship between her PDC and the SDC. She explained that the relationship always leaves her organization in the shadows of the better funded entity. She spoke specifically of an activity that her PDC had initiated and organized, but for which nearly all the credit went to the SDC, which played only a supportive role as sponsor (VT059). As it happens, the reality was complex as the SDC provides this PDC space on an ongoing basis. In consequence, it was not surprising the PDC enjoyed only limited purview concerning project branding.

As noted, the PDCs also depend on community philanthropy to continue their operations. These efforts require PDCs to mobilize social capital within their networks to attain desired support. As mentioned in chapter 3, PDCs also deliberately recruit persons who are able and willing to provide donations. One interviewee offered a very pointed response to the question of how PDC operations are funded: "We beg" (VT056). One PDC administrator paused in her interview comments to point out what she had acquired for her group by ingenuity and resourcefulness: "The equipment that you see here . . . comes from donation . . . when I heard that [an agency] was closing down, I wrote to them and beg office equipment and . . . that's how we got this computer, and when [a craft festival] came about, we got another computer through it" (VT059).

PDC members work to create social networks to help mobilize resources to realize their objectives, but those do not always match community needs. For example, when PDC participants were asked about the needs of their jurisdiction, those often did not match the projects they indicated they were pursuing. This reality stems from the tactic of identifying projects based partially on the resource contribution it can make to the PDC's survival. These projects might then focus on protecting the environment when citizens are asking for job creation ventures or better roads. However, in any community, there are so many needs that virtually any project will alleviate some concern. As one stakeholder explained: "Everything for the parish right now is priority because there is nothing going on" (VT029). So some projects PDCs undertake might not be at the top of the community request list, but they are nevertheless valuable. Here are some examples: "We got funding to set up a work centre . . . how they [are] planning to do it is to make part of it a shelter in case there is a disaster. . . . We got some funding now for a rainwater project to harness the rainwater. . . . They also got funding to fix the postal agency" (VT029).

These examples illustrate that sometimes priority is not a matter of perceived needs or concerns, but instead depends heavily on the availability of funding. The long-term sustainability of the experiment might, however, depend on the extent to which PDCs ultimately address citizen's priorities. In addition, goal displacement constitutes a real risk when keeping the organization afloat trumps meeting the mission of the PDCs.

PDC members, as a solution to the financial quandary they daily confront, absorb much of the everyday costs associated with keeping the experiment alive. This is the case as well across much of civil society in Jamaica, where necessity demands that members "pitch in". One interviewee said this goes beyond volunteering time, energy and skills to mean that "somebody will buy the water, somebody will buy some of the things to prepare the food, somebody would buy the cups and plates, somebody would buy the trophies that we will give out, somebody will do the banner, you know, and we solicit a place, and somebody to volunteer a hall large enough to hold several persons . . . the persons that sit on the committee" (VT060).

The level of philanthropy varies significantly. Examples abound of chairmen and other members donating items to their PDCs that range from cash to office space. One chairman explained that he has personally contributed in the past year "maybe fifty or sixty thousand US" dollars to his PDC (VT111). The PDCs less able to mobilize such individuals and convince them to serve will be less effective and perhaps fail or become inactive. In this sense, it appears likely that the inability to secure funding disproportionately affects PDCs serving the poorest areas. Not surprisingly, most members interviewed saw increased government support for the PDCs as the best possible solution to this dilemma (VT070).

The Complex Nature of Altruism

As argued previously, the strategic efforts of members to secure funding for their PDCs are typically coupled with their own altruistic steps to keep their PDCs afloat. In some cases, staff and members are able to arrange "twofers" in which the PDC and another civic group share resources, and both are aided by their common use. As one PDC administrator observed, "That machine [printer] over there is for the football because I volunteer with the football league. . . . The league bought it, but it is in here, and so it is used by the PDC, and the [the same with the] paying of the phone bill . . . with the football season, the phone bill is paid for by the league. That's how it goes" (VT059).

When this source of funds dries up after football season, the PDC reverts to tapping its parish council for help, which generally tries to provide some assistance to aid the PDC. This PDC's relationship with the sports league is mutually beneficial as the PDC office and staff becomes a de facto office for the athletic group during the season. The PDC keeps the printer and gains telephone service in the bargain.

Many PDCs strategically align themselves with existing parish projects rather than create costly new initiatives on their own. One PDC tackled the problem of school dropouts by partnering with a civil society organization already involved in addressing the concern (VT054). As positive as such efforts may be, they do run the risk of stifling the potential for new creative partnerships. A recently launched PDC is already benefiting from a network of state and civil society entities that meet and coordinate activities on a regular basis "so everybody is sharing information" (VT053). This suggests that this parish might soon fare better than long-established bodies in terms of successful project implementation because of its connected civil society presence. But, again, this will arise only if those participating think creatively about the possibilities their shared efforts might present.

Holding the State to Its Obligations and Other Strategies

For all the PDC leaders interviewed, a principal strategy for meeting funding obligations is to pressure the government to fund the participatory initiative adequately. The interview comments read like potential protest signs in front of Parliament, with stakeholders complaining that the lack of state support signalled a "lack of commitment" and further contending that the government needs to "accept that the PDCs have a critical role to play as it relates to governance" (VT032). The majority of interviewees referenced the PDCs' limited success in securing necessary funding from the state, and follow-up interviews a year later revealed that insufficient government aid remains a serious threat to PDC survival.

All failed attempts to identify alternative funding sources raise members' frustration levels, a turn that threatens the survival of the experiment as representatives, whether they leave or stay, are less motivated and effective. Some efforts to secure funding have definitively failed, such as collecting dues from members. Contributing as needed was one thing, but ongoing efforts to do so appear to be something else altogether. Fundraising initiatives are difficult, whether it is lobbying the state for funds or soliciting for support within a PDC's membership and the community. The frustration was palpable in this interviewee's comment: "There is only so many places you can ask. Can you give me for this, can you give me for the other? Really, you can do what you can do with what you have and what you are able to get, and recognize that you will not do all that you want to do, and it can be frustrating" (VT112).

All of this said, the PDC members persist in their fundraising efforts because successfully obtaining support offers the opportunity for a thriving programme.

The Result Is Worth the Effort

When a PDC successfully raises additional support, the outcome is obvious. PDCs can range from those operating out of a member's home to a few that have several offices, a technical team, a secretariat and enjoy sufficient funding for income-generating projects. One donor put the combined contribution to one PDC at well over J$60 million (VT012). This PDC's stakeholder conference featured remarks by PDC members, political representatives and prominent guests. This was possible because of funding from an international body sufficient to transport and house those individuals.

PDC members were keenly aware that funding sources can and do dry up. The same PDC that boasts a comprehensive development plan and extensive secretariat had a member who discussed their concern about what will happen when community development is no longer in vogue and its funders move on (VT056). This fact makes planning unpredictable and adds to members' frustration. Other PDCs have managed to keep their doors open and projects going when external support ceased, but they did not have as many activities as this entity had underway. Time will tell. Just one of the four PDCs examined (PDC 1) had an ongoing income-generating activity, and one other PDC (PDC 3) listed a revenue-generating project as in an "incubator" stage. Even the "established" project was still fairly new, and I observed no users for the service offered while I was there, which may suggest that, in the short term, that effort, too, will not prove a reliable source of funds.

The quest to secure needed resources will for some time remain a staple of PDC activity, but efforts to secure resources or circumvent shortfalls suggests that persistent financial gaps have not by themselves completely undermined PDC vitality. Pluralists have argued that there are other resources in addition to funds used in the exercise of power that might not be obvious, such as "social standing", "popularity, esteem, charisma", "ethnic solidarity", "time" and "personal energy", all of which can be applied "with greater or lesser skill".[39] This application remains at the heart of emancipatory politics, and ultimately PDC member ingenuity will play a key role in shaping the experiment's long-term chances for survival, despite its continuing financial difficulties. The PDCs examined were all operational despite a general insufficiency of public support, a fact that speaks to the tenacity and tactics their members have employed to keep them alive. The issues the PDCs face linked to partisan politics will require the same great ingenuity and determination to overcome.

Assumption 3: Jamaica's Political Culture Could Facilitate Participatory Democracy

If you yearry debil a come, clear de way.
(Keep clear of trouble.)

Perhaps the most obvious government assumption concerning Jamaica's participatory process was that it could be facilitated by the nation's political system and culture. MacKinnon asserted that "all the strengths and weaknesses of participatory democracy are vividly illustrated in culture".[40] Sives, Gray and Harrison all found that partisan decision-making and high levels of nepotism characterize the country's political system. In Jamaica, partisan allegiances influence policy formation as well as the distribution of political benefits.[41] PDCs, on the other hand, are supposed to be politically neutral and seek to assist all citizens regardless of their partisan association. In this sense, PDCs are expected to play a role in helping to mend the gaps caused by Jamaica's existing political culture. The nation's PDCs are still trying to realize this vision while navigating the formidable obstacle represented by the island's partisan political space. Partisan activity is embedded in the fabric of society, meaning that the nation's participatory experiment cannot escape it even with the best intentions. Stakeholders have sought to minimize its effects by using a variety of tactics, including some that run counter to the PDCs' democratic ideals. Stakeholders justify these actions by arguing that preserving the possibility the PDCs represent ranks higher than the current quality of the experiment, at least in the medium term. This speaks volumes about the determination of these groups to survive, but their very efforts to do so could, ironically, represent their undoing if they compromise their core principles and sacrifice their legitimacy in the process. This section examines the scope of the political culture challenge and surveys the strategies the PDCs have employed in response to it.

Politics and Participatory Democracy

In her survey of empirical accounts of democratizing efforts, Abers found that state-led experiments usually mask who is actually exercising power even though she was optimistic about a select few. She also questioned why legislators would hand over power to ordinary citizens, especially in light of the dangers of tyranny. She cited Brazil, for example, where participatory budgeting saw citizens quickly deplete available resources when accorded power to distribute them. Her answer to this concern was to contend that legislators must somehow benefit from devolution, and citizens must be prepared to exercise their responsibilities deliberatively. Her study of the participatory landscape led her to conclude that all stakeholders, from elected representatives to the bureaucracy, must be "motivated to support, take part in, and respect the EPG [empowered participatory governance] experiments [or] those policies are unlikely to become empowered or participatory".[42] The Communist Party of India/Marxist implemented a participatory experiment in Kerala, India, after campaigning on the basis of realizing that possibility. Both the populace and those governing supported the effort in a disciplined way, resulting in empowered local government.[43] In analysing Latin American cases, Baiocchi as well as Selee and Peruzzotti agreed on the importance of the legislators and legislatures to the success of participatory experiments.[44] But that role is not univalent. Kramer found, for example, that many residents viewed the legislature's involvement in the citizen engagement negatively because they saw legislators as the source of many of the problems that plagued society and therefore refused to participate.[45] On the other hand, the success of these experiments requires appropriate legislative support. The relationship between the PDCs and the legislature in Jamaica is often one of distrust or attempted co-optation, thereby making politics a major challenge to the nation's participatory experiment.

A few of the interviewees argued that many legislators see the PDC as a threat to entrenched partisan politics. Conversely, politics can pose a threat to the PDCs, particularly when members of the political class feel the power they hold is at risk due to some other group speaking for "the people". Consequently, when decisions serve to disrupt clientelist channels through non-partisan policy recommendations, and elected leaders perceive that the PDC has made gains that would usually be attributed to partisan efforts, they may view the effort with suspicion. These issues, to the extent they exist in a particular parish, act as impediments to the success of the participatory process.

PDCs Were "Created to Fail": The Role of Government

According to two PDC stakeholders, "PDCs were created to fail" (VT059; VT012). These critics cited limited support by the legislature during the implementation process, as evidence that strong, striving PDCs were never the lawmakers' objective. The frustration of one NAPDEC representative, who has been heavily involved in the participatory process for some time, was unmistakable: "Now the most important thing is if the government is really interested for the people to have a voice? . . . they figure that they know everything, politicians. You get me? Politicians believe that they know every friggin' thing, till they get out of office, then they start asking you what you would like to do" (VT029). It is evident that he had examined the contribution of elected representatives to the PDC and found them wanting.

As reported by a few stakeholders, some legislators have engaged in a form of Anansi politics by covertly impeding the success of the PDCs. Several interviewees provided a list of the obstructionist tactics used by elected representatives: not providing sufficient funds for the experiment (as explained earlier, some stakeholders this accepted due to the fiscal constraints faced by the government), not responding to invitations for meetings, ignoring PDC ideas and suggestions and delaying consideration of the same. There has been no audit to confirm nefarious intent on the part of the legislature, but a few PDC interviewees believe such is the case anyway. Whatever one chooses to believe, the outcome of parliamentary inaction or lack of support is less than effective PDCs.

Members across the interviews agreed that the stance of the two major political parties towards the PDCs is paramount to their success. A former PDC participant mentioned that the JLP in the early days of the experiment was not for the PDC or increased decentralization of power and authority to local governance. He recalled, "The early JLP would not be the one in favour of participatory governance. In fact, I can go further. In that regime, the only thing local government was left to manage was the cemetery. I am dead serious" (VT032).[46] Local governments have more responsibilities today, and it appears the JLP is no longer as antagonistic to their increased role.[47]

Interviewees in only one parish of the four in which interviews were conducted believed that legislators were sufficiently supportive of the nation's participatory experiment. Across PDC 2, interviewees consistently said that only one member of Parliament has ever attended a PDC meeting. A few members became emotional in interviews. As one noted, "I personally do not feel that there is that commitment to fast-track this thing" (VT084). Another stakeholder commented that members of Parliament and parish councillors "only show lip service" to the needs of the initiative (VT107). In several interviewees' views, there is a connection between legislators' disinterest in PDCs and citizens' lack of involvement with parliamentary inattention, which prompts "people (to) lose interest" (VT029).

In addition, according to a third-party leader, legislators only rarely mention the PDCs or Jamaica's other participatory organizations: "I have not heard anybody talking about how to empower the people, to give them a bigger voice, and to give them a bigger say. I don't hear any of those discussions on the national agenda at all" (VT033). In fact, one can find parliamentary speeches where the participatory experiment is discussed and promoted, but they are not normally highly publicized, and, empirically, as mentioned above, most citizens are not aware of the PDCs in any case.[48]

The legislators interviewed disagreed with the claim that the PDCs are not a priority. One declared that such claims are simplistic and ignore the significant progress the nation has made to date:

The PDC is high on the agenda and part of the focus that we want to get out there. So there is a collaborative effort [between local governments and the PDCs]. Now you know that community development is now part of the local government. . . . As I said, it is part of the whole reform process, and it is high on the agenda . . . but [we need] to ensure that we find ways to get these PDCs working and educate our groups, whether it is the community or the council, or the local authority or whatever, so that everybody has a good understanding of where they are and what their respective role and functions are. (VT086)

The official's statement suggests that much of the participatory experiment remains in its infancy. It also implies that the pace of the state's actions might never be satisfactory to a cynical populace. On the other hand, the responses from other elected officials suggest that there is not much internal discussion about the future of participatory democracy in Jamaica.

Perceived inaction and limited support from central government is mirrored at the level of the parish councils according to many of the stakeholders. One PDC member addressed the power of parish councils this way: "They are a critical part of how successful things can be in any community because, as you can imagine, an elected representative [parish councillor] can make things a little bit sticky for anybody who wants to come into their particular division and they are not in agreement" (VT084).

Yet, obstruction by parish councillors has declined over time, according to other stakeholders (VT032; VT053; VT084). Many members noted in interviews that the deep division between local governments and the PDCs witnessed at the beginning of the experiment has closed over time, although it has not been eliminated. Members still lamented, however, the continued presence or threat of local government partisan political interference or politics.

How Bad Is the "Politics"?

How bad are the politics really? One senior ministry official explained how entrenched partisan thinking is in Jamaica: "Major thing we have to look at before we move on is changing the mindset of those who have been elected. [They] still see their role in the classical clientelist view: give something to retain your vote right, and it is one of the hardest things to move" (VT038). Many sources shared this individual's concern, including former politicians who see clientelism as incompatible with the aims of participatory democracy, but see little signs of a shift away from it (VT099).

A few stakeholders declared that political support for the PDCs is often connected to party preference. One former PDC chairman was blunt when observing that "you [the PDC] can succeed or not succeed according to which administration is in, and they [the politicians] know which one you are aligned to" (VT099). I followed up by asking if the just-concluded dormancy of PDC 4, with which this chair was affiliated, could be explained by not being aligned politically correctly. The interviewee laughed and provided what I considered a less than adequate response. Such was something I often encountered and came to accept in interviews when discussing politics. The insights of this former chairman were key to this study, not only because his statement about the pervasive nature of politics in his parish was intriguing, but also because his arguments caused me to begin connecting several dots concerning one of the biggest puzzles encountered during my fieldwork. The parish in question is the one described earlier as having an extraordinary special election to restart the PDC after a period of inactivity, but answers as to why it had fallen into inactivity and had gone to such lengths to prevent supposed election-related "usurpation" proved elusive for some time.

Post-interview reflections concretized my view that politics had something to do with the elusive responses. Regardless, there was no doubt that the ubiquitous nature of partisan politics in Jamaica's parishes was a recurring theme of the interviews. The SDC representative for the same parish as that of the chair described just above described that jurisdiction's political culture by stressing that the "political process is very, very, very strong" (VT053). He stressed, however, that the current relationship between the PDC there and its parish council was "excellent" and went on to note that such had not always been the case (VT053). He pointed out, as had many of my interviewees, that "if you know the history of the PDC, when they were just formed and the way they went about their business, the parish councillors at that time probably saw the PDC as a threat" (VT053; VT072).

The SDC representative did not sufficiently explain the central question of the nature of the relationship between the withdrawal of legislative support and the inactivity at the highlighted PDC. Even more telling is that this representative is knowledgeable of the PDC's activities and played an integral part in orchestrating the extraordinary election that sought to breathe new life into the defunct PDC. His answer in the end was a vague "guess" as to what had gone wrong and included information about which I did not ask:

> Basically, I can't tell you. I have been here for [a few] years . . . but, basically, we had a system that really was not looked after that well. Sometimes things . . . just fall into disrepair. I think . . . that's what happened; it just went on, went on, the energy was not there you know, so basically you know, we try to reenergize it and try to put it back in such a way to energize it back to its role and function. (VT053)

The present chairman of PDC 4 was elected to office during this special election, and he indicated that the reason for the PDC's previous lack of activity was that the prior leadership was not pulling their weight sufficiently. Despite his explanation, another long-time member would not accept that the PDC had been inactive, but instead argued that it had just not been very active. None of these responses seemed to justify the very rigid and unique election procedure that occurred or why the group was doing so little in the first place. To gain a more complete picture, the interview with the former chairman was essential. By the time of that interview, I had configured my questions in such a way that they resulted in more fruitful and open responses. With experience, I learned to introduce the topic of politics much later in interviews, after I had built rapport, and I also decided not to shy away from pressing the issue or asking a leading question to ensure the interviewee opened up. Applying these strategies allowed me to get a better picture of why this particular PDC was inactive, the circumstances that led to the need for an extraordinary election and a clearer sense of the nature of the parish's politics. Vignette 4.3 contains a section of the interview with the former chairman that was particularly insightful.

Vignette 4.3

Chairman:	You can succeed or not succeed according to which administration is in, and they know which one you are aligned to, and I think in my case I had some of that.
Me:	You were not aligned properly, so it was a challenge?
Chairman:	[Laughs] It depends on when the change comes; you might be in one area where everything is going well, and then the government changes, and you are not there any more, and things don't go so well.
Me:	What would happen with a government not so supportive? What would the obstacles look like?
Chairman:	You get pushed aside, since what is carried out . . . a stumbling block is put in the way.
Me:	Examples?
Chairman:	I would say that more development could take place in an area. For instance, somewhere wants the place bushed? This [political] party wants to be praised; they want to be the one to say they are doing something, and if somebody from the other side who is in the organization is doing it, then they are not comfortable with it because they are the ruling administration. They can stop it from happening.

Vignette 4.3 (*continued*)

Me: Specific examples?

Chairman: More than once, for instance, I had said in one broadcast that the harbour was polluted, which it was, and my objective at the time was to get a central sewage system and if we had someone see and agree that the harbour is polluted, we can use all these things in order to get some funding . . . someone crying down the place; we don't want our dirty harbour to be shown up.

Me: Interesting. Politics is so deep that even if it is good for everyone, they will push it aside until their party is in power?

Chairman: Exactly! And it happens too often, too often, and therefore we are sometimes at a standstill, and I know of projects in our area that have been in the making for the past fifteen years, that same harbour problem being polluted.

Me: What was the reason for the four-year gap, and why did you leave?

Chairman: You heard what I said about politics? I saw clearly a political move, and a group of politicians descended on us, and I was pushed aside. The thing is, at the time, I had the company registered for the PDC . . . and as the director that really started that they said that I was no longer director, but they did not send in any of their new directors to the company's house; that is in a bad position with the company's office [today] because they did not pay the fees.

Me: Under what authority could they do that . . . these councillors?

Chairman: It was not just the councillors, it was a mixture of persons, because a gentleman came from the hierarchy of SDC, and he was the person who conducted most of the AGM meetings and made decisions on what should happen and how to go forward. . . . He is not there any more, and he is not part of us, and the mayor at the time had never attended a PDC meeting, not one for the four years, yet he came into that meeting and said what should happen, and because he is the mayor, some people said they had to listen to him, so a lot of disruption went on. When I realized that I was going to be working with people who have absolutely no knowledge at all of how a company [the PDC] works, I did not feel comfortable working with them any more either. Well I suppose they thought that they could do well, but they failed. (VT099)

This chairman went on to explain that the "new people" were ill-prepared to do all that was needed to keep the PDC going, which left the organization rudderless. Note that this actual hostile takeover is the only such example from all the interviews conducted, which makes it an outlier, but the episode captures what is possible within the realm of partisan politics. Importantly, one other PDC chairman expressed fear that a similar takeover might befall his group (VT111). This entire case, from the reluctance of the interviewees to describe the influence of elected representatives, to the nature of the political arena in the parish, is representative of experiences interviewees shared across the PDCs investigated. After examining this example, I could better gauge how detrimental partisan political action can be. The case of the chairman in vignette 4.3 showed how the level of "acceptable frustration" among that PDC's leaders had been surpassed due to the interference from political officials.

A common tactic of the legislature, as reported by members, was also highlighted in vignette 4.3: elected officials choosing to ignore even good ideas that arise from a PDC. Several individuals spoke of this phenomenon, including a member who had a pointed example to share. He recalled suggesting "some time ago that instead of having the market in the centre of the town, they should move [it to] Garvey Park.[49] . . . They say it will cost too much money. I remember at a meeting one councillor made the same suggestion, and they [gave] ear to it. You understand?" (VT072).

Another explained that the politicians do this while saying, "they are on board . . . they will not publicly say they are not listening to you" (VT070). The examples suggest a social trust deficit that makes it even more difficult for local government and PDC leaders to work together in the future.

Current efforts to reboot the PDC described in vignette 4.3 continue to be dogged by unresolved issues. For example, the PDC must find a way to pay the former group's unpaid fees, a circumstance that has slowed the process towards becoming certified under the nation's Friendly Societies Act. Achieving this status is important as funding agencies generally disburse only to registered entities. A check with the PDC a year later revealed that dealing with the negative legacy of the previous administration was still a major source of frustration added to the laundry list of other challenges this PDC faces daily. It is not just political parties that can serve as a stumbling block, but the attitudes of individual legislators can also make or break a local experiment.

A Legislator: Against the PDC

According to the interviewees, a few unsupportive legislators can essentially destroy a PDC. A former member of Parliament recalled that his primarily urban parish had a thriving PDC, but due to negative political interference, it is now dormant. He seemed near tears as he described how, after the JLP gained the majority in the parish council, a new mayor calculatedly oversaw the demise of the effort. The vignette 4.4 shows how he described the situation.

Vignette 4.4

Former member of Parliament:	I will go on the record . . . when we started and had a development plan, we had the parish development committee . . . we got some money from Cities Alliance, the World Bank and we did all the planning, everything, put all that together. . . . We had offices, we had Jamaica Social Investment Fund provide us with money, all of that, and we had an office advocator. I was able to get that, and then we had a leadership change . . . and the PDC was pretty much smashed! (VT107)
Me:	Was this after a change of mayors? (The individual no longer serves in that capacity.)
Former member of Parliament:	Exactly, and I have no problem saying that. The PDC was there ready to run with a business plan, surveys done; the World Bank gave us [a few hundred thousand US dollars], and we planned out everything . . . man you have no idea how much it hurts me! (VT107)

He gave me reports of studies commissioned by his office, documents outlining extensive overseas funding, and a well-defined structure as evidence that the participatory entity had a promising future, but he noted that none of this was pursued by the new mayor, whom he considered not philosophically aligned to the process. The PDC he referenced had not met for some time (at the time of my study) according to SDC representatives in the parish. The present PDC chairman, although he agreed to meet with me, never responded to subsequent calls. That group now exists largely in name only.

A NAPDEC official underscored the impediment that an elected representative can be to a PDC. He attributed the opposition by some elected officials not to ideological differences but to a lack of intelligence: "It depends on the councillor you see. If you have an intelligent councillor, it depends on him. If you have somebody with some sense, he will realize that you are working with him and not against him, but if you have a total ignoramus, they figure that you are trying to take away their job from them" (VT029). The frustration was obvious, as with many interviewees, when discussing the negative impact that political leaders can have.

A Legislator: For the PDC

Stakeholders were almost unanimous in interviews in their belief that a supportive legislator, whether member of Parliament or parish councillor, can boost the success prospects of a PDC. The present mayor of a parish with an inactive PDC said in an interview that legislative support is a significant factor in explaining resilient pockets of active participatory spaces within the parish. The mayor noted, "I believe that part of it has to do with the individuals who lead it and their relationship to other seats of power" (VT088). The elected official went on to explain "the truth is, both the MP and I are very strong advocates of participatory governance, and we have encouraged it . . . we have [encouraged] the discussions. I have been to the monthly meetings; I have been with them struggling through whether or not they have sufficient members participating" (VT088). This was not the only factor listed as she said the situation is explained as well by, "whether or not in those particular communities, individuals feel empowered . . . where people are in terms of how empowered they feel to take charge of their own communities" (VT088).

The most successful PDCs have benefited from supportive parish legislators, and less successful bodies have often faced substantial political opposition. At a conference for a PDC that most stakeholders interviewed considered a model for success, I conducted a joint interview with a PNP councillor and a JLP councillor. Considering Jamaica's well-known partisan political culture, this was surprising, but they explained that they could sit together for an interview because they worked together amicably on the PDC and were both openly in support of the experiment. One even had a formal role with the group. I asked what explained this, and they seemed unable to pinpoint a definitive reason other than to suggest that a celebrated political maturity exists among legislators in their parish. Maturity in this sense meant that they have accepted that they can accomplish more for the parish working together than as adversaries. They pointed to advances of their politically united council in the use of solar technology to reduce electricity costs within their parish and the use of geothermal mapping in planning as evidence that they are simply a more progressive legislative body than many of their counterparts elsewhere in the country (VT013). The term progress here underscores a process, as the congeniality and support they expressed with me was not always the case. The legislators' support for the experiment speaks to the work of that local PDC in gaining their confidence. This predominantly rural parish, however, is unique in that it has benefited from an influx of returning residents and export profits from a large multinational corporation. These facts imply there may be other reasons for the success of the participatory process in this jurisdiction. As with the successful Porto Alegre, few other areas in Jamaica can boast a similarly supportive socio-economic or political environment.

The interviews suggested that a supportive legislator has a particular profile. One PDC leader described helpful elected officials as roses among thorns, the only ones of the several in the parish to attend PDC meetings and who always were willing to help financially and otherwise. That now former member of Parliament was described this way: "Yes, she did a lot because when we want stationery for the office, it came out of her budget. I just get the invoice, and she did it" (VT059). PDC 2 asked every sitting member of Parliament in their parish for a donation from their constituency development fund, and only this particular official responded. A pattern emerged in which community vitality and participation are greatest where there is legislator support, even though the character of that aid may vary.[50] The essence of the portrait is someone who attends meetings, promotes the participatory process and supports the experiment financially.

This person, however, is an exception to the rule in most cases, as a former member of Parliament explained. He noted that within the political arena, winning re-election is the priority, not the participatory process. As such, resources and energy are usually spent on partisan efforts for which the elected representative is rewarded with votes in the next election. He explained: "I want everyone to be involved, yes I am willing to go out and do that, but with limited resources . . . I now have to always be thinking about being re-elected, and when I was MP, I can tell you, my wife left me because I used to spend my salary in the constituency, and we used to get only J$2.5 million per year" (VT107). He further recommended greater PDC autonomy from legislators (local or national), which is a stance that would ensure the stability of the experiment when someone not philosophically aligned to the aims of the experiment gets elected. He explained how he had previously proposed this be done: "we had suggested . . . that members of Parliament and councillors serve as ex officio members so they can come to meetings, [but] they would not have a vote. They came to meetings with the right to participate, and we encourage that. Once people get power, I tell you" (VT107). Another former member of Parliament echoed similar sentiments, "It is very difficult to get away from political leadership because that is where discretionary funds are" (VT057). As long as this is the case, elected officials will always have the upper hand in any negotiation with PDC leaders. I concluded that PDC members' critical sentiments were fuelled by frustration and that it perhaps is reasonable that members of Parliament and councillors, subject to popular election, carry greater political weight than members of an advisory body. On the other hand, these examples underscore the fact that representatives possess sufficient power to make or break a PDC.

One has to appreciate that a web of factors serves as the actant guiding the legislature's decision-making process. Scarce resources, for example, ensure that there is always extensive competition for available funds. Elected representative have to consider what they believe will be the most efficient and effective use of available funds while strategically ensuring their good standing in the upcoming election: "When you have a limited amount of funds and trying to put these things together with the right people, you sometimes get a conflict of interest between different projects, and sometimes that's a very challenging thing to deal with" (VT061). This reality leaves legislators engaging in their own brand of emancipatory politics in order to juggle all the factors and ensure that any decision made is beneficial to them as well as the community in the end.

Undercutting the Negatives: Some Solutions

Legislative support for the participatory experiment is often the result of efforts by members of a PDC to secure it. These activities are not linear and clear cut and may involve forging clientelist ties or having members convince elected officials that an alliance with the PDC would prove mutually beneficial. Pluralists, such as Polsby, complicated this picture by arguing that interests and concerns are not static and that coalitions typically form among interest groups as opposed to the rigidity of group values embraced in stratification theory.[51] Creative PDC leaders will seek to demonstrate to both local councillors and members of Parliament how they can advance mutually beneficial interests, such as identifying community needs and legislative priorities.

PDC members strategically signal to legislators how valuable the PDC can be to their objectives by hosting community meetings, retreats and collaborations involving citizens from both parties. A NAPDEC official discussed this approach: "We are trying to work with them to help them . . . if we get some information, we share it with them" (VT029). These efforts have yielded demonstrable results. An office administrator explained the change over time this way: "In the latter part, now you realize that they are now more informed and therefore they are now more or less supportive of the PDC and other community organizations at the community level. So there is greater support coming from the elected representatives, both at the council and member of Parliament" (VT081). Such collaboration has the additional benefit of reducing the perception that a particular activity or approach is partisan in character. This bodes well for a boost in the popular legitimacy of both camps.

One successful collaborative effort used by one PDC involved organizing and getting the community together for town hall–style meetings. This allows the elected representatives to address all of their constituents and not just the ones who voted for them, facilitating comprehensive dialogue on community needs. This initiative allowed the PDC to meet its need to interact and find out the needs of the community while also engendering a space for community dialogue and offering an invaluable forum for policymakers.

All attempts by the PDC to bridge the partisan divide are not created equal, but most PDC leaders with whom I spoke were resolute in their efforts to resist partisan infiltration. Such a resolve, as explained in interviews, included the most undemocratic of methods to achieve an apolitical body. In a clear example of emancipatory politics, at least one PDC chairman declared that they have chosen not to hold PDC elections for the sole purpose of denying political activists the opportunity to infiltrate. The chairman indicated in the interview that he wanted to leave but simply cannot: "I was going to walk away, but the problem was the people who were standing by to take it over would have just so politicized it that the whole purpose would have been aborted" (VT111). He justified his actions by noting that "the PDC requires the organization to be apolitical, and therefore the people that drive it has [sic] to maintain that, and we have to be very careful that it isn't politicized; that will just abort the whole process" (VT111). When asked for the source of his confidence that there would be political interference, he replied: "You know the individuals, and you know what their stance is; they have a history" (VT111). Interviewees were generally aware of who the political activists were and those who would take any opportunity to infiltrate organizations such as the PDCs.

Legislators' freighted relationship with the PDCs is symptomatic of the nation's larger political culture. Partisan politics in Jamaica is endemic and forms the core motivation behind the emergence of many of the community-based organizations that make up the participatory structure. Reflections on the interviews led me to consider examining partisan decision-making on the part of the citizenry, similar to the investigation of the legislators, and how such aligns with the goals of the participatory experiment.

The People and Politics

A clear assumption of the participatory process is that the Jamaican citizenry can be apolitical. Most PDC members vehemently support a non-partisan mantra. Indeed, just one PDC member mentioned an overt political association. The fact that two former PDC members interviewed had voluntarily stepped down to pursue elected office, and observations by ministry officials and members of Parliament that many of the affiliated groups emerged for partisan gain, shows that party politics is intertwined with the participatory environment. How PDC leaders adjust to this reality will determine the extent to which the experiment can thrive and fulfil the true purposes for which it was developed.

Can the Citizenry Be Apolitical?

The citizens can act without their decisions tilting in favour of their political party of choice, but Jamaica's partisan political culture limits this occurring consistently and across all PDCs. A member of the state bureaucracy who is very close to the process seemed to accept that the PDCs will have to adjust to this very real part of Jamaica's political culture. He explained that partisan politics "is embedded, and you will understand it from studying it already. It is a thing that obviously we have come to accept. . . . You have, honestly, you have operatives that are PDC chairmen or PDC executive members, you have operatives in the state, so it is not a sort of purist thing out of some egalitarian text. It is there" (VT038). When asked how far the politically connected pipeline goes, he replied as follows:

> Yes. Let me tell you usually at community level worse, if it is in a semi urban rural context . . . let us use Siasa.[52] People that come up for community leadership are also political activists. Those are the ones that are the runners and constituency executive chairpersons. . . . So there is no sort of even-handed plurality when it comes on to. . . . I am the political person, and I will deal with this at community level; you are civic volunteer you do your thing, and we will come together and discuss. Usually it is all intertwined.[53] (VT038)

Another ministry representative mentioned how universal this type of connection is, noting, "everybody knows because a lot of the PDCs you go [to], the people who you see there, in other words, are hard core in many of the things they do, they carry political lines. They carry party lines, you know how they operate, you know how the membership . . . the 'cliqueism' in terms of who sits where and how the thing is done" (VT042).

The presence of partisans, as raised by the ministry representative, carries the possibility that competent members are displaced, attempts to garner legitimacy within the community are strained and ultimately the survival of the experiment is threatened. As one member observed: "Governance . . . should include all sectors of our community from children to the elderly people with disabilities – persons whose voices are not heard. Marginalized communities, as well as those in the day-to-day mainstream, and those are often the communities that because they have a fear of being politically aligned, they shy away from it or help in obscure ways" (VT036).

As evidenced in vignette 4.3, these political activists are not always committed to the ideals and activities of the PDCs. Without commitment, a PDC organization is almost guaranteed to fail. One former development group member succinctly put it this way: "In most cases, you have many competent and capable persons in these communities who are better capable to handle the job. These persons [partisan political activists] are just put there, and they don't really function; most times they don't function" (VT035).

Handpicking candidates for leadership roles is used as a tactic to minimize partisan invasion by those so inclined, but it may also be used by those supportive of a partisan-led body. As one administrator explained, "when they have the AGM is handpicked people". The same administrator was prepared to be as candid as the ministry official above in saying that elections are "very political" (VT059). Both observations are not easily verified. One legislator agreed that the role of politics within the participatory process is real, but seemed to suggest that it does not overwhelm the process as participants "are all community people; some of them are political activists" (VT088). Similarly, a PDC administrator downplayed the negative presence of partisan individuals, explaining that the real problem is the lack of awareness and scepticism of the general population, and not that there is an epidemic of political activists in the PDCs. Is the real problem then the low levels of social capital in Jamaica? The extent to which the citizenry does not trust each other compromises the ability of the PDCs to have a dialogue on relevant issues as per its mandate.

PDCs Seek to Operate in the Midst of a Social Capital Deficit

Low social capital levels might mean distrust of PDC members and their intentions no matter what their motives or political connections might be. The issue with politics, one administrator asserted, is a reflection of the citizenry and not of the PDC: "[T]he people out there talking politics, they are the problem; they are the political ones. That is why they don't feel like they can come in and be neutral in what they do" (VT087). There is no proof of the validity of this claim. Nonetheless, it likely explains why some citizens will not participate. Social trust levels among the population in Jamaica might simply be insufficient to facilitate participatory democracy even though data exist which show that low levels of social trust can maintain a robust representative democracy.[54] The Jamaican participatory space has a clear challenge in the form of unhealthy social trust levels, and the government and the PDCs would do well to seek to improve this situation to create a more suitable environment for the participatory experiment.

Putnam stressed the importance of social capital to a vibrant democracy, and it appears that Jamaica is presently unable to obtain such benefits as its social capital levels are currently very low.[55] This situation is understandable in light of the nation's colonial history. Powell has noted that 83.3 per cent of Jamaicans reported that they did not trust each other, a level that is "disturbingly low".[56] At this level, any increase in social trust levels should aid the participatory process. Presently, dialogue across previously warring garrison communities is minimal. The urban areas show disjointed participatory structures, and the bombing incident referred to in chapter 3 together partially explain the unique nature of the participatory environment in these areas. You cannot meet where there is insecurity or work together where there is violence. Yet, violence has attracted a host of civil society actors on the ground with funding and expertise that have advanced the participatory process. This action contributes to disjointed development, and these groups are opportunistic in nature and have no allegiance; they often work in patches as they see fit.

Scholars such as Mutz and Dryzek argued that social trust is usually the outcome of participation and that engagement can potentially unite deeply divided societies.[57] Three scholars I interviewed suggested that higher levels of social trust would certainly aid the process and that increased levels of social trust can be an outcome of the PDC experiment (VT092; VT085; VT039). The garrison phenomenon and its attendant violence are limited to only a few communities, but more glaring is the disparity in incomes across the country, which stratifies the entire citizenry. According to Pickett and Wilkinson, it is this inequality that is the prime contributor to the low levels of social trust witnessed in many nations.[58]

Jamaica is one of the more unequal societies in its hemisphere, and this not only contributes greatly to low levels of social trust but also negatively affects involvement in community life.[59] Jamaica's Gini index was recorded at 45.5 in 2004,[60] and a 2011 International Monetary Fund report revealed that the country scored 59.9 on the Gini coefficient, which was worse than Haiti, the poorest country in the hemisphere, which scored 59.2. The same study reported that more than one million Jamaicans live in poverty when judged by the amount of the population earning less than US$2.50 per day.[61] These critical society-scale issues must be addressed if the PDC experiment is to survive and thrive. This leaves me to question the broad acceptance of the term "community" despite glaring socio-economic disparities among the citizenry. The gravity of the situation is not lost on the participatory policy's implementers, as a senior official with the SDC explained that PDCs are usually inactive in predominantly urban parishes where economic inequality is at its highest, and parishes with the most vibrant PDCs, are those with associational life and lower levels of economic disparity. This observation falls in line with Pickett and Wilkinson's 2011 study of American states and developed countries.[62] The solution, according to these scholars, involves a reduction in income disparities. The ability of PDCs to form and even flourish despite the near absence of social capital in many parts of Jamaica indicates that higher levels of social cohesion may be helpful but are not a prerequisite for participatory programmes.

Mending the Gap between the People and Their Politics

As emphasized earlier, almost all the interviewees declared that the PDCs should eschew partisan politics. Ameliorating economic disparities seems beyond the remit of the PDCs, at least in the short to medium term, but the selection of older, accomplished chairmen to signal even-handed competence is common. As a ministry official declared: "The chairpersons are really the champions of that; they are unbiased, at least publicly; they are even-handed; and they seek to benefit the entire parish based on their recommendations, based on how they represent the organization" (VT038). He suggested that while the problem of partisan activists infiltrating PDCs exists, it sometimes excludes the leadership, a view that accords with my earlier claim that special selections, though seemingly undemocratic, might in some cases serve to reduce overtly partisan figures from serving. Other techniques, such as a chairman not having elections, might have a similar near-term effect, but over time will undoubtedly create new problems of insularity and an entrenchment of ideas. Efforts by the government to build social trust among the citizenry and improve the way in which legislatures are perceived have also aided the participatory process. Said one member, "part of what [local government] reform tries to look at is trying to rebuild public order, public trust, public understanding; it is not necessarily happening at the pace that we want. There is a lot of cynicism out there" (VT038).

A few stakeholders explained that, in recent years, they have witnessed an improvement regarding the worst aspects of Jamaica's political culture. If sustained, this represents a positive sign for the PDC and its aims. These interviewees contended that the work of various civil society actors appears to be paying off, as the worst manifestations of partisan political activity, such as the high levels of violence and factional rifts within communities that dominated the island's politics in the 1970s, have subsided significantly in recent years. A civil society actor and scholar mentioned this shift and also suggested a type of political fatigue as the main reason. He explained that the benefit of partisan policies seems not to be worth the cost to the average Jamaican and especially to the youth of today. He cited the decline in election-related violence as a prime example and estimated that in "80% of the country, there [is] no partisan conflict now" (VT092). Politicians also gladly echo this sentiment. A member of Parliament told me to reflect on the 2011 "national elections . . . as a benchmark . . . nobody naw kill nobody [no one is killing anyone] over PNP, JLP, NDM or any other thing. I think people are dancing in the streets green or orange or any other colour so that in itself is a signal that we are beginning to move to another level" (VT086).

Partisanship is still very much a staple of Jamaica's culture, but such a positive move heralds well for the possibilities of dialogue and interaction needed to foster engagement and empathy in the participatory process.

Based on the interviews, I considered that the PDC stakeholders might be looking at the role of partisan politics too narrowly. Abers argued that self-interest brings individuals to the participatory table, and if active and motivated participants are partisan, they might very well offer some utility/capacity to a PDC, providing that proper mechanisms are in place to reject partisan policies and programmes.[63] Isaac and Heller also contended that partisan politics drive group formation for participation. They suggested that increases in participation could be seen as a positive, and competition within the experiment is more transparent and ultimately reduces the worst manifestations of partisan political culture, such as invisible clientelist relations. The authors noted that involvement in the experiment even led to an attack on partisan behaviour; their best explanation for this was the inexplicable "mischievous logic of social movements".[64] Almost all PDC members interviewed spoke critically of Jamaica's political culture, and all declared that PDCs should be apolitical. Over time, the "mischievous logic" hypothesis might explain the shift in the Jamaican experiment away from partisan connections. It could also be that Anansi politics might be at play, and the primary allegiance of these individuals is really with the advancement of their community and not with a particular political party.

Conclusion

This chapter highlighted the assumptions built into the design of the participatory experiment in Jamaica. These include the willingness and ability of the people to participate, the availability of funds to sustain the programme and the ability of the political climate in Jamaica to embrace and foster participatory democracy. These expectations to a great degree have not been met and have instead emerged as distinct challenges to the participatory process. Stakeholders expressed concern about citizen indifference and ignorance, insufficient funding for the experiment and legislative ambivalence, interference and obstruction. Some PDCs have been able to counter these negatives by working with small faithful groups while urging greater levels of participation. Some have also garnered funds from members as well as from foreign agencies, while other bodies have convinced their local legislators that supporting the participatory experiment is an asset. These steps explain the reasons some PDCs have survived, and indeed, why some have thrived.

5.

The Future of the Selected PDCs and the Link with Past Experiences

This chapter provides this study's conclusions and outlines the conditions that have advanced or impeded the ongoing participatory experiment in Jamaica. It explores stakeholders' optimism for the future of the democratization initiative, contextualizes the reasons for that optimism and offers recommendations for creating the institutional, infrastructural and superstructural conditions needed for the future success of participatory democracy in Jamaica. The chapter also addresses the value of the theoretical framework employed, critically assesses the limitations of this analysis and outlines fertile topics for future research.

The Future of the PDCs

In order to ascertain the factors that shape the stakeholders' outlook concerning the future of Jamaica's participatory democratic experiment, they were each asked how optimistic they were about the future of the PDC. Much of the data for this section emerged from that question. The majority of respondents declared that they were optimistic, but their optimism was often conditional. It hinged on the successful outcome of the strategies each was employing to combat daily challenges; therefore, any assistance towards removing or reducing those concerns should aid in the survival and ability to thrive of the PDCs. This section details prior knowledge ascertained through a review of the literature on participatory democracy and relates how this study's findings advance the field. Stakeholder recommendations concerning how to boost the prospects for the success of the experiment are also offered. This discussion should be of interest not only to PDC stakeholders but also to policymakers interested in designing future participatory initiatives for Jamaica.

Bring People In

Most PDC members cited the absence of the general citizenry from the participatory table as a vital concern. Several respondents suggested that their optimism about the future of the experiment hinges on the success of their efforts to attract the citizenry to become involved. After all, the engagement of the citizenry in matters of governance is the reason for these groups' existence. One past member explained that having an active engaged citizenry would yield even more positive results than the PDCs have created to date. He put it this way: "The more [the PDC] become[s] a more vibrant unit, I think that our impact will be greater" (VT070).

I entered my fieldwork expecting that low participation numbers might be a challenge for the PDCs. In support of that notion, Young has suggested that citizens are simply busy and cannot find the time to engage meaningfully in law-making. Lane, as cited previously, explained that most citizens rank personal and family issues above community engagement.[1] At the same time, Dahl asserted that participation numbers might be low as a result of citizens valuing consumerism, where such a culture is dominant, more than engaging in governance.[2] Anthropologist Deborah Thomas found Dahl's concern to be operative in Jamaica.[3]

The literature on participatory democracy also has captured how economic factors determine who is able to participate. One in five Jamaicans now lives in poverty,[4] and for these certainly, the daily struggle to subsist is likely to rank higher than participation in governance. Rousseau's admonition that there can be no substantial political equality without economic equality is an apt description of present-day Jamaica.[5]

The implications of the social reach of poverty constitutes a serious threat to the survival of the PDCs. The absence of a substantial share of the citizenry does not allow for planning inclusive of communal knowledge and, at a more basic level, facilitating constitutionally required quorums for meetings to occur. Notably, this situation conflicts with the premise on which the experiment was built, that is, that it would serve as a mechanism through which all, regardless of social, educational or financial status, would be able to inform government policy and help guide development at the community level.

This study complicates the narrative presented in previous works as it revealed that citizens do participate in governance, but not always in the formal manner PDC programme designers expected. The low numbers at formal PDC meetings mask the carving of "claimed spaces" (to borrow from Gaventa) in Jamaica for participation in governance.[6] The citizenry in true emancipatory fashion, according to interviewees, opted to address relevant members of Parliament or civil society organizations directly; engage in protests, including roadblocks; make calls to daytime talk shows; and pass requests to the PDC for action (VT033). All these alternatives are immediately cheaper and often more practical for many Jamaicans than attending PDC meetings. Gaventa explained that one manifestation of freedom is the demonstration of an ability to manipulate the boundaries that limit one's scope of political engagement.[7]

Overall, there were exceptions to the apathy regarding formal engagement with governance rule. Polsby argued that citizens usually mobilize to oppose an issue more readily than to support one,[8] and that was the case in at least one circumstance where opposition to the state applying toll charges to a previously free thoroughfare mobilized the community to take action (VT073). Abers had earlier found that "deliberative processes are most successful, when initiated, at least, by self-interest".[9] PDC members shared a similar sentiment when noting that they found citizens do come out, but when the issues are perceived as germane and where "sweeteners" are offered for participation. A former member of Parliament explained that small visible projects with immediate pay-offs, for example, sports, were a sweetener that often brought residents together (VT057).

Any effort, however, to reduce structural barriers to participation will go a long way in supporting the survival and thriving of the experiment. Present initiatives such as hosting meetings in various communities as opposed to the town or city centre will significantly reduce travel costs, but even more useful would be the focus on ensuring economic parity by engaging in resource redistribution which further engenders capacity development.[10] Navarro and Selee and Tulchin made the case that the immediate needs of the poor across Latin America must be met for participatory democracy to be effective, while Isaac and Heller contended that it was the efforts to improve the circumstances of many marginalized groups that explained the success of the Kerala participatory experiment.[11]

Reduce "Old School" Politics

A few interviewees suggested that their optimism about the future of the PDCs hinged on the extent to which Jamaica's partisan political culture improves. As was discussed, the island's politics historically has been less than conducive to participatory initiatives. As Sives, Gray and Harrison have argued, nepotism and policy decision-making based on partisan allegiances have long defined Jamaica's political culture. This situation has created a culture among voters of trading their support for political spoils.[12] A nationally representative survey a year before I entered the field to conduct my study found that 60 per cent of the Jamaican people held the view that the country would be better off under British rule than as an independent nation, suggesting that the citizenry is very dissatisfied with their present leadership and their socio-economic and political reality.[13] The government was cognizant of this, and along with several scholars, saw the introduction of PDCs as a cure. Caribbean scholars Munroe and Buddan have expressed hope that more direct forms of participation in Jamaica will provide a mechanism for closing the nation's democratic deficit.[14] Nonetheless, that deficit remains as I write.

Based on Isaac and Heller's finding that partisan politics drives group formation for participation,[15] I was not surprised to find that such was the case in Jamaica. As mentioned before, one ministry official referred to the presence of partisan operatives within the experiment as "embedded . . . so it is not a sort of purist thing out of some egalitarian text" (VT038). The official suggested that detaching the PDCs from such an entrenched part of the culture is unlikely to occur anytime soon. The PDCs might, therefore, need to include strong internal policy guidelines preventing participation by political activists.

I entered into my fieldwork cognizant of the importance of supportive legislators to the survival and success of participatory initiatives. Jamaican PDC stakeholders declared in interviews that legislators exhibit a general lack of support and, in some cases, even obstruction of their efforts.

A few interviewees expressed the view that the Parliament had no real intention of seeing the experiment succeed (VT059; VT012), while others questioned if elected officials truly wanted to give citizens a voice (VT029). Another individual noted that not even the rhetoric was sufficient: "I have not heard anybody talking about how to empower the people, to give them a bigger voice and to give them a bigger say. I don't hear any of those discussions on the national agenda at all" (VT033). A few interviewees explained that public officials routinely ignored good ideas, and when they offer support, it is often connected to party preference (VT099). The interviewees had a litany of complaints concerning their government representatives. In many cases, not providing sufficient funds for the experiment, not responding to invitations for meetings and ignoring ideas and suggestions from the PDCs were some of the most telling ones they listed. The worst of the lot was a single case of a hostile takeover by partisans, and another PDC member spoke of the fear of the same happening. A stakeholder explained that "all these cause people [to] lose interest" (VT029). In interviews, members explained that they have constantly reached out to the legislators and have little overall to show for their efforts as requests for increased funding and legal status remain unresolved more than a decade after implementation.

The government's contribution and plans for the PDC need to be documented with appropriate and verifiable milestones attached. One PDC representative mentioned that members of Parliament could show support for the work of the PDCs by offering project funding through their constituency development funds. But such has only rarely occurred. The extent to which this and other acts that members interpret as less than supportive occur, the frustration index for members rises. In some cases, this frustration reduces motivation and drive that can result in individuals disengaging with their PDC altogether.

The scenario in India stands in stark contrast to the Jamaican experience in terms of legislator support. In Kerala, India, the Communist Party of India/ Marxist implemented a participatory experiment and then offered extensive support for it. The Communist Party of India/Marxist also campaigned heavily on the initiative as its electoral victory was tied to its success. The result was that in India, Kerala became the state in which participatory governance was most evident.[16] This example suggests that elected officials must work with the PDCs to achieve Jamaica's democratization objectives.

PDCs still face legislators who are philosophically opposed to them. One urban PDC was driven out of existence by a mayor opposed to it (VT107). The political scientist interviewed underscored the importance of having legislators who support the model if it is to thrive. He explained that he is optimistic concerning the future of the PDCs largely because he believes key, philosophically aligned figures now lead the government:

> I believe the fact that Portia Simpson Miller is prime minister and that it was under her that the local government reform process – out of which the PDCs came – when she was minister of local government and community development. I think that's important because she has constantly been unshaken in her own commitment to community development. I believe that the current minister of local government and community development is similarly committed [and] for that reason why he was made the minister. So the fact that local government and community development has been restored as a ministry is more than just symbolic, it's a lot of substance, and in association with that, the prime minister has always maintained that local government is about community development and that is why those two must go together. Local government is not just about markets and parochial roads and those things that it is sometimes discussed as . . . it is about community. Portia has always wanted participatory budgeting; now that must be key to participatory governance. (VT039)

He further explained that his analysis skips the four years recently in which the JLP was at the helm, hinting strongly that the party remains less than committed to participatory democracy (VT039).

However, in true emancipatory political fashion, PDCs have not been observers of legislative action/inaction but have employed various tactics to win the hearts and minds of legislators. They have advised councillors that the PDCs are working with and not against them and demonstrated such through the sharing of information and hosting apolitical meetings from which the elected official benefits from being able to address the official's entire constituency. The PDCs that are doing well have been able to enlist politicians from both sides of the aisle as supporters in the form of financial aid, attendance at meetings and even serving in specific PDC posts.

Optimism Reflects Efficacy

Participatory democracy requires an active and engaged citizenry. Sirianni declared that all would and could have a role to play in governance. He noted that the role of the state therefore should include the creation of institutional designs that put citizens in a position to "co-produce" public goods, mobilizing their own assets, including localized knowledge for problem solving and promoting civic associations.[17] Lindblom and Cohen contended that local knowledge "does not owe its origin, testing, degree of verification, truth, status, or currency to distinctive . . . professional techniques, but rather to common sense causal empiricism, or thoughtful speculation and analysis".[18] Mitchell discussed the importance of local information to effective environmental governance, and Borkman's study of self-help groups documented how citizens assisted each other on the basis of the experiential knowledge they possessed.[19]

Sirianni further advised that the citizenry should benefit from capacity training in order to engage in governance efforts effectively. He explained that not all will be trained to do high-capacity tasks, as some would learn by doing, and he further suggested that less demanding tasks need no training, such as assisting in distributing food to the homeless.[20] All citizens could therefore have a role to play in community development.

This study found that most PDC members saw themselves as uniquely suited and situated to "save" their communities, and, by extension, they saw the PDC on which they serve as a conduit for such action. This optimism appears connected to an abiding confidence in the members' own ability. One stakeholder was adamant that Jamaica's communities need PDCs explaining, "As a matter of fact, I don't think the communities can do without us, without these organizations any more, because if these organizations stop functioning in these communities, then you know what the end result is . . . tragedy, right" (VT019). A former PDC member suggested that communities would be in a predicament if it were not for the PDCs: "Well, I am fairly optimistic. I believe that without these organizations, we are worse off; we are sort of like watch dogs to advance the parish council and local government and central government and communities" (VT064). This "saving" ideology for members was connected to the "us" versus "them" arguments documented in this study whereby the management of the PDC rests on the shoulders of highly educated individuals with extensive experience in community development and volunteerism, while the "others" comprise the rest of the community in need of aid. The extent to which this attitude persists into the future is likely to limit the ability of the citizenry to engage to co-produce public goods.

Present stakeholders have strategically sought to recruit persons already possessing the skills needed for the survival of the PDCs, as opposed to any or all citizens who might be interested in serving. This appears to be a manifestation of emancipatory politics, as strategic recruiting allowed for the emersion of PDCs and it also aided in their survival as more efficient and homogenous groups with fewer conflicts.[21] It is important to note, however, that particular views and values of the community are rejected when they run counter to the mission of engendering participation and ushering in sustainable development. One past member explained that such counterproductive values and thinking were rampant in the society and require an intervention: "Yes, it's just that people need to change their thinking . . . they have a mindset, and it is going take a lot of time and education" (VT035).

Optimism Reflects Tenacity and Resilience

Stakeholder optimism is also tied to a resilient commitment to their mission to inform and educate the population on governance matters. A civil society leader introduced this issue: "Those of us who understand how important it is for the people to be a part of the political process and the governance of the country, we have got to continue to call for that, and we have got to continue to educate the people for them to understand that they are a real power" (VT033).

Members are well aware that their mission is incomplete, and those interviewed were uniformly devoted to reaching a greater number of citizens. Each successful effort further boosted their optimism.

Every PDC Victory Is a Boost to Optimism

Abers determined that a demonstration effect occurs when others become attracted to outcomes.[22] In this view, self-interest provides the necessary adjustments to the calculus that would cause a citizen to participate in governance as opposed to engaging in some other activity. Abers's findings mirror what several interviewees declared as the basis for their optimism in the future of the PDCs.

A common theme across most interviews was that stakeholders were optimistic because they had witnessed tangible outcomes of the participatory approach. This experience led them to commit to the experiment's survival. As one stakeholder explained, "I am very optimistic. I think that there are still some challenges, but certainly the situation is better today than it was five years ago, and I think we are moving in the right direction" (VT041). The other side of the coin is that every loss increases PDC member frustration levels, which are manifest in a reduction in zeal among members or, at worst, lead to members leaving the PDC.

Win the Legal Case

PDCs seek formal legal status, which is strategic, in that such facilitates the securing of donor funds and partnerships and also augers well for the legitimacy and stability of the PDC. One stakeholder suggested that the stability explanation is paramount and necessary if the PDC is to attract members. He declared that some citizens are reluctant to engage the PDC for fear their work will be for naught if the PDC goes out of existence in a few years: "The PDC system will be entrenched . . . and at that time the PDC structures will have legal status through the local government reforms so we will be more recognized then; because one of the handicaps we have now is that plenty of people hear about [the] PDC but because we don't have that legal status as part of the process of governance, they take us lightly" (VT058).

An SDC representative was even more pointed in explaining that legal standing "is all the people in Jamaica [are] waiting on now because all these power brokers don't want to waste their time with an organization that might not go anywhere, so everybody is waiting on the entrenchment" (VT081). Having legal status, according to these stakeholders, has the potential to aid in tilting the pendulum of public opinion in favour of the PDCs.

Improve Levels of Social Trust

Putnam argued that the northern provinces of Italy have registered that nation's highest political and economic performance because their civic cultures have promoted active citizen commitment and horizontal relations of trust, tolerance and cooperation.[23] Both Putnam and Sirriani highlighted the importance of social capital to an association's lifespan, with Sirriani recommending that states invest actively in building social capital.[24] Unfortunately, according to Powell's 2008 survey, Jamaica has very little social capital on which to build. His research revealed that 83.3 per cent of Jamaicans did not trust each other.[25] Pickett and Wilkinson's study concluded that high-income inequality is correlated to low levels of social trust.[26] In these terms, Jamaica remains a deeply divided and unequal society.

More than one million Jamaicans live in poverty,[27] and, with a Gini coefficient of 59.9, Jamaica is one of the more unequal societies in its hemisphere. These sharp divides surely exist in Jamaica and have a direct impact on associational life. A senior government official explained that PDCs are usually inactive in urban parishes where economic inequality is at its highest but flourishes where economic divisions are less sharp. He noted:

> In urban areas, a next thing is from a community standpoint, you have more communities again, and the communities are less homogenous. These urban areas you might have a larger number of informal settlements, and you also have a larger number of

affluent communities as well, you follow where I am coming from . . . so they tend to not have that sort of unity among the civil society. In other areas, you still have affluent communities, but they tend to have a wider spread not so much of a sharp divide. For example, you are very familiar with St Catherine. In St Catherine, the only place you have to say is affluent is St Jago Heights, and even if you go St Jago Heights, you still have Tredegar Park and the Keystone and all those places around it, and all those middle-class people that slowly peters out into the Thompson Pens, Rivolies and Dela Vega City, and so you tend to have more homogeneity in other areas. So for civil society, they have common issues, common problems and common identity, so they tend to be stronger. It is easier for them to meet and to federate. (VT124)

Reducing socio-economic disparities would go a far way towards boosting levels of social capital and associational life in general in Jamaica. I interviewed three scholars who suggested that higher levels of social trust would certainly aid the democratic process, but each also contended that higher levels can produce such outcomes (VT092; VT085; VT039). I found, however, that several PDCs have survived and a few have even flourished despite Jamaica's epidemically low levels of social trust. This fact gives hope that participatory programmes can succeed in the long run.

Decreasing the trust deficit between elected representatives and the wider society should also increase optimism and serve to advance the interests of the PDCs. The often hostile character of Jamaica's politics dampens prospects for mass citizen participation. The PDCs can survive with few participants, but for them to thrive over time, they will require active involvement from a wider cross-section of the citizenry. This is hampered because of the population's broad distrust of the political process in all of its manifestations, including the PDCs. A ministry official echoed the sentiments of many members: "Because of how tribal our politics have been over the years, a lot of people want to stay away because they don't want to be labelled political" (VT042). This superstructural condition must change for the experiment to thrive. One scholar explained in an interview that efforts by civil society actors and others have contributed significantly to the decline of garrisons, and the general political maturity of the populace has manifested partly in the drastic reduction in violence during elections (VT092). A decline in partisan political activity should prove helpful for not only participatory efforts in Jamaica but also for the health of representative democracy and social relations in the nation.

Secure Sufficient and Reliable Funding

Sirianni demonstrated that governments can reduce costs when they invest in participatory initiatives.[28] The majority of PDC members, however, found the state's financial contribution to the groups to be inadequate, and their optimism for the future often hinged on resolution of this dilemma. Respondents pointed to several sources of PDC funding, but all members interviewed emphasized the state's role in supporting the democratization experiment. This focus was likely strategic, as Jamaican government officials are the most likely to read this work. One former PDC member was adamant that "the government needs to work with PDCs . . . right down the structure financially" (VT066). This individual went on to acknowledge that his PDC has not lacked public support, an assertion supported by all the PDC members with whom I spoke. That is, despite its relatively small size, there is an adequate supply of volunteers to serve on the PDCs: "I am optimistic . . . we still have people volunteering in communities working for nothing . . . it's just the support mechanism needs to be put in place" (VT066). Where PDCs face a gap is in their need for adequate and reliable funding sources, which perhaps can only be offered by the government. Chapter 4, in particular, outlined the reality that a lack of sufficient funds retards projects and raises member frustration. An interviewee gave a specific example of how the lack of resources such as office computers has resulted in the absence of meeting minutes (VT081). This anecdote does underscore the larger point that the viability of the experiment is threatened because of inadequate and unreliable funding.

Institute Comprehensive and Formalized Succession Planning

Having a succession plan is vital for the survival of the experiment. Rural areas, especially, have documented citizen migration to urban centres as a particular challenge to the longevity of the PDCs. For this reason, they have instituted measures, albeit often informal ones, to ensure that PDCs are less likely to have to continue for any period without a leader. I witnessed how the original selection of deputies to various posts served one PDC well, as one such individual was soon thrust into a main role when the person she was supposed to assist could no longer serve. A former PDC member explained how his experience with volunteer groups guided his philosophy towards always having persons ready to take on leadership roles: "You will have someone there to keep the group together, and when that person migrates or whatever, the group disintegrates . . . particularly in volunteer groups, it is very important also to have people trained in leadership to have succession planning" (VT034). Succession planning only mitigates the symptom of the larger superstructural problem of urban drift from rural areas and brain drain from the country generally.

Embrace New Leaders

Several key stakeholders from the ministry, the SDC and several PDC members shared in interviews that they saw regular leadership rotation as an essential element for a successful and thriving PDC. Few stakeholders openly celebrated the contributions of the present PDC in their parish while explaining that the future of the organization is best served through having seamless and consistent leadership transitions. To these members, new leadership meant the insertion of new ideas and energy. SDC representatives, as well as past members especially, took turns highlighting the intransigence of particular leaders as the principal cause of the stagnation of particular PDCs. As indicated in chapter 4, the character of the constellation of peculiar challenges confronting it best explains the vibrancy of any particular PDC, but the stakeholder interviews suggested that the lack of leadership rotation is very much a contributing factor as well. This is not true for all PDCs, however. For example, between 2012 and 2013, at least three PDCs held elections. Two of them selected new chairpersons while one retained its existing leader. Some PDC constitutions include term limits for officers, while others, such as in the case in which the chairman was retained, do not. Still, there are instances where leaders have been serving almost since the launch of the initiative, a fact that seemed to dampen the optimism of some stakeholders for the future. A former PCAC member explained:

> Yes, sir, I am optimistic about the PCAC. Optimistic, what does optimism mean here? Optimism means if you do the right things, you get the right results. As Einstein says, if you keep doing the same thing all the while and expect a different result, then you are a fool, so, therefore, we have to have people who are continually motivated. So this is why you can't wait until people sit down there and wait until they become a drag. (VT073)

Again, what is witnessed here is optimism tied to a caveat that includes putting structures in place to prevent compromising levels of lethargy among the group, a consequence this interviewee claims is almost inevitable if the group's leadership is not frequently changed.

"What's the Alternative?"

Government officials and PDC members past and present shared in interviews that they had no choice but to create a better Jamaica through the participatory process. From their responses, it became clear that there was a legitimate fear that not having this, even limited participatory space, would prove detrimental to Jamaica's future. One stakeholder explained the experiment was "the only way to go to develop the country" (VT052), and another opined: "It must work. It is part of the Jamaican thing, something must happen because if it doesn't, what's the alternative? We would have failed. . . . What do we owe the next generation? Why did we let it fail?" (VT038). This overt fear of limited options for a better future, perhaps explains the reason direct democratic tools, even those rarely used by constituents in the United States, are never repealed.[29]

"I Am Not as Optimistic"

A few stakeholders bucked the majority of my interviewees and focus group participants to declare that they were less optimistic about the future of the PDCs. One civil society actor with close ties to the participatory structure put it this way: "Optimistic is a strong word" (VT036). She pointed to conditions within communities as particular impediments to optimism about the PDC's future:

> If we go back to the initial conversation, CDCs that are most active are in response to some sort of social situation that is chronic, but chronic is relative, right, so if there is no upsurge of violence, quote, unquote, but you still have a lot of young persons who need engagement, but you have a lot of old persons who also need engagement, but it is not one of those hot-button items, then no funding comes in for it. But it is still an issue within the hierarchy and how people perceive it is not there. I think also there is a big fear, certainly among younger persons, of the political alignment that is implied with participation in CDC or any other such thing. It is assumed that if you are there, you are going to become targeted. In addition, you have to look at the perception of the community so when someone is on the CDC, it is implied that you have resources to give or you have access to resources. (VT036)

This response also raises the possibility that people might have been telling me what they thought I should hear. I do not believe so. I argued earlier that the optimism members espoused serves as a strategy to motivate themselves as well as others and that their hope is accompanied by conditions that must be met. The following individual serves as a good example. She is a PDC administrator who openly declared that she is not particularly optimistic about the future of the PDCs. She made that statement within earshot of a colleague and received a sharp glance as she spoke, yet she continued cautiously to explain that although she believes the initiative will survive in the short term, the fiscal plight of the PDCs ensures that their thriving and long-term survival is tenuous. Her comments are important in that her entity is perhaps one of the better funded PDCs, having received a substantial inflow of overseas donor funds. Her PDC, unlike many others, was able to hire technical staff and an extensive secretariat as well as engage in several development projects. In essence, this PDC had been able to overcome the challenge of adequate funding, at least in the short term. The office manager was not optimistic because she was aware of the temporal nature of the funds her group was then enjoying. The PDC in which she serves depends heavily on overseas benevolence, and she believes the organization will have to shut down when the funders withdraw. These supporters have facilitated many projects and even financed ventures aimed at filling the financial void after they withdraw, but with the date of withdrawal approaching, the business ventures are yet to be profitable. This led to her expressed fear that the organization would grind to a halt within the year (see R1 in vignette 4.5) (VT056).

Vignette 4.5 captures several comments from my interview with the staff member of a PDC with relatively strong external funding. Such assistance has enabled long-term planning, but the short-lived nature of this foreign assistance has raised the frustration index for PDC activists. Respondent 2's response in the vignette illustrates the "passion and drive", or as I argued earlier, the resilience and tenacity, of members, a manifestation of the nation's long tradition of emancipatory political action, which allows her to remain optimistic.

Vignette 4.5

Me: Are you optimistic about the future of the PDC?

R1   I will let her answer that because everybody knows my feelings on this.

R2:   I will speak for [PDC 1] because I can't speak for, I can probably speak a little about the other parishes, but for now I think we are on the path we are not going to back down; we are not going to if we are supposed to sit back, we will close the doors. . . . Yeah, but with the passion that we have and the drive that we have to get this thing working, we will survive. I think I can safely say that.

Me: [To R1] What are your views?

R1:   My view on it was that it makes no sense because we have to be dependent on foreign entities to survive. So we got to the point where I said to my boss, come . . . 2013, the PDC is going to be forced to close its doors if we don't do something about it and so . . .

Me: Why that date?

R1:   We, our funders. The agreement we have with our funding agency comes to an end and where they get their funding from that focus has changed, it is no longer about governance and capacity building and all of that stuff, so soon we probably won't fit their criteria any more to still be able to access that funding. However, being the type of persons that we are, we are trying to make sure that we stay afloat come then, so we are doing something that we can start generating our own income, because one of the things we did very early on when we realized what was happening, first, we registered as a legal entity. Some people will knock us for doing it, but that is the only way we could have managed to stay afloat . . . or stay relevant because we were registered, so we were able to attract funding outside of the government, so we got grant funding. So the next thing we did now was to register a business entity – another business entity now we are putting things in place.

Optimism Is Good Strategy

As noted above, the majority of those interviewed were optimistic, yet their hope was based on the success of the tactics they have employed (or utilized) to keep their organizations afloat. One stakeholder put it this way: "I am optimistic because it makes sense; what we have to do is to manage it and facilitate it . . . It could be resources, it could be capacity; there could be many reasons . . . we need to do more than what we have done" (VT042). Several other responses followed a similar pattern, in which interviewees followed their affirmation of optimism with a checklist of needed steps for the future. This suggests that PDCs must continue to engage in emancipatory tactics in order to overcome particular obstacles en route to meeting their aims, including, at the very least, keeping the experiment alive.

I concluded, following review of this section of the interviews, that optimism likely serves as a motivational tool for members. A stakeholder put it this way:

> You have to be [optimistic] because if you don't approach these activities with an optimistic outlook, then you are going to quit. So you always have to have a positive attitude, and a positive attitude, just like a negative attitude, is an infectious thing. So when you exhibit this kind of attitude, you encourage other persons to get involved, to be a part and to continue the work that we are doing. (VT060)

A senior bureaucrat appropriately tied this embrace of optimism to various emancipatory tactics when he explained that he "refuse[s] to take on the Hobbesian view. . . . The thing about it is if we want to stay with the political thing, some of it has to be Machiavellian as well, some of it has to be thinking outside the box, getting to sacrifice in some things that you really don't need. In other words . . . getting to the end by unusual means" (VT038).

He acknowledged here, as with most respondents, that action on the part of stakeholders underpins his optimism in the place the experiment will hold in Jamaica's future.

Lessons from This Study's Approach and Findings

PDCs and Emancipatory Political Action

My review of Jamaica's political history has led to the conclusion that emancipatory tactics seamlessly blend into daily life and became invisible. Scholars, including Scott and Marshall, recognized the resistance and fortitude implicit in even understated behaviour, such as shaming political representatives in efforts to pressure them to act in a community's best interest. Collins suggested that such calling out of a representative should be considered a political act.[30] This insight prompted me to portray those interviewed as they are – very complex beings acting in a field of competing and overlapping interests. I found that PDC members exercised agency and exhibited political efficacy yet did so in constantly evolving ways as they found their voice and identified better strategies to tackle issues. These efforts were necessary because of and despite immense challenges. The obstacles confronting the PDCs have resulted in some casualties, as not all PDCs are in operation. However, I found that even previously dormant bodies can and do re-emerge.

Challenging the Strategy

As mentioned, emancipatory tactics abounded across the PDCs examined, but, perhaps oddly, they often went unrecognized as political activities. This normalizing resulted in few criticisms of them. For example, a small number of interviewees challenged the less than democratic handling of elections by some PDCs. As outlined, some parishes have not held leadership elections for some time, and, in other cases, the electoral process has not been inclusive. The reasons for this situation range from the absence of funding to advertise meetings to fear of co-optation by partisan agents. The sustainability of such actions, however, is almost never raised. After all, the "problem" is invisible on many levels. In the case of the PDC member who suggested that his PDC has not held elections out of fear of political co-optation, a senior SDC representative suggested to me that his actions were not the result of such a fear but instead of a run-of-the-mill reluctance on the chairman's part to relinquish power. I concluded that both factors could be at play as the possibility of co-optation was real enough to lead to the employment of such a tactic by the chair, who may also be relishing his role so much as not to wish to relinquish it.

Once the problem of co-optation by partisan activists becomes visible to all stakeholders, a discussion can be had about policy prescriptions or programmes that could strengthen rules governing who can serve on PDCs. Some PDCs have already experienced the negative repercussions of attempted co-optation. A senior bureaucrat described the PDC whose chairman feared such a possibility, and a PDC administrator expressed serious concern in her interview about a woman "selected" to a particularly influential post when there was extensive evidence of her unsuitability (VT059). One scholar lamented the very narrow approach to development adopted by some PDCs (VT039). This "situation" might be alleviated if a wider variety of people could be attracted to participate. This concern cannot be separated from the superstructural issues already identified in that a much larger pool of applicants might not be available because of the financial state of the country as well as the low levels of social capital among the citizenry. I do not purport to have a solution to this dilemma, but it should remain a key fixture in future PDC discussions. It seems clear that some tactics that may have played a role in helping the PDCs to survive might in the long run jeopardize their capacity to thrive if insularity characterizes PDC operations or incompetent individuals comprise their leadership.

Highlighting the Complexity of the Battle

Emancipatory politics as a theoretical lens requires that the analyst sees the participatory political space as not a neutral or empty space to be filled, but instead one with overlapping competing interests. There is much debate in the literature on participatory democracy about how to circumvent entrenched interests, with some scholars suggesting that efforts at unifying groups with different aims are likely to yield limited rewards.[31] Dryzek and others have offered practical steps towards ensuring successful deliberative engagement.[32] His and other guidelines are less effective, however, when interests are not clearly demarked.

I observed, for example, a PDC's effort to referee a dialogue between a particular service provider and community members, from which participants departed feeling that their voice had been heard, but very little else in terms of their concerns was likely to be rectified. The general view across the representatives of the PDCs that I studied is that such engagements are worth undertaking even if the issues on the table are not resolved because individuals perceive that "at least they are heard" (VT052). While I accept the view that finding a voice counts as resistance, I nonetheless believe that it would be useful to consider creating an agenda for such discussions in the future. To use the service provider scenario as an example, I observed that the representative was unable to address several questions raised by audience members. That fact severely limited what could be accomplished at the gathering. Perhaps citizens could be encouraged to submit their questions in advance so that representatives could obtain answers from relevant personnel when necessary.

I also propose that members seeking citizen participation be educated about the history of power realities, government structures or identities within the country that might prohibit a handcart man from speaking up or being heard by a table of educated middle-class "development experts". That is, as Cornwall stressed, every effort must be put into "equipping ordinary people with the weapons of the powerful". Such is already the case when participatory action research or participatory rural appraisals aim directly at challenging experts and incorporating and documenting the lived experience of people.[33] Local and international bodies with such skill sets should be urged to contribute in the development of members through capacity building in these areas.

We Think, Therefore We Are

Gaventa stated that organizational efforts purporting increased inclusivity are often more rhetoric than substance.[34] The PDCs' efforts to thrive might also be compromised to some degree because of the "us" versus "them" dichotomy I observed. If a central aim of the PDCs is to bring elements of Jamaican society together, preconceived notions about "others" of that society among PDC members must be addressed. If it is assumed that young people, for example, simply do not want to participate, as many interviewees claimed, that view might be reflected in the extent of PDC efforts to incorporate them in the participatory process. This factor, coupled with the various other issues that limit citizen engagement, suggests that the PDCs face substantial challenges in their efforts to incorporate the citizenry in governance. These perception barriers will only be overcome through empathetic interaction between PDC members and citizens.

For this reason, Morell advocated for an infusion of emotions alongside the more familiar argument for reasoned debate within the public space. He sought to build on the work of Mansbridge, who argued that a combination of emotion and reason should be regarded as "public reason".[35] This idea is similar to the nature of the "talk" Barber argued must occur within participatory spaces.[36] The effect of this infusion of empathy through interaction was manifest in my interviews when some members expressed a more nuanced knowledge of the financial obstacles to participation than others because they had spoken directly with individuals struggling with such constraints. I suspect that once the engagement process begins to attract a larger pool of participants, this specific problem will resolve itself. Nonetheless, the PDC presently represents a middle-class space that "others" might find less than welcoming for a variety of reasons, ranging from the nature of the activities conducted within it to the stereotypes embraced by a share of its active members. To the extent that these conditions remain unaddressed, one should expect that efforts to attract greater numbers of citizens to become involved will remain difficult.

Enemies Without: Jamaica and the Global Economy

The 2003 award-winning documentary *Life and Debt* told the story of Jamaica's devastating experience with structural adjustment policies in the 1970s.[37] Instead of the development promised, the nation has gained an unsustainable debt burden via its participation in the initiative. The devaluation of the Jamaican currency and sharp reductions in social programme spending have produced negative repercussions that reverberate to the present day. Many

PDC stakeholders interviewed, however, place blame for insufficient state funding of their efforts squarely on Jamaica's government. The superstructural issues that surround the survival and thriving of the participatory experiment remained generally outside of the realm of discussion in meetings I attended as well as in the interviews I conducted.

Many stakeholders perceived a simple lack of will on the part of legislators for the limited funding they received. And they are likely correct, but not completely so. I have argued that a cluster of factors explain the insufficiency of public support, including the unsustainable debt burden the country presently faces. Debates concerning the state's budget capacity have generally ignored the uneven global economic playing field that underpins such crippling debt for countries such as Jamaica. This concern must be addressed before one may reasonably expect the nation to have the leeway to fund fully a range of programmes, including PDCs.

Post-Marxists contend that if today's inequitable economic system is not addressed, the social justice aims of the participatory approach will not be realized. Their argument highlights the flawed assumptions of the neoliberal agenda, which embraces the "top-down" notion of efficiency and participation honed from the harmony model of power. This frame asserts that "power resides with individual members of a community and can increase with the successful pursuit of individual and collective goals".[38] Such a perspective leaves existing power imbalances intact. Post-Marxists on the other hand, propose a direct challenge to hegemonic forces within the state from the "bottom-up". The conflict these analysts see as inherent in the power structure requires an overhaul of the political and economic system if social justice for those on the margins is to be attained.[39]

A global outlook should assist in, among other things, finding advocacy alliances in addition to needed financial support. Following Tarrow, and Batliwala and Brown,[40] Gaventa acknowledged that participatory initiatives must recognize the impact of globalization, which comes with, "shifting traditional understandings of where power resides and how it is exercised, transforming traditional assumptions of how and where citizens mobilize to hold states and non-state actors to account".[41] To the extent that PDCs acknowledge this change, they will possess the potential to embrace pragmatic and effective alliances. Envisioned social justice outcomes are more likely to be achieved when "social movements or social actors . . . are able to link the demands for opening previously closed spaces with people's action in their own spaces, to span across local and global action, and to challenge visible, hidden and invisible power simultaneously".[42]

Implications for Future Research

This analysis has implications for how scholars study democracy in Jamaica and other countries with similar history and socio-economic, political and cultural conditions. I argue that a traditional focus on idealized forms of democratic activity will immediately cast organizations such as the PDCs of Jamaica in a negative light. The NAPDEC report, for example, noted the general absence of regular elections among these entities and dubbed many of them undemocratic for not meeting that standard. The careful investigation of each entity at a granular level undertaken here, however, revealed many and diverse reasons for relatively few PDC elections. These included efforts to preserve the democratic space by negating partisan infiltration as well as waiting to identify a potential candidate who would not only be suitable by meeting constitutional expectations (being a citizen of voting age, for example) but also by meeting the organization's needs as stipulated by the on-the-ground realities it was confronting. Such might range from having the financial wherewithal to assist the group to possessing a reputation that could bring others to the participatory table. Sensitivity to each entity's organizational context is crucial to PDCs' surviving and ultimately thriving. Such an outcome would not be met by simply selecting an available candidate who could gain a majority vote on election day. More generally, I contend that the specific and contextual understanding of problems lends itself to the identification of more useful and sustainable solutions. Providing funds to permit all PDCs to advertise elections, for example, would not address the various reasons at the root of infrequent elections for some PDCs.

Similarly, as it pertains to research design, the identification of where women fall within an organization's hierarchy might serve to highlight gendered social forces at play, but such knowledge does little to show how these forces could be combatted. Far more empowering is to report on the actual observed role played by women; in the case of the PDCs, I found the women's roles to be far more powerful than their titles often suggested. As with gender analyses generally, Jamaica's culture must be incorporated into the study of any local phenomenon in the nation to be well understood. Jamaica's partisan political culture, for example, has alienated many residents from all aspects of politics. Nonetheless, many PDC members, in their interviews, described this absence as simply apathy. Similarly, it would not be sufficient to declare a "closed participatory space" if one class is over-represented without explaining that poverty creates a major barrier for many to engage in civic life in the first instance.

This study captured several other examples, which taken together, support my guidance for future researchers of Jamaican politics to examine each phenomenon under study within its local socio-economic, political and historical context. Doing so reveals complexities and nuances that result in a more complete accounting of organizational activities and processes. I left the research field with an expanded definition of political efficacy, in particular, where members analysed their local conditions and employed emancipatory political tactics to overcome obstacles. These actions might not always be democratic, such as when PDC leaders chose not to hold elections. These steps may also not always be sustainable, such as reaching out for small-scale donations. In other words, I found that some democratic principles were compromised but paradoxically served the immediate and priority needs of the PDCs to keep the participatory space they represented open to the citizenry.

I suspect as well that the methodology and findings of this project will influence the design of my future projects and that of others on the Caribbean and Latin America through its focus on capturing a rich contextual understanding of how people exert power from below and how democratic ideals are pursued sometimes by less than ideal means in an imperfect socio-economic and political environment.

Future Research

There is a story to tell about the nature of the PDCs and the lower layers of Jamaica's participatory organization structure. The inelastic time set for fieldwork of four months and the similarly restricted research budget did not allow me to pursue the nature of the connections among the PDCs, DACs, CDCs and community-based organizations extensively. I hope that future enquiry will specifically explore whether the experiences documented at the PDC, from limited resources to legislative inattention, are also characteristic of the lower levels of the experiment. This knowledge, as well as the strategies employed by those members to combat such challenges, will deepen understanding of the participatory experiment in Jamaica and should give stakeholders and policymakers insight into the elements that constitute an effective programme design for the nation.

I was also made aware from observation and interviews with stakeholders that there is a glaring absence of PDC activity within urban centres. I highlighted some of the reasons for this situation above, which include high crime rates, partisan political violence and a sharper socio-economic divide which keeps communities heavily dissected. I offer here, however, that a more in-depth understanding of this phenomenon is necessary and is only possible through a study which targets specifically former PDC members of these less active bodies. I am interested in engaging in such interviews, as they would shed light on challenges that might very well be unique to Jamaican urban spaces.

I would hope as well that this project sparks an interest in comparative research between Jamaica and other Caribbean countries. Girvan mused about the nature of participatory democracy in Cuba, as a visit forced him to come to terms with his assumptions regarding the country. He then asked himself "whether the ordinary Cuban citizen does not enjoy more democracy in Cuba – at least in the sense of participation – than I do in Jamaica".[46] He did not vote in Jamaica's local government elections and reasoned that such was a pertinent avenue for influencing policy. He recounted his experience in the meeting room with officers or staff directly elected to Cuba's provincial council:

> They appeared to range in age from their late 20s to their 50s with the majority clustered around the mid-point of this range. About one-third were women, and the ethnic balance appeared to be roughly representative of the Cuban population as a whole. Except for a small number of staff employed to the Council, all had been directly elected to the Provincial Assembly. The Assembly is made up of 326 delegates divided roughly equally between those elected directly by the population in the Municipalities, and those elected by the mass organisations (women, youth, workers, professional organisations) by voting every five years. . . . Apart from voting, Cubans can and do participate actively in meetings of the "Circunscripciones" (the basic units in the Municipalities, of which there are 1,510 in Havana City) as well as of the mass organisations to which they belong.[47]

He explained that such a rich participatory experience might be lost in the hostile rhetoric, which often accompanies discussion of that island's political realities by Western outlets. A comparison of Cuba's and Jamaica's experiences with participatory initiatives could provide rich insights into different approaches and lessons learned concerning how ordinary people participate in governance.

Conclusion

The Jamaican experience suggests that the state can and does have a role to play in the creation of spaces for participatory democracy. The nation's democratization process has reflected its history of emancipatory political action, as well as the efforts of a myriad of other actors. The PDCs I examined confront a number of ongoing challenges, including insufficient and unreliable funding, limited participation from the population and, frequently, a lack of political support or even overt obstruction from elected representatives. The degree to which Jamaica's participatory bodies can survive and move forward will depend on the degree to which they are able to overcome these persistent trials. The PDCs I studied have embraced various tactics in their efforts to combat or circumvent particular obstacles, some of which were undemocratic and unsustainable.

These efforts have included but are not limited to fundraising from a variety of sources, which often incorporated personal contributions from members, community businesses and international NGOs. PDCs combated citizenry apathy by pursuing their aims through a small, skilled group of elites experienced in community development while requesting greater levels of participation from the general population. PDC members addressed the "politics" challenge using various strategies. One PDC tackled legislative nonchalance towards its activities by highlighting the mutual benefits of a relationship, which might include sharing information between the bodies or by offering a non-partisan space for policy discussions. Another PDC, prompted primarily by the fear of partisan usurpation, opted not to have elections. Despite the challenges and the frustrations that accompany their involvement in these unique entities, most stakeholders I interviewed remained optimistic about the future of the PDCs. This optimism is due primarily to the faith they have in the emancipatory tactics they employ as well as their own skills and level of commitment to PDC aims.

Notes

Chapter 1. Planting the Seeds of Jamaica's Democracy

1. Keith Miller, "Parish Development Committees and the Emerging New Institutional Framework for Participatory Local Governance in Jamaica" (Office of the Prime Minister Department of Local Government, April 2008), 2.

2. Eris D. Schoburgh, "Local Government Reform in Jamaica and Trinidad: A Policy Dilemma", *Public Administration and Development* 27, no. 2 (1 May 2007): 163, https://doi.org/10.1002/pad.434.

3. Miller, "Parish Development Committees", 4; see also "Kingston and St Andrew Parish Development Committee (KSAPDC) Local Sustainable Development Planning Process: Processes, Best Practices and Lessons Learned" (report, December 2005), 8–9; Ministry of Local Government and Community Development, "Local Government Reform: A Regional Framework for Local Governance and Development"(report, n.d.), 6.

4. Miller, "Parish Development Committees", 2.

5. Robert Buddan, *Foundations of Caribbean Politics* (Kingston: Arawak, 2001), 15; Robert Buddan, "A New Time for Democracy", *Gleaner* (22 June 2003), http://old.jamaica-gleaner.com/gleaner/20030622/focus/focus1.html; Trevor Munroe, "Democracy and Democratization: Global and Caribbean Perspectives on Reform and Research", *Social and Economic Studies* 46, no. 1 (1 March 1997): 31–55.

6. Munroe, "Democracy and Democratization", 39.

7. Ibid., 32.

8. Ministry of Local Government and Community Development, "Local Government Reform", 29.

9. Sérgio Gregorio Baierle, "Porto Alegre: Popular Sovereignty or Dependent Citizens", in *Participation and Democracy in the Twenty-First Century City*, ed. Jenny Pearce (New York: Palgrave Macmillan, 2010), 52; Omar Uran, "Medellín Participative Creativity in a Conflictive City", in *Participation and Democracy in the Twenty-First Century City*, ed. Jenny Pearce (New York: Palgrave Macmillan, 2010), 150.

10. Andrew D. Selee and Enrique Peruzzotti, eds., *Participatory Innovation and Representative Democracy in Latin America* (Washington, DC, and Baltimore: Woodrow Wilson Center Press and Johns Hopkins University Press, 2009), 1.

11. Vertical accountability refers to the extent to which elected officials answer to the electorate; elected leaders inform the public of decisions and justifications for those decisions, and citizens are then able to reward or punish those officials as they see fit. Jonathan Hartlyn, "Democracy Consolidation in Latin America: Current Thinking and Future Challenges", in *Democratic Governance and Social Inequality*, ed. Joseph S. Tulchin and Amelia Brown (Boulder: Lynne Rienner, 2002), 21–49.

12. Horizontal forms of accountability references an autonomous judiciary and other institutions to ensure rule of law.

13. Selee and Peruzzotti, *Participatory Innovation*, 2.

14. Hartlyn, "Democracy Consolidation".

15. Larry Diamond, *Developing Democracy: Toward Consolidation* (Baltimore: Johns Hopkins University Press, 1999), 49.

16. Maxwell A. Cameron, Eric Hershberg and Kenneth E. Sharpe, "Voice and Consequence: Direct Participation and Democracy in Latin America", in *New Institutions for Participatory Democracy in Latin America: Voice and Consequence*, ed. Maxwell A. Cameron, Eric Hershberg and Kenneth E. Sharpe (New York: Palgrave Macmillan, 2012), 2.

18. Hartlyn, "Democracy Consolidation"; Andrew Selee and Joseph Tulchin, "Decentralization and Democratic Governance: Lessons and Challenges", in *Decentralization, Democratic Governance, and Civil Society in Comparative Perspective: Africa, Asia, and Latin America*, ed. Philip Oxhorn, Joseph S. Tulchin and Andrew D. Selee (Washington, DC: Woodrow Wilson Center Press, 2004), 295–320.

18. For a discussion on the various manifestations of clientelism across Latin America, see Tina Hilgers, *Clientelism in Everyday Latin American Politics* (New York: Palgrave Macmillan, 2012).

19. Hartlyn, "Democracy Consolidation", 21–49.

20. Selee and Tulchin, "Decentralization", 309. This is not to say that the goal is always achieved.

21. Carole Pateman, *Participation and Democratic Theory* (Cambridge: Cambridge University Press, 1976); Thomasina Borkman, *Understanding Self-Help/Mutual Aid: Experiential Learning in the Commons* (New Brunswick, NJ: Rutgers University Press, 1999). Borkman has argued that participation leads to the development of social capital and that engagement-related experiential learning becomes transformative. See also Kathleen P. Iannello, *Decisions without Hierarchy: Feminist Interventions in Organization Theory and Practice* (New York: Routledge, 1992). For a full discussion of the challenges that may accompany democratic participation at the micro level, the extent to which these can be overcome, as well as the conditions (for example, a homogenous group, small size, a clear organizational goal) that best facilitate such interactions, see J.E. Thomas, "'Everything about Us Is Feminist': The Significance of Ideology in Organizational Change", *Gender and Society* 13, no. 1 (1999): 101–19, https://www.jstor.org/stable/190242; Joyce Rothschild-Whitt, "The Collectivist Organization: An Alternative to Rational-Bureaucratic Models", *American Sociological Review* 44, no. 4 (August 1979): 509–27, https://doi.org/10.2307/2094585.

22. Susan Clark and Woden Teachout, *Slow Democracy: Rediscovering Community, Bringing Decision Making Back Home* (White River Junction, VT: Chelsea Green Publishing, 2012), 20.

23. Giles Mohan and Kristian Stokke, "Participatory Development and Empowerment: The Dangers of Localism", *Third World Quarterly* 21, no. 2 (April 2000): 247–68.

24. John Gaventa, "Finding the Spaces for Change: A Power Analysis", *IDS Bulletin* 37, no. 6 (November 2006): 23–33.

25. Mohan and Stokke, "Participatory Development".

26. Faranak Miraftab, "Making Neo-liberal Governance: The Disempowering Work of Empowerment", *International Planning Studies* 9, no. 4 (2004): 239–59.

27. Gaventa, "Finding the Spaces"; Andrea Cornwall, "Spaces for Transformation? Reflections on Issues of Power and Difference", in *Participation: From Tyranny to Transformation? Exploring New Approaches to Participation in Development*, ed. Samuel Hickey and Giles Mohan (London: Zed Books, 2004), 75–91.

28. Gaventa, "Finding the Spaces", 25–26.

29. Mohan and Stokke, "Participatory Development", 249–50.

30. Cornwall, "Spaces", 78.

31. Brent L. Pickett, "Foucault and the Politics of Resistance", *Polity* 28, no. 4 (July 1996): 445–66, https://doi.org/10.2307/3235341.

32. James Scott, *Domination and the Arts of Resistance Hidden Transcripts* (New Haven, CT: Yale University Press, 1990).

33. Cornwall, "Spaces", 87.

34. NAPDEC, "Assessment of Parish Development Committees" (2010), 28: "73% of the PDCs, that is, 10 of the 14, are active, meaning that they were holding regular executive meetings, which were planned and implemented by the[ir] members, during the six-month period prior to the assessment".

35. Dvora Yanow, "Thinking Interpretively: Philosophical Presuppositions and the Human Sciences", in *Interpretation and Method: Empirical Research Methods and the Interpretive Turn*, ed. Dvora Yanow and Peregrine Schwartz-Shea (Armonk, NY: M.E. Sharpe, 2006), 22; Henry Brady and David Collier, *Rethinking Social Inquiry: Diverse Tools, Shared Standards*, 2nd ed. (Lanham, MD: Rowman and Littlefield, 2010), 25.

36. David Brion Davis, *Inhuman Bondage: The Rise and Fall of Slavery in the New World* (New York: Oxford University Press, 2008), 207; Joseph J. Williams, *The Maroons of Jamaica* (Chestnut Hill, MA: Boston College Press, 1938).

37. Thomas Benjamin, *The Atlantic World: Europeans, Africans, Indians and Their Shared History, 1400–1900* (New York: Cambridge University Press, 2009), 414.

38. Davis, *Inhuman Bondage*, 207; Aggrey Brown, *Color, Class, and Politics in Jamaica* (New Brunswick, NJ: Transaction Books, 1979), 36–37. Brown argued that rebellion was a permanent feature of Jamaican society.

39. Sidney W. Mintz, "Reflections on Caribbean Peasantries", *Nieuwe West-Indische Gids/New West Indian Guide* 57, nos. 1–2 (January 1983): 1–17.

40. Anthony Harriott et al., *Political Culture of Democracy in Jamaica and in the Americas, 2012: Towards Equality of Opportunity* (Kingston: University of the West Indies/Nashville, TN: Vanderbilt University, 2012), http://www.vanderbilt.edu/lapop/jamaica/Jamaica_Country_Report_2012_W.pdf. In this report, a 2012 Latin American Public Opinion Project study suggested that more than 2 per cent of Jamaicans reported participating in protest actions within a year of the 2012 survey. The study's authors noted convincingly that a high interest in politics and one's position at the lower end of the economic ladder best predicted participation in protest action.

Chapter 2. The Space for and the Characteristics of Participatory Democracy

1. Cornwall, "Spaces"; Gaventa, "Finding the Spaces", 23–33; Mohan and Stokke, "Participatory Development", 247–68.

2. Cornwall, "Spaces", 87.

3. Editorial, "Give Us the Queen!" *Gleaner*, 28 June 2011, http://jamaica-gleaner.com /gleaner/20110628/lead/lead1.html.

4. Munroe, "Democracy", 32.

5. Benjamin Barber, *Strong Democracy: Participatory Politics for a New Age*, 20th anniv. ed. (Berkeley: University of California Press, 2004), xxi; Mark Lawrence Korn-bluh, *Why America Stopped Voting: The Decline of Participatory Democracy and the Emergence of Modern American Politics* (New York: New York University Press, 2000); Glenn C. Altschuler, *Rude Republic: Americans and Their Politics in the Nineteenth Century* (Princeton, NJ: Princeton University Press, 2000).

6. Gerhard Peters and John T. Woolley, "Voter Turnout in Presidential Elections: 1828–2012", American Presidency Project, UC Santa Barbara, 1999–2015, http://www .presidency.ucsb.edu/data/turnout.php.

7. Frank Newport. "Congressional Approval Sinks to Record Low", *Gallup Politics*, 12 November 2013, http://www.gallup.com/poll/165809/congressional-approval-sinks -record-low.aspx; Lydia Saad, "Congress Approval at 18%, Stuck in Long-Term Low Streak", *Gallup Politics*, 26 November 2012, http://www.gallup.com/poll/158948/congress -approval-stuck-long-term-low-streak.aspx. The public's congressional approval rating in 2012 was also 18 per cent.

8. Lawrence LeDuc, *The Politics of Direct Democracy: Referendums in Global Perspective* (Toronto: University of Toronto Press, 2003), 20.

9. Daniel C. Kramer, *Participatory Democracy: Developing Ideals of the Political Left* (Cambridge, MA: Schenkman, 1972), 11.

10. Ibid., 12–13.

11. Ibid., 14.

12. Jeremy Lott, *Citizen Centre Report* 30, no. 5 (3 March 2003).

13. Ibid.; Dalton Russell, Wilhelm Burklin and Andrew Drummond, "Public Opinion and Direct Democracy", *Journal of Democracy* 12, no. 4 (October 2001): 141–53, http:// www.socsci.uci.edu/~rdalton/archive/jod01.pdf.

14. Kevin Mattson, *Creating a Democratic Public: The Struggle for Urban Participatory Democracy during the Progressive Era* (University Park: Pennsylvania State University Press, 1998); Dan A. Chekki, ed., *Participatory Democracy in Action: International Profiles of Community Development* (Sahibabad, India: Vikas, 1979); Mark Bevir, *Democratic Governance* (Princeton, NJ: Princeton University Press, 2010), 257; John S. Dryzek, *Deliberative Global Politics: Discourse and Democracy in a Divided World* (Cambridge: Polity, 2006), 24; Clement Bezold, ed., *Anticipatory Democracy: People in the Politics of the Future* (New York: Vintage, 1978).

15. Barber, *Strong Democracy* (2004 ed.), 132.

16. Ibid., 307.

17. Matthew A. Crenson, *Neighborhood Politics* (Cambridge, MA: Harvard University Press, 1983), 23.

18. Barber, *Strong Democracy* (2004 ed.), 189.

19. R.K. Sinclair, *Democracy and Participation in Athens* (Cambridge: Cambridge University Press, 1988).

20. David Butler and Austin Ranney, "Theory", in *Referendums around the World: The Growing Use of Direct Democracy*, ed. David Butler and Austin Ranney (Washington, DC: AEI Press, 1994), 13.

21. Pateman, *Participation*; Peter Bachrach and Aryeh Botwinick, *Power and Empowerment: A Radical Theory of Participatory Democracy* (Philadelphia: Temple University Press, 1992); Barber, *Strong Democracy* (1984 ed.); Ross E. Mitchell, "Environmental Governance in Mexico: Two Case Studies of Oaxaca's Community Forest Sector", *Journal of Latin American Studies* 38, no. 3 (August 2006): 519–48; Michael Albert and Robin Hahnel, *Looking Forward: Participatory Economics for the Twenty First Century* (Boston: South End Press, 1991); Ronald M. Mason, *Participatory and Workplace Democracy: A Theoretical Development in Critique of Liberalism* (Carbondale: Southern Illinois University Press, 1982).

22. Kramer, *Participatory Democracy*, 36. Freedom is defined as not being the master of another. See: David Held, *Models of Democracy*, 3rd ed. (Stanford, CA: Stanford University Press, 2006).

23. Carol C. Gould, *Rethinking Democracy: Freedom and Social Co-operation in Politics, Economy, and Society* (Cambridge: Cambridge University Press, 1989); Kramer, *Participatory Democracy*, 159. We sometimes shape the world by acting on the circumstances presented to us through purposeful deliberate action. This is the human capacity for self-determination.

24. Charles Zueblin, *A Decade of Civic Development* (Chicago: University of Chicago Press, 1905), 22.

25. Michael J. Sandel, "Introduction", *Liberalism and Its Critics, Readings in Social and Political Theory*, ed. Michael J. Sandel (New York: New York University Press, 1984), 5.

26. Selee and Peruzzotti, *Participatory Innovation*, 6.

27. Selee and Tulchin, "Decentralization", 296.

28. Barber, *Strong Democracy* (1984 ed.), 171–73.

29. Barber, *Strong Democracy* (2004 ed.), 169–70.

30. Ibid., 173–88.

31. Diana C. Mutz, *Hearing the Other Side: Deliberative versus Participatory Democracy* (Cambridge: Cambridge University Press, 2006); Andrew J. Perrin, *Citizen Speak: The Democratic Imagination in American Life*, Morality and Society Series (Chicago: University of Chicago Press, 2006). George Lakoff, *The Political Mind: Why You Can't Understand 21st-Century American Politics with an 18th-Century Brain* (New York: Viking, 2008), 206–7, 267. Cognitive scientist George Lakoff contends that empathy is key if a reflexive brain is to supplant existing frames or positions.

32. Bezold, *Anticipatory Democracy*.

33. Karl-Oskar Lindgren, *Participatory Governance in the EU: Enhancing or Endangering Democracy and Efficiency?* (New York: Palgrave Macmillan, 2011).

34. World Bank Group, "Engaging with Citizens for Improved Results", 2014, http://consultations.worldbank.org/consultation/engaging-citizens-improved-results; S.P. Agrawal, *Information India: 1996–97: Global View* (New Delhi: Concept Publishing Company, 1999), 16: "Evidence is mounting that government programs work better when they seek the participation of potential users, and when they tap the community's reservoir of social capital rather than work against it. The benefits show up in smoother implementation, greater sustainability, and better feedback to government agencies. Higher returns from water-borne sanitation systems in Recife, Brazil; housing schemes for the poor in Port Elizabeth, South Africa; forest management efforts in Gujarat State, India; and health care in Khartoum, Sudan, are all testament to the power of partnership – the participation of local people. This is in contrast with top-down approaches, which often fail".

35. Carmen Sirianni, *Investing in Democracy: Engaging Citizens in Collaborative Governance* (Washington, DC: Brookings Institution Press, 2009), 43.

36. Ibid., 11.

37. Robert Putnam, "The Prosperous Community: Social Capital and Public Life", *American Prospect* 13 (1993): 35–42, Robert Putnam, "Bowling Alone: America's Declining Social Capital", *Journal of Democracy* 6, no. 1 (1995): 65–78.

38. Charles E. Lindblom and David K. Cohen, *Usable Knowledge: Social Science and Social Problem Solving* (New Haven, CT: Yale University Press, 1979), 12.

39. Mitchell, "Environmental Governance in Mexico".

40. Borkman, *Understanding Self-Help*, 38.

41. Kramer, *Participatory Democracy*; Pateman, *Participation*.

42. Pateman, *Participation*, 37–42; Kramer, *Participatory Democracy*, 18.

43. Pateman, *Participation*, 107.

44. Iannello, *Decisions without Hierarchy*, 22. The quote comes from a DuPont executive.

45. Thomas, "'Everything about Us Is Feminist'", 101–19.

46. Jeff Hyman, Paul Thompson and Bill Harley, eds., *Participation and Democracy at Work: Essays in Honour of Harvie Ramsay* (New York: Palgrave Macmillan, 2005).

47. Mason, *Participatory*; Marvin Elliott Olsen, *Participatory Pluralism: Political Participation and Influence in the United States and Sweden* (Chicago: Burnham, 1982); Lane Davis, "The Cost of Realism: Contemporary Restatements of Democracy", *Western Political Quarterly* 17, no. 1 (March 1964): 37–46, https://doi.org/10.2307/445369.

48. Davis, "Cost of Realism", 41.

49. Crenson, *Neighborhood Politics*, 18.

50. Ibid., 17.

51. Ibid., viii–x, 9–17. Locke and Rosseau argued that citizens should establish political bonds with each other within a local community before they made agreements with kings and legislators.

52. Ibid., 9.

53. Zander Navarro, "Porto Alegre: From Municipal Innovations to the Culturally Embedded Micro-Politics of (Un)Emancipated Citizens: The Case of Rubbish Recyclers," in *Participation and Democracy in the Twenty-First Century City*, ed. Jenny Pearce (New York: Palgrave Macmillan, 2010), 80.

54. Gianpaolo Baiocchi, *Militants and Citizens: The Politics of Participatory Democracy in Porto Alegre* (Palo Alto, CA: Stanford University Press, 2005); Anny Rivera-Ottenberger, "Against All Odds: Participatory Local Governance and the Urban Poor in Chile", in *Participatory Innovation and Representative Democracy in Latin America*, ed. Andrew D. Selee and Enrique Peruzzotti (Washington, DC: Woodrow Wilson Center Press, 2009), 89–125. Rivera-Ottenberger addressed how benefits could be lost if the participatory approach is not institutionalized. Kramer, *Participatory Democracy*, 113, 118–19. Kramer offered an American example where the Mayors designed the project that way, as they feared a loss of political clout if they had limited control over the dissemination of jobs created by the programme. This result was a lack of participation that could be interpreted as apathy without deeper examination of the context. In some cases, residents stayed away because they distrusted the public officials they had to work with on the programme. In fact, they saw these individuals as a cause of their problems. Jonathan Pugh, "Social Transformation and Participatory Planning in St Lucia", *Area* 37, no. 4 (December 2005): 384–92. Pugh's study revealed that elite programme designs produce different outcomes than when programme elements arise from those they aim to serve.

55. Juan J. Linz and Alfred Stepan, *Problems of Democratic Transition and Consolidation: Southern Europe, South America, and Post-Communist Europe* (Baltimore: Johns Hopkins University Press, 1996), 186–87. The authors explained that the pay cheques were not necessarily personal ones as many individuals received as many as seven consistent pay cheques.

56. Ibid., 186–87.

57. Sirianni, *Investing in Democracy*, 21–28.

58. Ibid., 14–17.

59. Mohan and Stokke, "Participatory Development".

60. Gaventa, "Finding the Spaces", 28.

61. Navarro, "Porto Alegre", 86.

62. Ibid., 97; Selee and Tulchin, "Decentralization", 313.

63. See Bradley J. Young, *TABOR and Direct Democracy: An Essay on the End of the Republic* (Golden, CO: Fulcrum, 2006); Kramer, *Participatory Democracy*, 124. Bradley Young suggested that citizens are simply busy and cannot find the time to engage meaningfully in law-making.

64. Quoted in Kramer, *Participatory Democracy*, 130–32.

65. Ethan J. Leib and Baogang He, eds., *The Search for Deliberative Democracy in China* (New York: Palgrave Macmillan, 2006).

66. Rothschild-Whitt, "Collectivist Organization".

67. Sirianni, *Investing in Democracy*; Simone Chambers, *Reasonable Democracy: Jürgen Habermas and the Politics of Discourse* (Ithaca, NY: Cornell University Press, 1996); Steve Martinot and Joy James, eds., *The Problems of Resistance: Studies in Alternate Political Cultures*, vol. 2 (Amherst, NY: Humanity Books, 2001).

68. Chambers, *Reasonable Democracy*; Martinot and James, *Problems of Resistance*.

69. Frank MacKinnon, *Postures and Politics: Some Observations on Participatory Democracy* (Toronto: University of Toronto Press, 1973).

70. Crenson, *Neighborhood Politics*, 17

71. Cornwall, "Spaces", 79.

72. Ibid., 79, 84; Robert A. Dahl, *On Political Equality* (New Haven, CT: Yale University Press, 2006), 85–86.

73. Nici Nelson and Susan Wright, *Power and Participatory Development: Theory and Practice* (London: Practical Action, 1995), 1–18.

74. Sirianni, *Investing in Democracy*, 3, 20–21.

75. Guy Gran, *Development by People: Citizen Construction of a Just World* (New York: Praeger, 1983).

76. Lawrence Powell, "Are We Experiencing an Epidemic of Distrust?" *Gleaner*, April 7, 2010, http://jamaica-gleaner.com/gleaner/20100407/cleisure/cleisure3.html. In summarizing his research on social capital in Jamaica, Powell noted "the overall atmosphere of trust within Jamaican society is disturbingly low at present".

77. Diamond, *Developing Democracy*, 122–23; Charles Tilly, *Democracy* (New York: Cambridge University Press, 2007), 59; Arend Lijphart, *Patterns of Democracy: Government Forms and Performance in Thirty-Six Countries* (New Haven, CT: Yale University Press, 1999); Joseph V. Montville, *Conflict and Peacemaking in Multiethnic Societies* (Lexington, MA: Lexington Books, 1989); John S. Dryzek, "Deliberative Democracy in Divided Societies: Alternatives to Agonism and Analgesia", *Political Theory* 33, no. 2 (April 2005): 223; Rothschild-Whitt, "Collectivist Organization"; Mutz, *Hearing*, 148.

78. Powell, "Are We Experiencing".

79. Edward N. Muller and Mitchell A. Seligson, "Civic Culture and Democracy: The Question of Causal Relationships", *American Political Science Review* 88, no. 3 (September 1994): 546–47, https://doi.org/10.2307/2944800.

80. Pamela Paxton, "Social Capital and Democracy: An Interdependent Relationship", *American Sociological Review* 67, no. 2 (April 2002): 254–77, https://doi.org/10.2307/3088895. Using data from the World Values Survey as well as the Union of International Associations in a cross-lagged panel design led Paxton to conclude that social capital affects democracy and that democracy shapes social capital.

81. Tilly, *Democracy*, 74.

82. Ibid., 74–76.

83. Jenny Pearce, introduction to *Participation and Democracy in the Twenty-First Century City*, ed. Jenny Pearce (New York: Palgrave Macmillan, 2010), 12.

84. Terry Lynn Karl, "Dilemmas of Democratization in Latin America", *Comparative Politics* 23, no. 1 (October 1990): 1–21, https://doi.org/10.2307/422302. Karl recommends instead clarifying how the mode of regime transition (itself conditioned by the breakdown of authoritarian rule) sets the context within which strategic interactions can take place; examining how these exchanges, in turn, help to determine whether political democracy will emerge and survive; and analysing what type of democracy will eventually be institutionalized.

85. Ibid., 13–14.

86. Ibid., 16.

87. James C. Scott, *Weapons of the Weak: Everyday Forms of Peasant Resistance* (Princeton, NJ: Yale University Press, 1987), 29; Scott, *Domination*; Michel de Certeau, *The Practice of Everyday Life*, trans. Steven F. Rendall (Berkeley: University of California Press, 2011).

88. Benjamin, *Atlantic World*; Davis, *Inhuman Bondage*; Brown, *Color*.

89. Brown, *Color*, 15.

90. R.B. Sheridan, "The Wealth of Jamaica in the Eighteenth Century", *Economic History Review*, new ser., 18, no. 2 (January 1965): 292–311, https://doi.org/10.2307/2592096.

91. Trevor Burnard, "A Failed Settler Society: Marriage and Demographic Failure in Early Jamaica", *Journal of Social History* 28, no. 1 (October 1994): 64.

92. Richard S. Dunn, "The Demographic Contrast between Slave Life in Jamaica and Virginia, 1760–1865", *Proceedings of the American Philosophical Society* 151, no. 1 (March 2007): 43.

93. Davis, *Inhuman Bondage*, 207.

94. Williams, *Maroons of Jamaica*.

95. Brown, *Color*, 36–37.

96. Benjamin, *Atlantic World*, 414.

97. Davis, *Inhuman Bondage*, 207. Rebellion was a permanent feature of Jamaican society according to Brown (*Color*, 36–37).

98. Brown, *Color*, 50–52.

99. Eric Williams, *The Negro in the Caribbean* (New York: Haskell House, 1971), 16; Howard Johnson and Karl S. Watson, eds., *The White Minority in the Caribbean*, illus. ed. (Princeton, NJ: Markus Wiener, 1997), xiv.

100. Mintz, "Reflections", 1–17.

101. Williams, *Negro*, 49.

102. Ibid., 52.

103. Emily Zobel Marshall, *Anansi's Journey: A Story of Jamaican Cultural Resistance* (Kingston: University of the West Indies Press, 2012), 94.

104. Ibid., 167.

105. Ibid., 134; Gaventa, "Finding the Spaces", 28.

106. Marshall, *Anansi's Journey*, 174.

107. Hume N. Johnson, "Incivility: The Politics of 'People on the Margins' in Jamaica", *Political Studies* 53 (October 2005): 592, https://doi.org/10.1111/j.1467-9248.2005.00545.x.

108. Richard L. Bernal, "The IMF and Class Struggle in Jamaica, 1977–1980", *Latin American Perspectives* 11, no. 3 (July 1984): 53–82; Anders Danielson, "Economic Reforms in Jamaica", *Journal of Interamerican Studies and World Affairs* 38, nos. 2–3 (July 1996): 97–108, https://doi.org/10.2307/166362; Helen McBain, "Government Financing of Economic Growth and Development in Jamaica: Problems and Prospects", *Social and Economic Studies* 39, no. 4 (December 1990): 179–212.

109. Diane J. Austin, "Culture and Ideology in the English-Speaking Caribbean: A View from Jamaica", *American Ethnologist* 10, no. 2 (May 1983): 223–40.

110. Schoburgh, "Local Government Reform", 159–74.

111. Department of Local Government, "Final Report of the National Advisory Council on Local Government Reform" (report for Office of the Prime Minister, November 2009), 9–10.

112. Schoburgh, "Local Government Reform".

113. Ministry of Local Government and Community Development, "Local Government Reform", 7.

114. Philip D. Osei, "Strengthening Local Fiscal Capacity in Jamaica, 1993–2002", *Social and Economic Studies* 51, no. 4 (December 2002): 32–34.

115. Ibid.

116. Ibid., 32–34; Ministry of Local Government and Community Development, "Local Government Reform", 9. The JLP oversaw the dissolution of the St Catherine Parish Council in 1949, Trelawny Parish Council in 1954, Portland Parish Council in 1963 and KSAC in 1964 and 1984.

117. Osei, "Strengthening", 32–34.

118. Carlene J. Edie, "From Manley to Seaga: The Persistence of Clientelist Politics in Jamaica", *Social and Economic Studies* 38, no. 1 (March 1989): 16–17. According to surveys carried out by Jamaican pollster Carl Stone, an overwhelming majority of workers in all sectors supported, in principle, the concepts of (1) workers sharing ownership in the enterprises to which they sell their labour; (2) profit-sharing between workers and the company; (3) management of workers by committees instead of by one boss; (4) direct worker representation as opposed to that through trade unions; and (5) having a larger voice in managing the enterprises where they work.

119. Ministry Paper 51. Six officers of the commission were granted scholarships overseas to pursue studies in specialized fields of interest. In addition, UNESCO provided technical support to some of these initiatives.

120. Ministry Paper 52, 5.

121. Edie, "From Manley to Seaga", 16.

122. Issa G. Shivji, *Silences in NGO Discourse: The Role and Future of NGOs in Africa* (Nairobi: Pambazuka Press, 2007). There was a radical shift in the 1980s and 1990s, when international financial institutions and development agencies began giving money to NGOs and less to governments.

123. Osei, "Strengthening", 32–34, 46; "Kingston and St Andrew Parish Development Committee", 20: "In November 2002, KSA, through the KSAC and KSA PDC, became the first Caribbean City to receive funding from the World Bank's Cities Alliance Programme toward the development of a Sustainable Development Plan". United Nations Development Programme, "Country: Jamaica Project Document: Building Civil Society Capacity to Support Good Governance by Local Authorities" (report for United Nations, 2010).

124. Horace Levy, "Community in Jamaica", typescript (n.d.).

125. Gaventa, "Finding the Spaces".

126. Miller, "Parish Development Committees", 3; See also: Cabinet Office, "Local Government Policy" (policy statement to reinforce the state's commitment to participatory democracy, 1 July 2011); Ministry Paper Number 56, 19: Note the key objectives of public sector reform: confirming the role and functions of government as well as improving "the ways in which Jamaica is governed, through sharing the exercise of power and increasing participation in decision-making".

127. "Kingston and St Andrew Parish Development Committee", 9.

128. Ministry Paper 56, 7–8; Department of Local Government, "Final Report", 9–10. There is some confusion in the literature about the launch date. At least one report mentions that the first PDC was officially launched in Portland in 2000. "Kingston and

St Andrew Parish Development Committee", 8; Colin Fagan, "Transforming Communities", Ministry of Local Government and Community Development Contribution to the Sectoral Debate 2012–2013 (11 July 2012). Legislator support was declared early: "As such Mr Speaker, we shall place primary focus on building the capacity of our Parish Development Committees (PDCs) and other civil society partners to work even more closely with their Local Authorities in fashioning and building a broader collective planning and development mechanism, that utilizes all the diverse natural, professional, cultural and creative resources available to each parish."

129. Damion Keith Blake, "Direct Democracy and the New Paradigm of Democratic Politics in Jamaica", *Social and Economic Studies* 53, no. 4 (December 2004): 163–90. Damion Blake documented how the implementation of PDCs reflected a shift in Jamaica towards engaging the citizenry in governance.

130. Miller, "Parish Development Committees", 5–6.

131. Ministry Paper No 56 (September 2002), 17. The other principles include the facilitation of investment and trade; pro-poor policies; equitable provision of services; justice for all; open and accountable, as in free from corruption; and promoting of partnerships with civil society and the private sector.

132. Miller, "Parish Development Committees", 2.

133. Ibid., 6–8; Lois A. Jackson, "Canadian Bilateral Aid to Jamaica's Agricultural Sector from 1972–86", *Social and Economic Studies* 41, no. 2 (June 1992): 83–101.

134. Osei, "Strengthening", 31–62.

135. Miller, "Parish Development Committees", 3–4. The state having designed the PDCs did not convey to them the rights and privileges as a registered agency of the state.

136. Communications Unit, Office of the Prime Minister, *The Councillor's Handbook: A Guide for Jamaican Councillors* (Kingston: Department of Local Government, 2009), 35; "Kingston and St Andrew Parish Development Committee", 16: "The objectives of the PDC were never made very clear, and in the early stages of their formation, Parish Councils (PCs) were very wary of them. They were viewed by PCs as competitors who were there to replace them. The creation of the PDCs came from the national level, without sufficient sensitization of the local authority on its roles and responsibilities. Consequently, the relationship between the PCs and the PDCs has not been fully resolved."

137. Social Development Commission, "Corporate Plan, 2012–2015", 5–9, 13, 15.

138. NAPDEC, "Assessment of Parish Development Committees", 28.

139. Ibid., 28, 46.

140. Ibid., 36.

141. Ibid., 29–30, 32–35, 45.

142. Ibid., 45, 29.

143. "Kingston and St Andrew Parish Development Committee", 1–2.

144. NAPDEC, "Assessment of Parish Development Committees", 29–30, 32–35, 45, 53–54.

145. Ibid., 25.

146. Gaventa, "Finding the Spaces", 25.

Chapter 3. The People and Paradigm of the PDC Process

1. This body includes a representative, usually a minister of religion, from each church in a particular geographic area.

2. Ministry of Local Government and Community Development, "Structure, Role and Functions of the Local Authority", Government of Jamaica, accessed 3 October 2014, https://www.localgovjamaica.gov.jm/roles-and-functions/.

3. Ministry of Local Government and Community Development, "Local Government Reform", 29.

4. Local Authorities of Jamaica, "Parish Development Committees", Ministry of Local Government and Community Development, 2014, http://www.localauthorities.gov.jm /parish-development-committees.

5. Lindsay Prior, *Using Documents in Social Research* (Thousand Oaks, CA: Sage, 2003), 28; Jane Bennett, *Vibrant Matter: A Political Ecology of Things* (Durham, NC: Duke University Press, 2010), viii, 27. The term "vibrant matter" as used here is understood primarily through the work of Bennett who articulated a powerful and pragmatic agenda. She has sought "to encourage more intelligent and sustainable engagement with vibrant matter and lively things" (viii). Her aspiration is to articulate a "vibrant materiality that runs alongside and inside humans to see how analyses of political events might change if we gave the force of things more due" (viii). If we can acknowledge that the human body, for example, is a thing, comprised of various material constructs (the minerals that make up our bones or the electricity that makes our neurons functional are good examples), we would then be able to accept similar "assemblages" in the world, from an electric grid to a polity.

6. Harriott et al., *Political Culture*. A 2012 Latin American Public Opinion Project study suggested that just over 2 per cent of Jamaicans report participating in protest actions within a year of the 2012 survey. The study notes convincingly that a high interest in politics and one's position at the lower end of the economic ladder best predicted participation in protest action. K.W.J. Post, "The Politics of Protest in Jamaica, 1938: Some Problems of Analysis and Conceptualization", *Social and Economic Studies* 18, no. 4 (December 1969): 374–90; Johnson, "Incivility".

7. Katherine Butler, "Jamaica Erupts in Fuel Price Rioting", *Independent* (22 April 1999), http://www.independent.co.uk/news/jamaica-erupts-in-fuel-price-rioting-1088840 .html. Entrepreneur Gordon "Butch" Stewart, who owns the Sandals hotel resort chain, described the gas riots this way: "It's a hell of a signal to the government that enough is enough."

8. Ministry of Local Government and Community Development, "Local Government Reform", 1; Portia Simpson Miller, "A Modern System of Local Government Is Essential to Good Governance in Jamaica", Ministry of Local Government, Community Development and Sport Contribution to the Sectorial Debate 2004 (June 2004), 4. The former prime minister's observation also figured in the 2004 Sectorial Debate by the Hon. Portia Simpson Miller.

9. World Education Forum, "The Education for All (EFA) 2000 Assessment: Country Reports. Jamaica", *UNESCO*, http://www.unesco.org/education/wef/countryreports /jamaica/rapport_2.html; "This is a programme designed to employ 40,000 people aged

18–30 by the end of the year 2000 at a cost of JA $2.5 billion. The long-term objective is to socialize young people into accepting the value and importance of working according to time, quality, teamwork and accountability. There are three basic features of the programme, which if achieved, will have significant impact on national development: (a) It is aimed at harnessing and improving the infrastructural capacity of the island (for example, rehabilitating watersheds, maintenance of roads, restoration of buildings), (b) Compulsory training is a pre-condition for employment and (c) The identification of projects and individuals recruited is done through a process of consultations with all relevant sectors of the society". See also: Editorial, "Lift Up Jamaica Programme Boosting Work Ethic – UDC", *Gleaner*, 15 August, 2000, https://gleaner.newspaperarchive.com/kingston-gleaner/2000-08-15/page-5/.

10. Schoburgh, "Local Government Reform", 169.

11. Barber, *Strong Democracy* (20th anniv. ed.), 309.

12. NAPDEC, "Assessment of Parish Development Committees", 28.

13. Barber, *Strong Democracy* (1984 ed.); Pateman, *Participation*, 24–25; Mason, *Participatory*, 192; Olsen, *Participatory Pluralism*.

14. Clark and Teachout, *Slow Democracy*, 20. See also Mutz, *Hearing*; Perrin, *Citizen Speak*; Bezold, *Anticipatory Democracy*.

15. Miller, "Parish Development Committees", 2.

16. Sirianni, *Investing in Democracy*, 43; Clark and Teachout, *Slow Democracy*, 9–19, 25–27, 35–37; Crenson, *Neighborhood Politics*.

17. Ministry of Local Government and Community Development, "Local Government Reform", 29.

18. Portmore Citizens Advisory Council, "The National Association of Parish Development Committees (NAPDEC), 2011–2012". PCAC is "an organization through which the citizens of Portmore are given the opportunity to participate in the governance process of the municipality". In essence, this is a PDC for a unique municipality in the parish of St Catherine. They also have a representative on NAPDEC.

19. The Department of Co-operatives and Friendly Societies (DCFS), "Get Your Facts on Friendly Societies", Ministry of Industry, Investment and Commerce, Government of Jamaica, 2007. The Friendly Societies Act of 1968 allows for a broad range of organizations to register as a legal entity for operation within Jamaica. It incorporates PDCs according to clauses allowing groups with any benevolent or charitable purpose or a focus on community development.

20. Miller, "Parish Development Committees", 6–8.

21. Gaventa, "Finding the Spaces", 23–33.

22. Avagay Simpson, "Survey on the Status of the Local Public Accounts Committee (LPAC) in Jamaica" (report for the Building Civil Society Capacity to Support Good Governance by Local Authorities Project, June 2011), 5. This project is funded by United Nations Development Programme Jamaica under the Democratic Governance Thematic Trust Fund (DGTTF). Most PDCs have been invited and do serve as watchdogs of the finances of parish councils though the Local Public Accounts Committee (LPAC). "The Local Public Accounts Committee of the Parish Council is established in accordance with provisions of the Parish Councils Act or Municipalities Acts (KSCAC & Portmore)

and procedures and bylaws of the Council. The LPAC's main function is to provide ongoing oversight and examination of all financial activities and the management and performance of the Local Authority."

23. Editorial, "Unemployment Biggest Concern for Jamaicans", *Jamaica Observer*, 21 September 2010.

24. NAPDEC, "Assessment of Parish Development Committees", 28. The 2010 assessment of all PDCs by NAPDEC revealed that there were eleven active PDCs, two partially active and one inactive body.

25. Gaventa, "Finding the Spaces", 26–27. PDCs might then be unintentionally closed spaces, where, according to Gaventa, decisions are made by representatives without the input of the masses. See also the discussion on participatory space in Cornwall, "Spaces", 75–91.

26. Each parish council determines the number and composition of these committees.

27. To offer some perspective, in 2012, Jamaica's smallest parish population comprised 69,874 citizens, according to the Statistical Institute of Jamaica, "Population by Parish, 2012", http://statinja.gov.jm/Demo_SocialStats/populationbyparish.aspx.

28. NAPDEC, "Assessment of Parish Development Committees", 36.

29. Clark and Teachout, *Slow Democracy*.

30. Name changed.

31. Adrian Frater, "Living at Risk in St James", *Gleaner*, 13 October 2013, http://jamaica-gleaner.com/gleaner/20131013/lead/lead65.html; T.K. Whyte, "Dirty Rodney Memorial Complex Irks Parish Development Committee Chairman", *Jamaica Observer*, 9 May 2007.

32. Cornwall, "Spaces", 78.

33. Sirianni, *Investing in Democracy*, 14–17.

34. Shaun Bowler, "'Hybrid Democracy' and Its Consequences", in *Direct Democracy's Impact on American Political Institutions*, ed. Shaun Bowler and Amihai Glazer (New York: Palgrave Macmillan, 2008), 4. The author shows that the threat of citizen activism causes legislators to act differently; the proverbial "gun behind the door" leads to policies that are closer to voter needs.

35. Selee and Tulchin, "Decentralization", 296.

36. Clark and Teachout, *Slow Democracy*; Sirianni, *Investing in Democracy*; Jonathan Pugh and Robert B. Potter, eds., *Participatory Planning in the Caribbean: Lessons from Practice* (Aldershot, UK: Ashgate, 2003).

37. Navarro, "Porto Alegre", 81; Kimberly Nettles, "Learning, But Not Always Earning: The Promise and Problematics of Women's Grassroots Development in Guyana", in *Participatory Planning in the Caribbean: Lessons from Practice*, ed. Jonathan Pugh and Robert B. Potter (Aldershot, UK: Ashgate, 2003), 175–76. Participation, for a variety of reasons, tends to be limited. Red Thread Women's Development Organization geared towards income-generating projects for rural Guyanese women engaged between two hundred and four hundred women at its peak in the mid-1980s, but only twenty-five women were considered active in 1996.

38. M.G. Smith, "Education and Occupational Choice in Rural Jamaica", *Social and Economic Studies* 9, no. 3 (September 1960): 347; Nassau A. Adams, "Internal Migration in Jamaica: An Economic Analysis", *Social and Economic Studies* 18, no. 2 (June 1969): 137–51.

39. Rothschild-Whitt, "Collectivist Organization", 509–27.

40. Irving L. Janis, *Groupthink: Psychological Studies of Policy Decisions and Fiascos*, 2nd ed. (Boston: Cengage Learning, 1982), 5. The inclination in such cases involves a group rejecting the views of nonconformists.

41. Barber, *Strong Democracy* (1984 ed.), 171–73.

42. "The KSA Parish Development Committee", Kingston and St Andrew Parish Development Committee, accessed 10 June 2013, http://www.ksapdc.com/about-us.html.

43. A few PDC members I interviewed pointed out that at the lower levels (DACs and CDCs), there is greater class diversity among members. Race is still an important factor in Jamaican life, but not overtly so. This is due to the mass exodus of whites following Emancipation, which explains why Jamaica presently has a population of 2,683,707, of which only 4,365 are white. Race today is covert in the sense that its influence lingers without a formal declaration. Whites are disproportionately owners of the means of production, and even though they are increasingly based off the island, they continue to retain their influence. The lack of diversity with regard to class stands out more in the present day than in the past and is particularly salient as it reflects partly the value system which determines one's positions on the issues faced by the PDCs.

44. NAPDEC, "Assessment of Parish Development Committees", 45.

45. Editorial, "Partisan Politics and Job Allocation", *Gleaner*, 8 February 2004. "Clientelism in the Jamaican context constrains genuine democratic forms associated with parliamentary democracy, promotes personalised authority and therefore weak, non-autonomous and partially bureaucratised institutions, encourages low levels of accountability in political life and high concentrations of personal power, retards the development of a civic sense of a national interest independent of party political interests, discourages independent individual and group participation in public life. . . . It represents a species of authoritarian democracy the democratic content of which is anchored on the ballot box and competitive elections." Carl Stone, *Democracy and Clientelism in Jamaica* (New Brunswick, NJ: Transaction Books, 1980), 109. PNP Policy Commission Report (10 November 2003), https://rightstepsandpouitrees.files .wordpress.com/2016/06/kerr-report.pdf. See also "Report of the National Committee on Political Tribalism" (23 July 1997), https://rightstepsandpouitrees.files.wordpress.com /2016/06/kerr-report.pdf; Miller, "Parish Development Committees", 2.

46. Harriott et al., *Political Culture*, 142.

47. Faith Webster, "Gender Mainstreaming: Its Role in Addressing Gender Inequality in Jamaica", *Caribbean Quarterly* 52, nos. 2–3 (June 2006): 104–20.

48. Julie L. Hotchkiss and Robert E. Moore, "Gender Compensation Differentials in Jamaica", *Economic Development and Cultural Change* 44, no. 3 (April 1996): 657–76.

49. Annelle Bellony, Alejandro Hoyos and Hugo Nopo, "Gender Earnings Gaps in the Caribbean: Evidence from Barbados and Jamaica", *Inter-American Development Bank* (August 2010): 1–33, https://www.econstor.eu/bitstream/10419/89065/1/IDB-WP-210.pdf.

50. Nettles, "Learning".

51. Belinda Robnett, *How Long? How Long? African-American Women in the Struggle for Civil Rights* (New York: Oxford University Press, 1997), 19–21.

52. Carl Stone, "Class and Status Voting in Jamaica", *Social and Economic Studies* 26, no. 3 (September 1977): 279–93. Carl Stone uncovered increasing class voting among the

Jamaican electorate during the 1970s. Edwin Jones, "Class and Administrative Development Doctrines in Jamaica", *Social and Economic Studies* 30, no. 3 (September 1981): 17–18. The class divide is so entrenched in Jamaica that fear "of incurring bureaucratic wrath and discontent" has prevented the electorate from applying necessary correctives to the state's administrative bureaucracy.

53. Rebekah Nathan, *My Freshman Year: What a Professor Learned by Becoming a Student* (Ithaca, NY: Cornell University Press, 2005), 65.

54. Gaventa, "Finding the Spaces", 29.

55. R. Robert Huckfeldt, *Political Disagreement: The Survival of Diverse Opinions within Communication Networks*, Cambridge Studies in Political Psychology and Public Opinion (Cambridge: Cambridge University Press, 2004).

56. Pierre Bourdieu, *Pascalian Meditations* (Palo Alto, CA: Stanford University Press, 2000), 81–96. "Habitus" here refers to actions and practices that individual's evidence who have been socialized to perpetuate a particular construct. This distinction is explained through the conceptual framework of the nomos. According to Bourdieu, the nomos, or law, is irreducible to and incommensurable with any other law or "regime of truth".

57. Wilma Bailey, Clement Branche and Aldrie Henry-Lee, "Gender Relations and Conflict Management in Inner-City Communities in Jamaica: The Importance of Community Participation", in *Participatory Planning in the Caribbean: Lessons from Practice*, ed. Jonathan Pugh and Robert B. Potter (Aldershot, UK: Ashgate, 2003), 152.

58. Jodi Halpern and Harvey M. Weinstein, "Rehumanizing the Other: Empathy and Reconciliation", *Human Rights Quarterly* 26, no. 3 (August 2004): 561–83; Dahl, *On Political Equality*, 37.

59. Dryzek, *Deliberative Global Politics*; Ulrich Beck, *Power in the Global Age: A New Global Political Economy* (Cambridge: Polity, 2014), 23, 119.

60. Rothschild-Whitt, "Collectivist Organization".

61. Sirianni, *Investing in Democracy*, 47.

62. Ibid., 43.

63. Zueblin, *Decade*.

64. Name changed.

65. Borkman, *Understanding Self-Help*.

66. Huckfeldt, *Political Disagreement*, 4.

67. Barber, *Strong Democracy* (2004 ed.), 169–70.

68. Eugene Linden, *The Alms Race: The Impact of American Voluntary Aid Abroad* (New York: Random House, 1976); Dorothy L. Hodgson, *Once Intrepid Warriors: Gender, Ethnicity, and the Cultural Politics of Maasai Development* (Bloomington: Indiana University Press, 2004); Dambisa Moyo and Niall Ferguson, *Dead Aid: Why Aid Is Not Working and How There Is a Better Way for Africa* (New York: Farrar, Straus and Giroux, 2010).

69. Linden, *Alms Race*, 266–68; Hodgson, *Once Intrepid Warriors*, 8; Moyo and Ferguson, *Dead Aid*; Shivji, *Silences*.

70. Etzioni, "Towards an I & We Paradigm", xi.

71. Charles Price, *Becoming Rasta: Origins of Rastafari Identity in Jamaica* (New York: New York University Press, 2009). Price offers detailed accounts of the extent of the persecution faced by many Rastafarians by the state and even family members.

72. Name changed.

73. Linz and Stepan, *Problems*, 186–87. The state of Ceara, headed by two reform governors, created an award-winning grassroots preventative medicine health programme which led to a fall in infant mortality of 32 per cent in just four years. These executives also created a successful participatory self-housing programme.

74. Only one interviewee mentioned that his group had term limits.

Chapter 4. Rowing against the Tide of Assumptions: Testing the Limits of Survival and Creativity

1. Powell, "Are We Experiencing".

2. Amanda Sives, *Elections, Violence and the Democratic Process in Jamaica 1944–2007* (Kingston: Ian Randle, 2010); Obika Gray, "Predation Politics and the Political Impasse in Jamaica", *Small Axe*, no. 13 (March 2003): 72–95; Faye V. Harrison, "The Politics of Social Outlawry in Urban Jamaica", *Urban Anthropology and Studies of Cultural Systems and World Economic Development* 17, nos. 2–3 (July 1988): 259–77.

3. Harriott et al., *Political Culture*, 30.

4. Mohan and Stokke, "Participatory Development", 252.

5. Young, *TABOR*; Kramer, *Participatory Democracy*.

6. Robert Lane, *Political Ideology: Why the American Common Man Believes What He Does* (New York: Free Press of Glencoe, 1962).

7. *Jamaica Survey of Living Conditions* (Kingston: Planning Institute of Jamaica and the Statistical Institute of Jamaica, 2008, 2009 and 2012).

8. Dahl, *On Political Equality*.

9. Deborah A. Thomas, *Modern Blackness: Nationalism, Globalization, and the Politics of Culture in Jamaica* (Durham, NC: Duke University Press, 2004), 229.

10. Ibid., 250.

11. Ibid., 249–51.

12. T.M. Thomas Isaac and Patrick Heller, "Democracy and Development: Decentralized Planning in Kerala", in *Deepening Democracy: Institutional Innovations in Empowered Participatory Governance*, ed. Archon Fung (London: Verso, 2003), 81.

13. Robert Lane, *Political Life: Why People Get Involved in Politics* (New York: Free Press, 1959); Angus Campbell et al., *The Voter Decides: A Study of the Voter's Perceptions, Attitudes, and Behaviors . . . Based on a Survey of the 1952 Election* (Evanston, IL: Row, Peterson, 1954); Nelson W. Polsby, *Community Power and Political Theory*, Yale Studies in Political Science 7 (New Haven, CT: Yale University Press, 1965), 116.

14. Jane Jacobs, *The Death and Life of Great American Cities* (New York: Random House, 1961).

15. Crenson, *Neighborhood Politics*, 297–98, 303.

16. Rivera-Ottenberger, "Against All Odds". Even in the most destitute of locations, participatory democracy has been able to find a foothold. See also the cases surveyed in Fung, *Deepening Democracy*.

17. Crenson, *Neighborhood Politics*, 197–200.

18. Clement Dodd and Greg Rose, "Hand Cart Boy" (recorded by Perfect), *Serious Times* (XL Recordings, 2006).

19. Dahl, *On Political Equality*, 85–86.

20. Crenson, *Neighborhood Politics*, 201–2.

21. Gaventa, "Finding the Spaces", 27.

22. A third-party leader explained: "Here is what we do know: we know that the people have the talk shows. One of the reasons why talk shows have become popular we have over twenty-one of them is because really it is the only forum where ordinary people can get an opportunity to voice their opinions." My reflection on this interview led to the realization that calling a radio show from the convenience of one's house is perhaps cheaper, quicker and more convenient than going into the town square for a meeting. One also has a captive audience of sorts, and the intimidation factor of a middle-class space is eliminated. The proliferation and success of talk radio suggest that if the other more formal avenues are publicized or accommodative, they might be better utilized.

23. Polsby, *Community Power*, 130–31.

24. Howard Campbell. "Portmore Toll Road Controversy: Residents Vow to Fight On", *Gleaner*, 31 July 2005, http://old.jamaica-gleaner.com/gleaner/20040731/lead/lead1.html.

25. Young, *TABOR*.

26. Rebecca Abers, "Reflections on What Makes Empowered Participatory Governance Happen", in *Deepening Democracy: Institutional Innovations in Empowered Participatory Governance*, ed. Archon Fung (London: Verso, 2003), 200–207.

27. Isaac and Heller, "Democracy", 102.

28. Abers, "Reflections", 205–7.

29. Abraham Maslow, "A Theory of Human Motivation", *Psychological Review* 50, no. 4 (1943): 370–96, http://psychclassics.yorku.ca/Maslow/motivation.htm.

30. Name changed.

31. Name changed.

32. Maslow, "Theory".

33. MacKinnon, *Postures and Politics*, 8–9, 12.

34. Dryzek, "Deliberative Democracy", 223; Michael E. Morrell, *Empathy and Democracy: Feeling, Thinking, and Deliberation* (University Park: Pennsylvania State University Press, 2010), 139; Lakoff, *Political Mind*; Jean Decety and Philip L. Jackson, "A Social-Neuroscience Perspective on Empathy", *Current Directions in Psychological Science* 15, no. 2 (April 2006): 54–58; Halpern and Weinstein, "Rehumanizing the Other", 561–83.

35. Miller, "Parish Development Committees", 6–8.

36. Based on the lowest payment allowed on the government's payroll for secretaries, that figure could only pay for one such employee. See Ministry of Finance and the Public Service, "Government of Jamaica Revised Salary Scales", Ministry of Finance and Planning, last modified 16 March 2015, http://www.mof.gov.jm/documents/documents -publications/document-centre/file/390-goj-revised-monthly-salary-scale.html.

37. Sirianni, *Investing in Democracy*, 21–28.

38. Crenson, *Neighborhood Politics*, 295–96.

39. Polsby, *Community Power*, 33–34, 136–37.

40. MacKinnon, *Postures and Politics*, 225.

41. Sives, *Elections*; Gray, "Predation Politics", 72–95; Harrison, "Politics of Social Outlawry", 259–77.

42. Abers, "Reflections", 200–202.

43. Isaac and Heller, "Democracy and Development", 78–80. The other factors include the move to devolve planning and implementation to the local level, allowing for practical solutions to community problems, and that the experiment was "consciously deliberative".

44. Baiocchi, *Militants and Citizens*; Selee and Peruzzotti, *Participatory Innovation*.

45. Kramer, *Participatory Democracy*; Pugh, "Social Transformation", 384–92. Pugh's study revealed that elite programme design produces a different outcome than when the design is from the peasants, in this case.

46. Ministry of Local Government and Community Development, "Local Government Reform", 9. The JLP oversaw the dissolution of the St Catherine Parish Council in 1949, Trelawny Parish Council in 1954, Portland Parish Council in 1963 and KSAC in 1964 and 1984.

47. Ministry of Local Government and Community Development, "Structure, Role and Functions".

48. See Simpson Miller, "Modern System of Local Government", 4.

49. Name changed.

50. Crenson, *Neighborhood Politics*, 289–94.

51. Polsby, *Community Power*, 115. See also Ernesto Laclau, *Hegemony and Socialist Strategy: Towards a Radical Democratic Politics* (London: Verso, 1985).

52. Name changed.

53. He explained, however, that he has seen improvement. "This is a small island developing state; you can't escape, right, but to their credit, they have over time become less dependent on the political ideal . . . because you will have to learn it and understand that don't work all the time."

54. Muller and Seligson, "Civic Culture and Democracy", 546–47.

55. Putnam, "Bowling Alone", 65–78.

56. Powell, "Are We Experiencing", 23–25.

57. Dryzek, *Deliberative Global Politics*, 223; Mutz, *Hearing*, 148; See also Gran, *Development*; Martinot and James, *Problems of Resistance*.

58. Kate Pickett and Richard Wilkinson, *The Spirit Level: Why Greater Equality Makes Societies Stronger* (New York: Bloomsbury Press, 2011).

59. Ibid.

60. "GINI Index (World Bank Estimate)", World Bank Group, 2015, http://data.world bank.org/indicator/SI.POV.GINI?page=1

61. Editorial. "Poverty, Income Inequality on the Rise in Jamaica", *Gleaner*, 9 October 2011, http://jamaica-gleaner.com/gleaner/20111009/business/business8.html.

62. Pickett and Wilkinson, *Spirit Level*.

63. Abers, "Reflections", 205–7.

64. Isaac and Heller, "Democracy and Development", 108.

Chapter 5. The Future of the Selected PDCs and the Link with Past Experiences

1. Young, *TABOR*; Lane, *Political Ideology*.

2. Dahl, *On Political Equality*.

3. Thomas, *Modern Blackness*, 229.

4. UNDP in Jamaica, "Eradicate Extreme Hunger and Poverty: Where Are We?" (United Nations Development Programme, 2014), http://www.jm.undp.org/content/jamaica /en/home/mdgoverview/overview/mdg1/; "Annual Reports and Statement of Accounts", Statistical Institute of Jamaica, 2013, 8, http://statinja.gov.jm/CD%20Annual%20Report %202011-2012%20FINAL.pdf.

5. Pateman, *Participation*, 37–42.

6. Gaventa, "Finding the Spaces", 27.

7. Ibid., 26.

8. Polsby, *Community Power*, 130–31.

9. Abers, "Reflections", 205–7.

10. Fung, "Deliberation", 5.

11. Navarro, "Porto Alegre", 97; Selee and Tulchin, "Decentralization", 313; Isaac and Heller, "Democracy", 81.

12. Sives, *Elections*; Gray, "Predation Politics"; Harrison, "Politics of Social Outlawry".

13. Editorial, "Give Us the Queen!" *Gleaner*, 28 June 2011, http://jamaica-gleaner.com /gleaner/20110628/lead/lead1.html

14. Buddan, *Foundations*, 15; Buddan, "New Time"; Munroe, "Democracy", 31–55.

15. Isaac and Heller, "Democracy", 108.

16. Ibid., 78–80.

17. Sirianni, *Investing in Democracy*, 43.

18. Lindblom and Cohen, *Usable Knowledge*.

19. Mitchell, "Environmental Governance in Mexico"; Borkman, *Understanding Self-Help*, 38.

20. Sirianni, *Investing in Democracy*, 21–28.

21. Rothschild-Whitt, "Collectivist Organization".

22. Abers, "Reflections", 205–7.

23. Putnam, "Prosperous Community", 35–42; Putnam, "Bowling Alone", 65–78.

24. Putnam, "Bowling Alone"; Sirianni, *Investing in Democracy*, 20–21.

25. Powell, "Are We Experiencing". See also Harriott et al., *Political Culture*, 23–25.

26. Pickett and Wilkinson, *Spirit Level*.

27. Editorial, "Poverty, Income Inequality on the Rise in Jamaica", *Gleaner*, 9 October 2011, http://jamaica-gleaner.com/gleaner/20111009/business/business8.html.

28. Sirianni, *Investing in Democracy*, 14–17.

29. John G. Matsusaka, "Direct Democracy Works", *Journal of Economic Perspectives* 19, no. 2 (April 2005): 185–206. Since South Dakota first accepted and implemented the use of the initiative and referendum in 1898, not a single state has sought to repeal it.

30. Scott, *Weapons*; Marshall, *Anansi's Journey*; Patricia Hill Collins, *Black Feminist Thought: Knowledge, Consciousness, and the Politics of Empowerment* (New York: Routledge, 1990).

31. Andrew Knops, "Delivering Deliberation's Emancipatory Potential", *Political Theory* 34, no. 5 (October 2006): 594–623; Dryzek, "Deliberative Democracy", 223.

32. Dryzek, "Deliberative Democracy".

33. Cornwall, "Spaces", 85–86.

34. Gaventa, "Finding the Spaces", 23–33.

35. Morrell, *Empathy and Democracy*, 8–11.

36. Barber, *Strong Democracy* (2004 ed.), 169–70.

37. *Life and Debt*, directed by Stephanie Black; narrated by Belinda Becker (2001; Kingston: Tuff Gong Pictures, 2003), DVD.

38. Mohan and Stokke, "Participatory Development", 249.

39. Ibid.

40. Sidney Tarrow, *The New Transnational Activism* (New York: Cambridge University Press, 2005); Srilatha Batliwala and L. David Brown, eds., *Transnational Civil Society: An Introduction* (Bloomfield, CT: Kumarian Press, 2006).

41. Gaventa, "Finding the Spaces", 28.

42. Ibid., 30.

43. Norman Girvan, "'Ours Is an Autonomous Revolution': Impressions from a Visit to Cuba, March–April 1999" (typescript).

47. Ibid., 10–11.

Selected Bibliography

Abers, Rebecca. "Reflections on What Makes Empowered Participatory Governance Happen". In *Deepening Democracy: Institutional Innovations in Empowered Participatory Governance*, edited by Archon Fung, 200–207. London: Verso, 2003.

Adams, Nassau A. "Internal Migration in Jamaica: An Economic Analysis". *Social and Economic Studies* 18, no. 2 (June 1969): 137–51.

Agrawal, S.P. *Information India: 1996–97: Global View*. New Delhi: Concept Publishing, 1999.

Albert, Michael, and Robin Hahnel. *Looking Forward: Participatory Economics for the Twenty-First Century*. Boston: South End Press, 1991.

Alpern, Jodi, and Harvey M. Weinstein. "Rehumanizing the Other: Empathy and Reconciliation". *Human Rights Quarterly* 26, no. 3 (August 2004): 561–83.

Altschuler, Glenn C. *Rude Republic: Americans and Their Politics in the Nineteenth Century*. Princeton, NJ: Princeton University Press, 2000.

Austin, Diane J. "Culture and Ideology in the English-Speaking Caribbean: A View from Jamaica". *American Ethnologist* 10, no. 2 (May 1983): 223–40.

Bachrach, Peter, and Aryeh Botwinick. *Power and Empowerment: A Radical Theory of Participatory Democracy*. Philadelphia: Temple University Press, 1992.

Baierle, Sérgio Gregorio. "Porto Alegre: Popular Sovereignty or Dependent Citizens". In *Participation and Democracy in the Twenty-First Century City*, edited by Jenny Pearce, 51–75. New York: Palgrave Macmillan, 2010.

Bailey, Carol A. *A Guide to Qualitative Field Research*. 2nd ed. Thousand Oaks, CA: Pine Forge Press, 2007.

Bailey, Wilma, Clement Branche and Aldrie Henry-Lee. "Gender Relations and Conflict Management in Inner-City Communities in Jamaica: The Importance of Community Participation". In *Participatory Planning in the Caribbean: Lessons from Practice*, edited by Jonathan Pugh and Robert B. Potter, 138–54. Aldershot, UK: Ashgate, 2003.

Baiocchi, Gianpaolo. *Militants and Citizens: The Politics of Participatory Democracy in Porto Alegre*. Palo Alto, CA: Stanford University Press, 2005.

Barber, Benjamin R. *Strong Democracy: Participatory Politics for a New Age*. Berkeley: University of California Press, 1984.

———. *Strong Democracy: Participatory Politics for a New Age*. 20th anniversary ed. Berkeley: University of California Press, 2004.

Batliwala, Srilatha, and L. David Brown, eds. *Transnational Civil Society: An Introduction*. Bloomfield, CT: Kumarian Press, 2006.

Beck, Ulrich. *Power in the Global Age: A New Global Political Economy*. Cambridge: Polity, 2014.

Bellony, Annelle, Alejandro Hoyos and Hugo Nopo. "Gender Earnings Gaps in the Caribbean: Evidence from Barbados and Jamaica". *Inter-American Development Bank* (August 2010): 33.

Benjamin, Thomas. *The Atlantic World: Europeans, Africans, Indians and Their Shared History, 1400–1900*. New York: Cambridge University Press, 2009.

Bennett, Jane. *Vibrant Matter: A Political Ecology of Things*. Durham, NC: Duke University Press, 2010.

Bernal, Richard L. "The IMF and Class Struggle in Jamaica, 1977–1980". *Latin American Perspectives* 11, no. 3 (July 1984): 53–82.

Bezold, Clement, ed. *Anticipatory Democracy: People in the Politics of the Future*. New York: Vintage, 1978.

Blake, Damion Keith. "Direct Democracy and the New Paradigm of Democratic Politics in Jamaica". *Social and Economic Studies* 53, no. 4 (December 2004): 163–90.

Borkman, Thomasina. *Understanding Self-Help/Mutual Aid: Experiential Learning in the Commons*. New Brunswick, NJ: Rutgers University Press, 1999.

Bourdieu, Pierre. *Pascalian Meditations*. Palo Alto, CA: Stanford University Press, 2000.

Bowler, Shaun. "'Hybrid Democracy' and Its Consequences". In *Direct Democracy's Impact on American Political Institutions*, edited by Shaun Bowler and and Amihai Glazer, 1–19. New York: Palgrave Macmillan, 2008.

Brady, Henry, and David Collier. *Rethinking Social Inquiry: Diverse Tools, Shared Standards*. 2nd ed. Lanham, MD: Rowman and Littlefield, 2010.

Brown, Aggrey. *Colour, Class, and Politics in Jamaica*. New Brunswick, NJ: Transaction Books, 1979.

Buddan, Robert. "A New Time for Democracy". *Gleaner*, 22 June 2003. http://jamaica-gleaner.com/gleaner/20030622/focus/focus1.html.

———. *Foundations of Caribbean Politics*. Kingston: Arawak, 2001.

Burnard, Trevor. "A Failed Settler Society: Marriage and Demographic Failure in Early Jamaica". *Journal of Social History* 28, no. 1 (1 October 1994): 63–82.

Butler, David, and Austin Ranney. "Theory". In *Referendums around the World: The Growing Use of Direct Democracy*, edited by David Butler and Austin Ranney, 11–23. Washington, DC: AEI Press, 1994.

Butler, Katherine. "Jamaica Erupts in Fuel Price Rioting". *Independent*, 22 April 1999. http://www.independent.co.uk/news/jamaica-erupts-in-fuel-price-rioting-1088840.html.

Cameron, Maxwell A., Eric Hershberg and Kenneth E. Sharpe. "Voice and Consequence: Direct Participation and Democracy in Latin America". In *New Institutions for Participatory Democracy in Latin America: Voice and Consequence*, edited by Maxwell A. Cameron, Eric Hershberg and Kenneth E. Sharpe, 1–20. New York: Palgrave Macmillan, 2012.

Campbell, Angus, Gerald Gurin, Warren E. Miller, Sylvia Eberhart and Robert O. McWilliams. *The Voter Decides: A Study of the Voter's Perceptions, Attitudes, and Behaviors . . . Based on a Survey of the 1952 Election*. Evanston, IL: Row, Peterson, 1954.

Campbell, Howard. "Portmore Toll Road Controversy: Residents Vow to Fight On". *Gleaner*, 31 July 2005. http://jamaica-gleaner.com/gleaner/20050731/lead/lead6.html.

Chambers, Simone. *Reasonable Democracy: Jürgen Habermas and the Politics of Discourse*. Ithaca, NY: Cornell University Press, 1996.

Clark, Susan, and Woden Teachout. *Slow Democracy: Rediscovering Community, Bringing Decision Making Back Home*. White River Junction, VT: Chelsea Green, 2012.

Collins, Patricia Hill. *Black Feminist Thought: Knowledge, Consciousness, and the Politics of Empowerment*. New York: Routledge, 1990.

Communications Unit, Office of the Prime Minister. *The Councillor's Handbook: A Guide for Jamaican Councillors*. Kingston: Department of Local Government, 2009.

Cornwall, Andrea. "Spaces for Transformation? Reflections on Issues of Power and Difference". In *Participation: From Tyranny to Transformation? Exploring New Approaches to Participation in Development*, edited Samuel Hickey and Giles Mohan, 75–91. London: Zed Books, 2004.

Crenson, Matthew A. *Neighborhood Politics*. Cambridge, MA: Harvard University Press, 1983.

Dahl, Robert A. *On Political Equality*. New Haven, CT: Yale University Press, 2006.

Danielson, Anders. "Economic Reforms in Jamaica". *Journal of Interamerican Studies and World Affairs* 38, nos. 2–3 (July 1996): 97–108. https://doi.org/10.2307/166362.

Davis, David Brion. *Inhuman Bondage: The Rise and Fall of Slavery in the New World*. Oxford: Oxford University Press, 2008.

Davis, Lane. "The Cost of Realism: Contemporary Restatements of Democracy". *Western Political Quarterly* 17, no. 1 (March 1964): 37–46. https://doi.org/10.2307/445369.

de Certeau, Michel. *The Practice of Everyday Life*. Translated by Steven F. Rendall. Berkeley: University of California Press, 2011.

Decety, Jean, and Philip L. Jackson. "A Social-Neuroscience Perspective on Empathy". *Current Directions in Psychological Science* 15, no. 2 (April 2006): 54–58.

Diamond, Larry. *Developing Democracy: Towards Consolidation*. Baltimore: Johns Hopkins University Press, 1999.

Dryzek, John S. "Deliberative Democracy in Divided Societies: Alternatives to Agonism and Analgesia". *Political Theory* 33, no. 2 (April 2005).

———. *Deliberative Global Politics: Discourse and Democracy in a Divided World*. Cambridge: Polity, 2006.

Dunn, Richard S. "The Demographic Contrast between Slave Life in Jamaica and Virginia, 1760–1865". *Proceedings of the American Philosophical Society* 151, no. 1 (March 2007): 43–60.

Edie, Carlene J. "From Manley to Seaga: The Persistence of Clientelist Politics in Jamaica". *Social and Economic Studies* 38, no. 1 (March 1989): 1–35.

Etzioni, Amitai. "Towards an I & We Paradigm". *Contemporary Sociology* 18, no. 2. (March 1989).

Frater, Adrian. "Living at Risk in St James". *Gleaner*, 13 October 2013. http://jamaica-gleaner.com/gleaner/20131013/lead/lead65.html.

Frosh, Stephen. *Psychoanalysis Outside the Clinic: Interventions in Psychosocial Studies*. New York: Palgrave Macmillan, 2010.

Fung, Archon. "Deliberation before the Revolution: Towards an Ethics of Deliberative Democracy in an Unjust World". *Political Theory* 33, no. 3 (June 2005): 397–419.

——, ed. *Deepening Democracy: Institutional Innovations in Empowered Participatory Governance.* London: Verso, 2003.

Gaventa, John. "Finding the Spaces for Change: A Power Analysis". *IDS Bulletin* 37, no. 6 (November 2006): 23–33.

Girvan, Norman. "'Ours Is an Autonomous Revolution': Impressions from a Visit to Cuba, March–April 1999". Typescript.

Gould, Carol C. *Rethinking Democracy: Freedom and Social Co-operation in Politics, Economy, and Society.* Cambridge: Cambridge University Press, 1989.

Gran, Guy. *Development by People: Citizen Construction of a Just World.* New York: Praeger, 1983.

Gray, Obika. "Predation Politics and the Political Impasse in Jamaica". *Small Axe*, no. 13 (March 2003): 72–95.

Halpern, Jodi, and Harvey M. Weinstein. "Rehumanizing the Other: Empathy and Reconciliation". *Human Rights Quarterly* 26, no. 3 (August 2004): 561–83.

Harriott, Anthony, Balford Lewis, Kenisha Nelson and Mitchell Seligson. "Political Culture of Democracy in Jamaica and in the Americas, 2012: Towards Equality of Opportunity". University of the West Indies/Vanderbilt University, 2012. http://www.vanderbilt.edu/lapop/jamaica/Jamaica_Country_Report_2012_W.pdf.

Harrison, Faye V. "The Politics of Social Outlawry in Urban Jamaica". *Urban Anthropology and Studies of Cultural Systems and World Economic Development* 17, nos. 2–3 (July 1988): 259–77.

Hartlyn, Jonathan. "Democracy Consolidation in Latin America: Current Thinking and Future Challenges". In *Democratic Governance and Social Inequality*, edited by Joseph S. Tulchin and Amelia Brown, 21–49. Boulder: Lynne Rienner, 2002.

Held, David. *Models of Democracy.* 3rd ed. Palo Alto, CA: Stanford University Press, 2006.

Hilgers, Tina. *Clientelism in Everyday Latin American Politics.* New York: Palgrave Macmillan, 2012.

Hodgson, Dorothy L. *Once Intrepid Warriors: Gender, Ethnicity, and the Cultural Politics of Maasai Development.* Bloomington: Indiana University Press, 2004.

Horace Levy, "Community in Jamaica". Unpublished manuscript.

Hotchkiss, Julie L., and Robert E. Moore. "Gender Compensation Differentials in Jamaica". *Economic Development and Cultural Change* 44, no. 3 (April 1996): 657–76.

Huckfeldt, R. Robert. *Political Disagreement: The Survival of Diverse Opinions within Communication Networks.* Cambridge Studies in Political Psychology and Public Opinion. Cambridge: Cambridge University Press, 2004.

Hyman, Jeff, Paul Thompson and Bill Harley, eds. *Participation and Democracy at Work: Essays in Honour of Harvie Ramsay.* New York: Palgrave Macmillan, 2005.

Iannello, Kathleen P. *Decisions without Hierarchy: Feminist Interventions in Organization Theory and Practice.* New York: Routledge, 1992.

Isaac, T.M. Thomas, and Patrick Heller. "Democracy and Development: Decentralized Planning in Kerala". In *Deepening Democracy: Institutional Innovations in Empowered Participatory Governance*, edited by Archon Fung, 77–110. London: Verso, 2003.

Jackson, Lois A. "Canadian Bilateral Aid to Jamaica's Agricultural Sector from 1972–86". *Social and Economic Studies* 41, no. 2 (June 1992): 83–101.

Jacobs, Jane. *The Death and Life of Great American Cities*. New York: Random House, 1961.

Janis, Irving L. *Groupthink: Psychological Studies of Policy Decisions and Fiascos*. 2nd ed. Boston: Cengage Learning, 1982.

Johnson, Howard, and Karl S. Watson, eds. *The White Minority in the Caribbean*. Illustrated edition. Princeton, NJ: Markus Wiener, 1997.

Johnson, Hume N. "Incivility: The Politics of 'People on the Margins' in Jamaica". *Political Studies* 53, no. 3 (October 2005): 579–97. https://doi.org/10.1111/j.1467-9248.2005.00545.x.

Jones, Edwin. "Class and Administrative Development Doctrines in Jamaica". *Social and Economic Studies* 30, no. 3 (September 1981): 1–20.

Karl, Terry Lynn. "Dilemmas of Democratization in Latin America". *Comparative Politics* 23, no. 1 (October 1990): 1–21. https://doi.org/10.2307/422302.

Knops, Andrew. "Delivering Deliberation's Emancipatory Potential". *Political Theory* 34, no. 5 (October 2006): 594–623.

Kornbluh, Mark Lawrence. *Why America Stopped Voting: The Decline of Participatory Democracy and the Emergence of Modern American Politics*. The American Social Experience Series 39. New York: New York University Press, 2000.

Kramer, Daniel C. *Participatory Democracy: Developing Ideals of the Political Left*. Cambridge, MA: Schenkman, 1972.

Laclau, Ernesto. *Hegemony and Socialist Strategy: Towards a Radical Democratic Politics*. London: Verso, 1985.

Lakoff, George. *The Political Mind: Why You Can't Understand 21st-Century American Politics with an 18th-Century Brain*. New York: Viking, 2008.

Lane, Robert. *Political Ideology: Why the American Common Man Believes What He Does*. New York: Free Press, 1962.

———. *Political Life: Why People Get Involved in Politics*. New York: Free Press, 1959.

LeDuc, Lawrence. *The Politics of Direct Democracy: Referendums in Global Perspective*. Toronto: University of Toronto Press, 2003.

Leib, Ethan J., and Baogang He, eds. *The Search for Deliberative Democracy in China*. New York: Palgrave Macmillan, 2006.

Lijphart, Arend. *Patterns of Democracy: Government Forms and Performance in Thirty-Six Countries*. New Haven, CT: Yale University Press, 1999.

Lindblom, Charles E., and David K. Cohen. *Usable Knowledge: Social Science and Social Problem Solving*. New Haven, CT: Yale University Press, 1979.

Linden, Eugene. *The Alms Race: The Impact of American Voluntary Aid Abroad*. New York: Random House, 1976.

Lindgren, Karl-Oskar. *Participatory Governance in the EU: Enhancing or Endangering Democracy and Efficiency?* New York: Palgrave Macmillan, 2011.

Linz, Juan J., and Alfred Stepan. *Problems of Democratic Transition and Consolidation: Southern Europe, South America, and Post-Communist Europe*. Baltimore: Johns Hopkins University Press, 1996.

Lott, Jeremy. *Citizen Centre Report* 30, no. 5 (March 3, 2003).

MacKinnon, Frank. *Postures and Politics; Some Observations on Participatory Democracy*. Toronto: University of Toronto Press, 1973.

Marshall, Emily Zobel. *Anansi's Journey: A Story of Jamaican Cultural Resistance*. Kingston: University of the West Indies Press, 2012.

Martinot, Steve, and Joy James, eds. *The Problems of Resistance: Studies in Alternative Political Cultures*. Radical Philosophy Today, vol. 2. Amherst, NY: Humanity Books, 2001.

Maslow, Abraham. "A Theory of Human Motivation". *Psychological Review*, 50, no. 4 (1943): 370–96. http://psychclassics.yorku.ca/Maslow/motivation.htm.

Mason, Ronald M. *Participatory and Workplace Democracy: A Theoretical Development in Critique of Liberalism*. Carbondale: Southern Illinois University Press, 1982.

Matsusaka, John G. "Direct Democracy Works". *Journal of Economic Perspectives* 19, no. 2 (April 2005): 185–206.

McBain, Helen. "Government Financing of Economic Growth and Development in Jamaica: Problems and Prospects". *Social and Economic Studies* 39, no. 4 (December 1990): 179–212.

Mintz, Sidney W. "Reflections on Caribbean Peasantries". *Nieuwe West-Indische Gids/ New West Indian Guide* 57, nos. 1–2 (January 1983): 1–17.

Miraftab, Faranak. "Making Neo-Liberal Governance: The Disempowering Work of Empowerment". *International Planning Studies* 9, no. 4 (2004): 239–59.

Mitchell, Ross E. "Environmental Governance in Mexico: Two Case Studies of Oaxaca's Community Forest Sector". *Journal of Latin American Studies* 38, no. 3 (August 2006): 519–48.

Mohan, Giles, and Kristian Stokke. "Participatory Development and Empowerment: The Dangers of Localism". *Third World Quarterly* 21, no. 2 (April 2000): 247–68.

Montville, Joseph V. *Conflict and Peacemaking in Multiethnic Societies*. Lexington, MA: Lexington Books, 1989.

Morrell, Michael E. *Empathy and Democracy: Feeling, Thinking, and Deliberation*. University Park: Pennsylvania State University Press, 2010.

Moyo, Dambisa, and Niall Ferguson. *Dead Aid: Why Aid Is Not Working and How There Is a Better Way for Africa*. New York: Farrar, Straus and Giroux, 2010.

Muller, Edward N., and Mitchell A. Seligson. "Civic Culture and Democracy: The Question of Causal Relationships". *American Political Science Review* 88, no. 3 (September 1994): 635–52. https://doi.org/10.2307/2944800.

Munroe, Trevor. "Democracy and Democratization: Global and Caribbean Perspectives on Reform and Research". *Social and Economic Studies* 46, no. 1 (March 1997): 31–55.

Mutz, Diana C. *Hearing the Other Side: Deliberative Versus Participatory Democracy*. Cambridge; New York: Cambridge University Press, 2006.

Nathan, Rebekah. *My Freshman Year: What a Professor Learned by Becoming a Student*. Ithaca, NY: Cornell University Press, 2005.

Navarro, Zander. "Porto Alegre: From Municipal Innovations to the Culturally Embedded Micro-Politics of (Un)Emancipated Citizens: The Case of Rubbish Recyclers". In *Participation and Democracy in the Twenty-First Century City*, edited by Jenny Pearce, 76–99. New York: Palgrave Macmillan, 2010.

Nelson, Nici, and Susan Wright. *Power and Participatory Development: Theory and Practice*. London: Practical Action, 1995.

Nettles, Kimberly. "Learning, But Not Always Earning: The Promise and Problematics of Women's Grassroots Development in Guyana". In *Participatory Planning in the Caribbean: Lessons from Practice*, edited by Jonathan Pugh and Robert B. Potter, 173–202. Aldershot, UK: Ashgate, 2003.

Newport, Frank. "Congressional Approval Sinks to Record Low". *Gallup*. 12 November 2013. http://www.gallup.com/poll/165809/congressional-approval-sinks-record-low .aspx.

Olsen, Marvin Elliott. *Participatory Pluralism: Political Participation and Influence in the United States and Sweden*. Chicago: Burnham, 1982.

Osei, Philip D. "Strengthening Local Fiscal Capacity in Jamaica, 1993–2002". *Social and Economic Studies* 51, no. 4 (December 2002): 31–62.

Oxhorn, Philip, Joseph S. Tulchin and Andrew D. Selee, eds. *Decentralization, Democratic Governance, and Civil Society in Comparative Perspective: Africa, Asia, and Latin America*. Washington, DC: Woodrow Wilson Center Press, 2004.

Pateman, Carole. *Participation and Democratic Theory*. Cambridge: Cambridge University Press, 1976.

Paxton, Pamela. "Social Capital and Democracy: An Interdependent Relationship". *American Sociological Review* 67, no. 2 (April 2002): 254–77. https://doi.org/10.2307 /3088895.

Pearce, Jenny, ed. *Participation and Democracy in the Twenty-First Century City*. New York: Palgrave Macmillan, 2010.

Perrin, Andrew J. *Citizen Speak: The Democratic Imagination in American Life*. Morality and Society Series. Chicago: University of Chicago Press, 2006.

Pickett, Brent L. "Foucault and the Politics of Resistance". *Polity* 28, no. 4 (July 1996): 445–66. https://doi.org/10.2307/3235341.

Pickett, Kate, and Richard Wilkinson. *The Spirit Level: Why Greater Equality Makes Societies Stronger*. New York: Bloomsbury Press, 2011.

Polsby, Nelson W. *Community Power and Political Theory*. Yale Studies in Political Science 7. New Haven, CT: Yale University Press, 1965.

Post, K.W. J. "The Politics of Protest in Jamaica, 1938: Some Problems of Analysis and Conceptualization". *Social and Economic Studies* 18, no. 4 (December 1969): 374–90.

Powell, Lawrence. "Are We Experiencing an Epidemic of Distrust?" *Gleaner*, 7 April 2010. http://jamaica-gleaner.com/gleaner/20100407/cleisure/cleisure3.html.

Price, Charles. *Becoming Rasta: Origins of Rastafari Identity in Jamaica*. New York: New York University Press, 2009.

Prior, Lindsay. *Using Documents in Social Research*. Thousand Oaks, CA: Sage, 2003.

Pugh, Jonathan. "Social Transformation and Participatory Planning in St Lucia". *Area* 37, no. 4 (December 2005): 384–92.

Pugh, Jonathan, and Robert B. Potter, eds. *Participatory Planning in the Caribbean: Lessons from Practice*. Aldershot, UK: Ashgate, 2003.

Putnam, Robert D. "Bowling Alone: America's Declining Social Capital". *Journal of Democracy* 6, no. 1 (1995): 65–78. https://doi.org/10.1353/jod.1995.0002.

———. "The Prosperous Community: Social Capital and Public Life". *American Prospect* 13 (1993): 35–42.

Rivera-Ottenberger, Anny. "Against All Odds: Participatory Local Governance and the Urban Poor in Chile". In *Participatory Innovation and Representative Democracy in Latin America*, edited by Andrew D. Selee and Enrique Peruzzotti, 89–125. Washington, DC, and Baltimore: Woodrow Wilson Center Press and Johns Hopkins University Press, 2009.

Robnett, Belinda. *How Long? How Long?: African-American Women in the Struggle for Civil Rights*. New York: Oxford University Press, 1997.

Rothschild-Whitt, Joyce. "The Collectivist Organization: An Alternative to Rational-Bureaucratic Models". *American Sociological Review* 44, no. 4 (August 1979): 509–27. https://doi.org/10.2307/2094585.

Russell, Dalton, Wilhelm Burklin and Andrew Drummond. "Public Opinion and Direct Democracy". *Journal of Democracy* 12, no. 4 (October 2001): 141–53. http://www.socsci.uci.edu/~rdalton/archive/jod01.pdf.

Saad, Lydia. "Congress Approval at 18%, Stuck in Long-Term Low Streak". *Gallup Politics*. November 26, 2012. http://www.gallup.com/poll/158948/congress-approval-stuck-long-term-low-streak.aspx.

Sandel, Michael J., ed. *Liberalism and Its Critics: Readings in Social and Political Theory*. New York: New York University Press, 1984.

Schoburgh, Eris D. "Local Government Reform in Jamaica and Trinidad: A Policy Dilemma". *Public Administration and Development* 27, no. 2 (May 2007): 159–74. https://doi.org/10.1002/pad.434.

Scott, James C. *Domination and the Arts of Resistance Hidden Transcripts*. New Haven, CT: Yale, 1990.

———. *Weapons of the Weak: Everyday Forms of Peasant Resistance*. New Haven, CT: Yale University Press, 1987.

Selee, Andrew D., and Enrique Peruzzotti, eds. *Participatory Innovation and Representative Democracy in Latin America*. Washington, DC, and Baltimore: Woodrow Wilson Center Press and Johns Hopkins University Press, 2009.

Selee, Andrew D., and Joseph Tulchin. "Decentralization and Democratic Governance: Lessons and Challenges". In *Decentralization, Democratic Governance, and Civil Society in Comparative Perspective: Africa, Asia, and Latin America*, edited by Philip Oxhorn, Joseph S. Tulchin and Andrew D. Selee, 295–320. Washington, DC: Woodrow Wilson Center Press, 2004.

Sheridan, R.B. "The Wealth of Jamaica in the Eighteenth Century". *Economic History Review*, new ser., 18, no. 2 (January 1965): 292–311. https://doi.org/10.2307/2592096.

Shivji, Issa G. *Silences in NGO Discourse: The Role and Future of NGOs in Africa*. Nairobi: Pambazuka Press, 2007.

Simpson, Avagay. "Survey on the Status of the Local Public Accounts Committee (LPAC) in Jamaica". Building Civil Society Capacity to Support Good Governance by Local Authorities Project. A project funded by UNDP Jamaica under the Democratic Governance Thematic Trust Fund (DGTTF), June 2011.

Sinclair, R.K. *Democracy and Participation in Athens*. Cambridge: Cambridge University Press, 1988.

Sirianni, Carmen. *Investing in Democracy: Engaging Citizens in Collaborative Governance*. Washington, DC: Brookings Institution Press, 2009.

Sives, Amanda. *Elections, Violence and the Democratic Process in Jamaica 1944–2007*. Kingston: Ian Randle, 2010.

Smith, M.G. "Education and Occupational Choice in Rural Jamaica". *Social and Economic Studies* 9, no. 3 (September 1960): 332–54.

Stone, Carl. "Class and Status Voting in Jamaica". *Social and Economic Studies* 26, no. 3 (September 1977): 279–93.

Tarrow, Sidney. *The New Transnational Activism*. New York: Cambridge University Press, 2005.

Thomas, Deborah A. *Modern Blackness: Nationalism, Globalization, and the Politics of Culture in Jamaica*. Durham, NC: Duke University Press, 2004.

Thomas, Jan E. "'Everything about Us Is Feminist': The Significance of Ideology in Organizational Change". *Gender and Society* 13, no. 1 (1999): 101–19. https://www.jstor.org/stable/190242.

Tilly, Charles. *Democracy*. New York: Cambridge University Press, 2007.

Uran, Omar. "Medellín Participative Creativity in a Conflictive City". In *Participation and Democracy in the Twenty-First Century City*, edited by Jenny Pearce, 127–53. New York: Palgrave Macmillan, 2010.

Webster, Faith. "Gender Mainstreaming: Its Role in Addressing Gender Inequality in Jamaica". *Caribbean Quarterly* 52, nos. 2–3 (June 2006): 104–20.

Whyte, T.K. "Dirty Rodney Memorial Complex Irks Parish Development Committee Chairman". *Jamaica Observer*, May 9, 2007. http://www.jamaicaobserver.com/news/122751_Dirty-Rodney-Memorial-complex-irks-parish-development-committee-Chairman.

Williams, Eric. *The Negro in the Caribbean*. New York: Haskell House, 1971.

Williams, Joseph J. *The Maroons of Jamaica*. Chestnut Hill, MA: Boston College Press, 1938.

Yanow, Dvora. "Thinking Interpretively: Philosophical Presuppositions and the Human Sciences". In *Interpretation and Method: Empirical Research Methods and the Interpretive Turn*, edited by Dvora Yanow and Peregrine Schwartz-Shea, 5–26. Armonk, NY: M.E. Sharpe, 2006.

Young, Bradley J. *TABOR and Direct Democracy: An Essay on the End of the Republic*. Golden, CO: Fulcrum, 2006.

Zueblin, Charles. *A Decade of Civic Development*. University of Chicago Press, 1905.

Index

www.ingramcontent.com/pod-product-compliance
Lightning Source LLC
Chambersburg PA
CBHW021817270326
41932CB00007B/230